Give us a King

(Legal-Religious Sources of Jewish Sovereignty)

Give us a King

(Legal-Religious Sources of
Jewish Sovereignty)

By Rabbi David Polish

KTAV PUBLISHING HOUSE
Hoboken, NJ
1989

Library of Congress Cataloging-in-Publication Data

Polish, David.
"Give us a king" : legal-religious sources of Jewish sovereignty / by David Polish.
p. cm.
ISBN 0-88125-309-X
1. Kings and rulers—Biblical teaching. 2. Kings and rulers in rabbinical literature. 3. Jewish nationalism. 4. Religious Zionism. I. Title.
BS1199.K5P64 1989
296.3'877—dc20
89-15626
CIP

Manufactured in the United States of America

To Aviva and our children
Daniel, Loretta, Jonathan, and Ari
Judy, David, Amy, Abby, and Noah

Contents

Preface

For almost two thousand years Jews yearned for sovereignty, and having attained it they are now torn on how to define it and how to use it. In part, this inner conflict is rooted in Jewish tradition. For Jews today, sovereignty can be perceived through the Book of Kings or through the utopian visions of prophets. Suddenly the theoretical speculations of ancient scholars take on compelling and intimidating relevance. Although early warnings existed even before the creation of the Jewish state, a culture conflict has engulfed Israel and the Jewish people with unexpected intensity. Both the state and the people are polarized along political and religious lines. For some, national sovereignty means the possession of "the entire Eretz Israel," the land encompassed both by the Bible and by contemporary history. Among them are those who would expel Palestinians in order to consolidate their claims. For others it means historical compromise in which peaceful resolution of issues (if this is possible) is preferable to expanded borders. For them sovereignty is the instrument of national transformation, not expansion.

On the religious front, there have been steadily escalating demands for two kinds of concessions by the government: first, the use of its coercive power to enforce rabbinic law in the lives of Israelis; second, the increasing subjection of the state to the authority of rabbinic law in political affairs. This is presently embodied in a proposal by some scholars for a second chamber in the Knesset where state law would be tested by the standards of rabbinic law. Political and religious coalitions, particularly on the right, press for a virtual theocratic version of Jewish statehood. An extreme example is the agitation for the total elimination of secular law and democratic government in favor of biblical and rabbinic rule. Offsetting this, but to a lesser extent, is the assertiveness of political and Orthodox forces representing the ethical and conciliatory components in Jewish tradition.

All this roils around the fundamental issue of the nature of Jewish sovereignty. The issue is not merely personal status but, far more significantly, who truly governs Israel. It beats against the traditional revulsion toward being "like all the nations." This phrase, used only four times in the Bible, cites this principle three times as a popular model for the people of Israel, although the text views it negatively. Thus, from the start, the confrontation over the nature of Jewish nationhood has vexed the people and its thinkers. The vexation continues, down to those who court a religious war by agitating for the removal of a Moslem presence on the Temple Mount; and contrarily, to the Neturei Karta, who categorically reject the Jewish state in whose midst they dwell, who refuse to serve in its army, who openly defy it with impunity, and who would, if they could, put themselves under Jordanian protection.

Yet, notwithstanding this apparently irreconcilable conflict, Jewish sovereignty in the person of the king was not quite "like all the nations" conceptually. The Jewish king, unlike other monarchs in the region, was not a divine being, or derived from divinity. He was not informed with absolute power. Even David submitted to the wrath of a prophet and the curses of an opponent. Kings came last in Israel, after the priests, the prophets, the judges. Only concerning kings is the mandate, if that is what is, questionable or at best ambiguous.

The sole legalistic reference to kingship in the Bible contains restrictions on the king's power, so much so that he is circumscribed from the beginning. A long struggle in Israel was waged until kingship was accepted. Thus, kingship did not conform exactly to kingship among "all the nations."

The wariness toward this institution continues and intensifies in rabbinic literature; and the age-old wariness continues with the modern Jewish state, on two levels. On the first level, the biblical confrontation between the primal impulses of aggression toward the native population and the coexisting drives for national morality has broken out after millenia of apparent decay of the former and ascendancy of the latter. The confrontation has taken extreme forms and tears at the state's viability. The religious claim to all the territories and the impulse by many to subordinate or expel the Arab population of the West Bank draws its authority from biblical law. The symbol of the state as the instrument of absolute power or as the agent of a now vanishing Jewish society is contested. It is perceived by partisans as a conflict between collective ego and superego, or in kabbalistic terms between the sacred and the *sitra achra* (the other, demonic, side).

On the second level, the renewed struggle over sovereignty follows the biblical and rabbinic search for alternatives by which to curb political power. With varying degrees of urgency, rabbinic thought, even when it endorsed the legitimacy of kingship, was concerned with restraining it through existing, divinely ordained instruments. These instruments were intended from the first not only to share power with kingship but to serve as deterrents to absolute power. Through the centuries, rabbinic scholarship devoted great attention to this issue. It anticipated national restoration and it anticipated the full reinstatement of rabbinic law as the sole means of governance. The Rabbis' perceptions of sovereignty were limited. They could not envision a modern state, nor could they envision a future secular state in which the majority would not feel bound by rabbinic law. Nor could they have understood or tolerated religious pluralism. Nevertheless, they must be credited with religious radicalism dedicated to curbing royal absolutism, a political assumption in the ancient and early medieval world. This radicalism has no precedent in ancient religion. It was accompanied by violent hostility to non-Jewish tyranny and was identified with the abomination of idolatry.

The attempt in these times to disinter the violence and intolerance of biblical law arouses revulsion (understanding as we do that it was based on a total rejection of idolatry). Yet the corallary commitment to restraining the king must not be overlooked. When it is disentangled from ancient xenophobia, we observe a unique commitment to the restraint of political power. Admittedly, this could easily become an alternative power, with all the excesses of absolutist monarchy. It could substitute theocracy for autocracy with the justification that it has divine sanction, as indeed contemporary Jewish theocracy affirms. Still, at the center of a doctrine that is proving to be destructive is an inheritance of resistance to political absolutism and the quest for an alternative or a corrective. It represents a conviction that conventional political authority is not the final form of human polity. For this, rabbinic Judaism deserves understanding and credit. It searches not only for a *syag* (fence) for the Torah but also for a deterrent to human power. It must be understood that this was more than a theoretical quest alone. In fact it found a practical solution in the expansion of the judicial institution. Don Isaac Abravanel and Ha-Ran raised this to a systematic level.

Rabbinic Judaism believed in a unique kind of sovereignty based on a convenantal existence that transcends politics alone. While those who would impose the most repressive aspects of biblical law on the state and those who reject the state altogether may derive from their predecessors, their distrust of political absolutism emanates from a legitimate source. Through the "who is a Jew" debate and similar halachic challenges, they raise the essential issue around which Jewish life is joined—what is the ultimate source of political power in Israel and in Jewish life?

From a secular perspective, certain aspects of classical Zionism also perceived Jewish statehood warily. It also saw the hoped-for Jewish state as different. While much of the Zionist hope has proved to be romantic and illusory, the essential content of the hope was based on the rabbinic commitment to *tikun olam* (mending of the world) and to Jewish prophecy as embodied in Israel's Declaration of Independence. It is not surprising that the archsecularist David Ben-Gurion, responding to a query by a British Commission of Inquiry on Palestine concerning the source of the Jewish claim to the land, responded "the bible."

Like rabbinic Judaism itself, Zionism was split between "like all the nations" factions and those who held to the moral uniqueness of Jewish nationalism. So Nachman Syrkin, a socialist Zionist, could write:

> As longing and hope, as mystical belief, . . . the confluence of thoughts and feelings contained in Socialist Zionism is rooted in all of Jewish history. The struggle against the world . . . for the spiritualization and moralization of life, is the basic theme of Jewish history. The transformation of natural and historical reality in order to bring down the Holy Presence runs like a scarlet thread through . . . Jewish history. In the ideas of "return to Zion", "the advent of the Messiah", "Redemption", "the end of days" . . . revolves the historical originality of Judaism . . . The unique spirit of "tikun olam" . . . pervades all epochs of Jewish history. . . . In all manifestations of the Jewish spirit . . . , there is expressed this unique Jewish individuality that wishes to conquer the world of nature and build the kingdom of the spirit. . . . The modern Jewish renaissance-aspiration is more than a socio-political movement, more than a national uplifting.[1]

So Chaim Weizmann, preeminent leader of the Zionist movement and first president of the State of Israel, could say:

> I speak as a deeply religious man, although not a strict observer of the religious ritual. I make a sharp distinction between the present realities and the messianic hope, which is part of our very selves, a hope embedded in our traditions and sanctified by the martrydom of thousands of years, a hope which the nation cannot forget without ceasing to be a nation. A time will come when there shall be neither enemies nor frontiers, when war shall be no more, and men will be secure in the dignity of man. Then Eretz Israel will be ours.[2]

That secularist side in Zionist thought that has wrestled with the issue of national sovereignty derives some of its values from Jewish tradition. At the same time, the awareness that contemporary, spiritual, moral Jewish thought is informed with those values cannot escape the notice of Jewish religious modernists. So Martin Buber could say:

> There is no reestablishing of Israel, there is no security for it save one: It must assume the burden of its own uniqueness; it must assume the yoke of the kingdom of God. Since this can be accomplished only in the rounded life of a community, we must reassemble, we must again root in the soil, we must govern ourselves. But these are mere prerequisites. Only when the community recognizes and realizes them as such in its own life will they serve as the cornerstones of its salvation.[3]

In such values, drawn out of the Jewish past and transmitted into new idioms, Jewish sovereignty is challenged to find its way back to its ancient spiritual sources.

It would be well to begin our study by questioning the notion that there is no connection between modern political Zionism and Judaism's earlier religious thought. This notion deprives Zionism of an older an authentic past and of its inherently Jewish character. The chief argument for the relative newness of Zionism is that older Jewish aspirations for redemption were just that—passive aspirations, and that Zionism placed the burden for deliverance upon Jews, not upon God. This argument ignores instances from antiquity until the seventeenth century when Jews did resort to efforts at self-emancipation. When these efforts were repeatedly crushed, the people did indeed subside into passivity. The fact that at last Jews did seize upon a historical opportunity for self-liberation suggests the power of long-suppressed national aspirations, fused, to be sure, to nineteenth century nationalism. But the earlier yearnings were prerequisites.

Another connection between the past and the present reflects a conflict in Jewish thought over the desirability of kingship. This climaxed in the early 1940s over the necessity of Jewish nationhood. The analogy is inexact because in no ancient time was the concept of a claim to Jewish sovereignty in question. The only issue was, how and by whom should that sovereignty be administered? Modern anti-Zionism rejected any form of political-territorial Jewish autonomy. Still, the biblical and rabbinic issue over kingship and the later struggle over Zionism dealt with Jewish political power. The struggle in both instances centered on both the claim and its rejection that the people should be "like all the nations." Could and can the Chosen People adopt what was considered an idolatrous form of political hegemony and still be a chosen people? And, in contemporary context, can the people remain without political autonomy and survive, much less as a chosen people? In both instances, the antinationalists lost out. The nationalists triumphed, and this time they are determined that the fate of their predecessors should not overtake us.

Perhaps the most intriguing element uniting sovereignty in ancient Israel and in contemporary Israel is the concept of *malchut shamayim*, the Kingdom of Heaven." Subsumed under this concept was the biblical desire to differentiate Israel from other nations and yet to be like them through kingship. This contradiction was reconciled by placing restraints upon the king, including his selection by God. Even in sanctioning the king, Jewish thought placed him under a higher jurisdiction and subjected him to the jurisdiction of appointed officials. The issue is power and the restraint of power. *Malchut shamayim* subordinates the rule of the king to the absolute authority of God. The transcendant God alone is the true King. The earthly king rules at God's pleasure. Ideally this subjected the human king to the control of God's agents—the Torah, the prophets, the judges. The relativistic position of the kings was perhaps the most significant characteristic of Jewish sovereignty. Today, in a time when the absoluteness of the state is undergoing the challenge of both historical and philosophical reevaluation, biblical and much of rabbinic insight on sovereignty can be instructive. The American slogan "one nation, under God" is a rhetorical relic of a once-potent theological principle.

But just as the idea of *malchut shamayim* was buttressed with human instruments, so the very thought of the need for transcending the state requires a search for more enduring structures to serve that purpose.

Reborn Jewish statehood has brought unresolved questions to the center of Jewish existence. While kingship is no longer an issue, the uses of power do challenge us. The question of ultimate loyalties, to the state or to a higher authority, persists. Despite their mischievous aberrance, pietistic rejectors of Israel as an enemy of God's Kingdom speak out of a tradition that cannot be ignored. Essentially the problem is reduced to this: Is statehood the product of historical necessity alone, incurred by millennial suffering, or is it an inherent and indispensible Jewish value, a mitzvah required by our religious heritage? If the former, need a Jewish state, in exercising power, be inhibited by special considerations in a brutal world? If the latter, can a Jewish state be true to the restraints demanded by our tradition? The issues that vex Jewish life cannot be adequately addressed without exploring those aspects of Jewish thought that never ceased to be concerned with the problem.

For modernity no less than for antiquity, the issue of power, an issue that may never be resolved, becomes a continuing challenge to search for a higher absolute, both within a Jewish state and in the world order. That search must be tempered by the awareness that restraints on power often become absolutes of their own, as theocratic manifestations in our time and in Israel demonstrate. Yet the search cannot be abandoned.

Notes

1. *Der Tog*, March 19, 1918, translated from Yiddish by Jeffrey V. Mallow.
2. Arthur Hertzberg, *The Zionist Idea*, New York, 1959, p. 587.
3. Ibid., p. 457.

Acknowledgements by the author

I thank the following for their helpful and critical reading of all or portions of my manuscript:

Daniel Elazar, Yaakov Elman, Stephen Passamaneck, Daniel Polish, Hayim Goren Perelmuter, Yechiel Poupko, and Norbert Samuelson.

I thank the following for making possible the publication of this book:

Dr. Richard and Marian Kaufman
Sol and Ruth Weiner
Earle and Lorraine Iverson
Mason and Jeanette Loundy
Howard and Anne Gottlieb
Leonard and Diane Sherman
Hilton and Shirley Leibow
William and Anne Goldstein

All the elders of Israel assembled and came to Samuel at Ramah, and they said to him, "You have grown old, and your sons have not followed your ways. Therefore appoint a king for us, to govern us like all other nations." Samuel was displeased that they said "Give us a king to govern us." Samuel prayed to the Lord, and the Lord replied to Samuel, "Heed the demand of the people in everything they say to you. For it is not you that they have rejected; if is Me they have rejected as their king. Like everything else they have done ever since I brought them out of Egypt to this day—forsaking Me and worshiping other gods—so they are doing to you. Heed their demand; but warn them solemnly, and tell them about the practices of any king who will rule over them."

(Samuel 8:4–9)

When thou art come unto the land which the Lord thy God giveth thee, and shalt possess it, and shalt dwell therein; and shalt say: 'I will set a king over me, like all the nations that are round about me'; thou shalt in any wise set him king over thee, whom the Lord thy God shall choose.

(Deuteronomy 17:14–15)
(Jewish Publication Society Translation, 1916)

If, after you have entered the land that the Lord your God has given you, and occupied it and settled in it, you decide, "I will set a king over me, as do all the nations about me," you shall be free to set a king over yourself, one chosen by the Lord your God.

(Deuteronomy 17:14–15)
(Jewish Publication Society, 1962)

Give us a King

(Legal-Religious Sources of Jewish Sovereignty)

I

A People Divided—An Historic Overview

In the year 63 B.C.E., three years after being dispatched to the Middle East by Rome to quell an uprising by Mithradates of Pontus, Pompeii was approached in Damascus by representatives of the brothers Hyrcanus and Aristobulus for his support in their struggle for kingship of the Jews. This rivalry by two members of the priestly class for royal power was to give Pompeii a pretext for imposing Roman dominion over Judea, which would experience declining sovereignty and would eventually suffer destruction. In Damascus Pompeii heard not only from the partisans of the warring brothers but also from "the nation against them both, which did not desire to be under kingly government, because the form of government they received from their forefathers was that of subjection to the priests of that God whom they worshipped; and [they complained], that though these two were of the posterity of priests, yet did they seek to change the government of their nation to another form, in order to enslave them."[1]

In succeeding years, delegations of Jews to Syria and to Rome persisted, in the face of bloody reprisals, in appealing to Roman authorities for the abrogation of the Jewish state. "How deep was the desire of the Pharisees for the extinction of the Jewish State . . . [that they regarded] the state as an instrument of evil when it subverts or overshadows the interests of religion and nationality."[2]

These observations raise compelling questions. Did "the nation" indeed oppose the political aspirations of its divided leaders? Was the nation indeed threatened with an unprecedented "change of government? Assuming that in this as in other instances Josephus hyperbolized, did a significant body like "the Pharisees," as Baron argues, resist Jewish political sovereignty? In posing a priestly regime to a monarchy, did they accurately perceive that it was the authentic form of Jewish government and that the monarchists, in attempting to change it, as Josephus tells, were imposing an alien form of government? Most important for our study, did opposition to political statehood (or kingship) reflect a pragmatic response to an unacceptable historical condition, or was it based upon a set of religious principles rooted in Jewish thought that gave theological and legal validation to Jewish nationalism's opponents? Which form of government enjoyed divine sanction—kingship or priesthood? Is kingship paramount, expendable, or subordinate?

It should not be surprising that in our time this issue has assumed urgent relevance. Today, too, there are Jewish pietists who declare that Jewish statehood is "diametrically opposed to Judaism."[3] No less surprising is it that during the ages of Jewish statelessness and kinglessness this issue was discussed and disputed with considerable intensity. But today, when statehood in general is being critically scrutinized, when various political regimes have been replaced or are being challenged by theocratic systems, and when in Israel as well as in Jewry the confrontation over the relationship of religious law to national policy has become acute, the ancient debate becomes real. As in Roman times, the confrontation represents more than a power struggle between opposing and essentially political forces. It represents in one case a commitment to a well-documented perception of how a Jewish society in the land of Israel should be governed and who should govern. The structure of Jewish government was conceived ages ago. The rise of the modern State of Israel made it possible for that conception to make its claims upon the people.

The debate has its origins in two classical biblical texts—Deuteronomy 17:14–20 and I Samuel 8, whose echoes can be heard in ensuing Jewish history. The struggle in the Hasmonean period is illustrative. The antimonarchical strain in Pharisaic Judaism was rooted in great measure in the impulse toward separation from the nations. Its antithesis, the urge for monarchy, was predicated on "let us be like all the nations." Schalit, in *Hordos Ha-Melech,* suggests that Jewish Hellenism was a derivative (albeit corrupt) of prophetic universalism that reached out into the world, while the anti-Hellenistic spirit in Judaism was rooted in prophetic particularism that sought to preserve the people's spiritual integrity by withdrawal from a morally polluted world. The initial motive of the Maccabees was to achieve separation by overthrowing the external enemy and destroying the Jewish Hellenizers. The Maccabean goal was the defeat of anyone, Jew or Gentile, who sought to join Israel to the corrupting gentile world. This is why the early Chassidim were at first among the most zealous supporters of the Maccabees. But following the victory, they withdrew out of concern that political power would lead to immersion in and defilement by the pagan world.

The Hasmoneans who had fought to free their people from foreign domination and influence were nevertheless increasingly driven to political entanglements as the only way of preserving their hard-won independence. They had gained sovereignty in order to be free, but through sovereignty they exposed themselves to the very dangers against which they had rebelled. The Hasmoneans hoped to escape the fearful dilemma of power by counting on national strength as a deterrent against aggression, and even as a means of imposing the will and the doctrines of Israel upon all non-Jews under their jurisdiction.

The Chassidim, however, rejected this course with all of its obvious pitfalls and separated themselves from the center of power when the national crisis had passed. They reasoned that in a hard decision between religious and political considerations, between religious integrity and international involvement, the latter would prevail, and they feared it as an ever-present danger. Schalit finds corroboration for this in the Book of Daniel, which he considers a product of chassidic thought. Most significant, in Daniel, is found the distinction between the preordained role of the nations and that of Israel. Political power had been granted by God to the nations of the earth from the earliest times. "The history of this world is the history of the nations." In this category, Israel had been assigned no role. It was part of the divine plan that Israel was to be subjugated as long as the domination of the nations persisted. This would prevail only for a time, but with the fall of the last tyranny the rule of nations would cease, and the Kingdom of God would ensue, bringing redemption to Israel, and all the nations would then serve God. Thus, Israel was reserved by God and kept separate for a special purpose.

This mystery for which the world was created was not to be made clear to all until the end of days; in the interim, it was known to the chosen ones, the Chassidim. Therefore, "Israel is not like all the nations. The place of Israel is outside the normal course of life which obtains among the nations of the world. This course, that of the

State, does not apply to Israel. The effort to force the Jewish people into the cast of a political state is a perversion of its spiritual image and a constriction of its task in creations as conceived by God."[4] To apply political criteria to the people was to render its position untenable in the midst of greater and overpowering nations. The Hasmonean intent was therefore a violation of the divine will that intended Israel to be apart from the nations, not reduced to the level of a nation among the nations. The apprehensions of the Chassidim were not unjustified. The Hasmonean dynasty increasingly took on the aspects of power in its external and internal affairs. It imposed taxes, shed blood in the conquest of territory, hired mercenary warriors. The Chassidim considered all this to be contempt of God. Israel was ruled by God alone, not men. Thus began the alienation of the Chassidim and ultimately their opposition to the Hasmonean dynasty.

By the very immersion of the Hasmoneans in power politics attracted even as it repelled. Ultimately, those forces in the community who saw Israel's destiny as bound up with its national aspirations, who increasingly stressed the possibilities of this world, were drawn into what came to be known as the Zadokite party. In contrast to them, the Chassidim eventually evolved into the Pharisaic party, dedicated to overcoming the influence of the Hasmonean dynasty. The early idealism of the Maccabees had deteriorated into the growing ruthlessness of their successors. The early misgivings of the Chassidim were substantiated by many of their successors among the Pharisees. Thus the conflict, which was to mold the course of Jewish history and belief, was joined.

Maimonides was to concur, however, with the early "nationalists." He explained the significance of Chanukah not in terms of the traditional miracle of the oil, but rather in terms of the Hasmonean victory. "They rescued Israel from [their] enemies and established a King among the priests; kingship was restored to Israel for more than 200 years until the second destruction.[5] This statement is almost exultant, but even more, the inclusion is particularly significant in the reign of King Herod, so great was Maimonides' dedication to the concept of kingship. As will become evident, he considered Bar Kochba a legitimate king, despite his disastrous failure: "He was a great king."[6] The position of Maimonides is reinforced as follows: "When a prophet designates a king from the other (non-Davidic) tribes of Israel, and he goes in the way of the Torah and wages the wars of God, he is an (authentic) king and all the laws of kingship apply to him although the primary kingship is Davidic."[7]

Why did many members of the Pharisaic party oppose the Hasmonean dynasty? They clung steadfastly to the conviction that the King-Messiah would be a descendant of David. His everlasting kingdom would be accompanied by an era of peace, while the Hasmonean kingdom, supported by bloodshed, was a usurper because it was both non-Davidic and transitory like all human kingdoms. It was a defilement, usurping a divine prerogative that was primordially ordained and repudiating Israel's authentic task: "to live in holiness and to prepare for the true kingdom which is yet to come."[8] Thus, Pharisaic opposition was to the usurpation by Hasmonean kings, not to legitimate kingship from the house of David.

While Pharisaic Judaism would seem to be uniformly opposed to kingship, there are enough exceptions to warrant a nonmonolithic perception. When we discuss "the Pharisees" we must qualify the term by recognizing first that, like religious and political systems generally, Pharisaism was not thoroughly unitary. Although he consistently refers to "the Pharisees," Marcel Simon advances the case for a less than monolithic Pharisaism. He approvingly cites Guignebert[9]: "When we have described a man as a Pharisee we have not really said very much about him, for there are Pharisees and Pharisees."[10] Second, like other religious systems, Pharisaism responded differently to changing historical conditions. This accounts for the contrasting changes in Pharisaic attitudes toward Jewish monarchy and foreign rule. While Pharisaism opposed Hasmonean rule, and awaited the return of the Davidic line, there were those who "did not oppose [Hasmonean] rule . . . and even took part in the affairs of state during the reign of Shlomit Alexandra, wife of Jannai."[11]

Thus, Pharisaism seems to have strongly rejected the Hasmonean dynasty, yet there were significant exceptions. It hoped for the restoration of the Davidic dynasty, yet its commitment to the kingdom of God was central. While there was allegiance to national rule, there was also growing resignation to foreign domination. There was much uniformity; there was also diversity. Out of such diversity came the unfolding debate over the nature of kingship in Israel. The persistent adherence to the ultimate disclosure of God's kingdom made it possible for the Pharisees, and earlier for the Chassidim, to tolerate foreign rule as long as it was not oppressive. During the

Seleucid reign (which began in 312 B.C.E.), Israel managed to achieve an accommodation by living under Syrian hegemony, yet in a state of spiritual withdrawal from it. When rebellion came under the leadership of the Maccabees, it was not against foreign rule but against the special tyranny of Antiochus.

The Pharisees saw the fall of the dynasty (in 63 B.C.E.) as retribution by God, against whom the Hasmonean house had rebelled. The subjection of the Jewish people to ensuing Roman rule restored the divine order of the world, according to many of the faithful. Worldly power, ordained from the beginning, had been imposed over Israel, and Israel would endure under its domination until the advent of the Messiah and the Kingdom of God. Thereafter, it would live a holy existence in absolute separation from the outside world, as befits the Chosen People. The divine plan required Israel's subjugation so that it might be purified for the events of the End of Days. Aside from this, the Imperium of Rome had no special function assigned to it by God. Israel had nothing in common with it, and Rome as much played no part in advancing the coming of the Messiah. Pharisaism "came to terms with the Roman occupation," an adaptability that was "a victory of the Pharisees . . . and of the Jews in the dispersion."[12] Many Pharisees hoped only that Rome would be no different from the other kingdoms that ruled Israel (except for the tyranny of Antiochus) so that the people might not be driven to rebel. Thus the people could avoid arousing the wrath of Rome while separating itself from the power of Rome, from "the defilement of the nations," and prepare itself for the authentic Kingdom of God.

The land was to be the scene of Israel's deliverance, which can come about only through the return of exiles. "Gather together the despised of Israel. . . . Gird (the son of David) to purge Jerusalem from the nations that trample her down to destruction."[13]

If Pharisaic leaders could have rid Palestine of its Roman masters without violence, they would gladly have done so. They did not see any inherent benefit in being subject to foreign power. But if the cost of keeping the sacred community inviolate on its own soil was submission to Rome as a political power, they were ready to pay the price. One may question the wisdom or even the morality of such a course, but we can understand it only in terms of the Pharisees' ultimate allegiances. The allegiances simultaneously transcended the political pretensions of the Maccabean dynasty and the claims of imperial Rome. The (probably non-Pharisaic) "Psalms of Solomon" condemn the reign of the Hasmoneans, who are denounced as evil, corrupt, and ungodly. "They left no sin undone, wherein they surpassed not the heathen" (Psalms of Solomon, 8:9–13). (Although "Psalms" is no longer considered Pharisaic,[14] its dissent against kingship demonstrates continuing Jewish ambivalence on the issue.)

The Pharisaic position was ultimately anchored in the sovereignty of God—*malchut shamayim.* The radicalism of their allegiance to God as King is best understood against the background of a world where kings were regarded as gods. The Jewish breach of this concept is significant because it rejects both the divinity of foreign kings and the primacy of the kings of Israel. The rabbinic declaration "Praised be His name whose glorious kingdom is forever and ever" was an affirmation that the only kingdom worthy of ultimate fealty is God's.

It would be misleading to identify the Pharisees as opposed to national Jewish existence in Palestine. They did not reject the sacred land and the sacred community, bound to one another and inescapably joined to God's promise and God's covenant with Israel. But the Pharisees made clear that their ultimate loyalty was not to the state. In addition, unlike their opponents, they manifested a great concern for the Diaspora, which they sought to incorporate into the universal hierarchy of Judaism. Even before the destruction of the Temple, Pharisaic Judaism was already developing a system of observances and institutions that could encompass Jewish life everywhere, unlike the Palestine-moored Temple and priestly cult. The ubiquitous synagogue, the mobile Torah—these were the products of Pharisaic outreaching to the Disapora.

But did not the wars against Rome, culminating in the destruction of the Temple in 70 and the annihilation of national existence in 135 C.E. manifest intense nationalism? A close look at history reveals sharp conflicts over the policy of resistance. Great segments of the people, including Sadducees who had abandoned their nationalist fervor after a century of submission to Rome, were reluctant to be drawn into a war for statehood. Josephus tells us hyperbolically but not altogether falsely that the most influential men in the land attempted to dissuade the rebellious elements from insurrection and even engaged in a futile deterrent attack upon them.[15] (While the historiography of Josephus is sometimes suspect, his portrayal of his own values and convictions is useful as reflecting an aspect of his times. He tended to distort popular opinion during the anti-Roman rebellion, but he was certainly not alone in his antirevolutionary views.)

THE CROWNS OF GOVERNMENT

Despite the ambivalence over kingship, and predating kingship, a polity emerged in Israel and it came eventually to incorporate the king as part of an interlocking system metaphorically referred to as the "three crowns" of Torah, priesthood, and kingship. Pirke Avot 4:13 employs these terms as symbols of the tripartite nature of the Jewish polity. While it does not literally reflect a specific period of Jewish governance, it is a helpful paradigm for assessing Jewish self-rule. The polity has its origins in the earliest development of the Jewish people, whose constitution is contained in the Torah, and whose leader Moses governed as its first ruler. Each "crown" *(keter)* occupied a theoretically equivalent, autonomous, and interdependent role in relation to the others. All this was based on a covenantal relationship by which the people, as equal members of the polity, acquiesced to the governance under which they lived.[16]

There is one issue, however, that disturbs the tripartite equilibrium, an issue over which the Bible reflects inner tension and over which rabbinic thought found itself in confrontation. That was the role of kingship. While the crown of Torah and the crown of priesthood were not only ordained and legislated but accepted as normative (even when they reflect internal struggles over authority), the place of kingship in the polity is subject to debate, at times even challenge, and in extreme cases outright rejection. Even after the destruction of the Temple, the legitimacy of priesthood, past or future, did not come into question in Jewish thought, nor certainly did that of Torah until modern times. Strictly speaking, Stuart Cohen's observation is correct: "Classic Jewish records . . . do (not) indicate the successful attempt on the part of one Keter to indicate that the existence of any other is either illegitimate or unnecessary."[17] The attempt may not have been "successful" but it was pronounced, and it left its mark. When rabbinic champions of *keter* Torah insisted on its "inherent supremacy"[18] they often came close to considerably reducing kingship and even rejecting it. Abravanel and Ha-Ran delegated even political matters to the realm of *keter* Torah (i.e., judges). This was a predictable development in a constitutional system where "the rule of law tends to elevate judges to a position of special authority within the body politic."[19] Maimonides saved kingship from possible attrition and so codified it that in effect it became the dominant element in the triad. Rabbinic thought was preoccupied with the legitimacy only of kingship.

Kingship alone is the *keter* whose claim to divine mandate is in dispute and whose bona fides are shrouded in ambiguity. While empirically it functions as a fully accredited entity, its legal credentials are ultimately subject to the fiat of rabbinic authorities and are not unequivocally fixed in biblical law. Hence, kingship must be examined as an entity uniquely differentiated from the others.

Our study essentially concerns *malchut* (kingship) in the context of the king's rule. The term is sometimes used in connection with Jewish government in general, but our attention is directed to the governing of Jewish polity by the king. *Malchut* is intended to be equated not with statehood but rather the king's rule over the state or the people. We shall be dealing with the extent and limitations of the king's authority as perceived in Jewish thought, primarily in a postmonarchical setting in which contemporary statehood could not be envisioned. Nevertheless, the issue is far from irrelevant, insofar as the authority and power of kingship have been transferred to the ruling powers in present day Israel. So have some of the issues concerning that authority.

In turning to our issue, we must also distinguish the term "state" as applied today from its use in the context of early Jewish experience. The term "state" is recent, invoked to conform to contemporary realities that require a centralized political system, and it would disqualify a premonarchical decentralized political entity. Yet that entity did function as a polity, and under crisis conditions as an organized political system. Elazar properly cautions that "there is no 'state' in the Jewish political tradition in the sense of a reified political entity complete in and of itself. . . . Jewish political tradition does not recognize State sovereignty in the modern sense of absolute independence. . . . Classically, only God is sovereign, and He entrusts the exercise of His sovereign powers to the people as a whole, mediated through His Torah as constitution as provided through His covenant with Israel."[19]

The eminence and authenticity of kingship in biblical and rabbinic thought is not at issue. That is a given. Its legal status is, however, at issue. The same literature presents a wide range of critical perceptions of kingship, correcting and at times even rejecting it. We address this aspect primarily with the intent of tracing a single ambiguous law on which the issue hangs.

"LIKE ALL THE NATIONS"

The events of I Samuel 8 and the law of Deuteronomy 17:14ff, linked in both style and content, raise common profound issues: What was the nature of kingship among "all the nations" whom many in Israel wished to emulate? How was the role of kingship perceived? What was the biblical response to the impulse for kingship in Israel?

The thrice-voiced popular call in I Samuel and in Deuteronomy for a king "like all the nations" seems to present an invidious contrast between governance in Israel and in the neighboring kingdoms. Although the kings of "all the nations" are not characterized, Yahweh complains to Samuel that He rather than Samuel was being abandoned for foreign kings. Later commentators would seize upon this as a clear indication of idolatry. The popular request is followed by Samuel's negative description of the repressive king and by Deuteronomy's insistence that Yahweh alone will choose, if necessary, the longed-for king. "Like all the nations" becomes a token of the incompatibility between Israel and the nations with respect to kingship.

When the desire for kingship was first voiced in Israel, neighboring nations had long been governed by kings while Israel still lived under a loosely federated tribal system led by judges during critical times.

Basic institutions in Israel—the priesthood, the judicial system—had already been legislated and established, but not monarchy. Other than the sole Deuteronomy passage, there is no suggestion of any prior legal reference to kingship, and as we shall see, its meaning is unclear, certainly more ambiguous than the mandates for priests and judges. The roles of priests and judges are minutely delineated. The *role* of the king carries more restrictions and proscriptions of his authority than positive definitions of his task. Somehow, he appears more intrusive than ordained.

When kingship in Israel was finally established in response to continuing national peril, which a looser confederation of tribes could no longer contain, it nevertheless proved to be no mere copy of prevailing monarchies.

The most striking difference was that, unlike Egyptian tradition, the king in Israel was neither a deity nor of divine origin. Kingship did not "descend from heaven," as in Babylonia.[20] Nor did the king have sacred origins. In Egyptian texts, the pharaoh is referred to as "the god," expressing the belief that he was endowed with supernatural powers. He also served as priest in the sanctuary.[21] As god, the king was the "intermediary between men and nature" even after his death. Through him the "powers of nature flowed into the body politic. . . . (He) exercises a never ending mysterious activity (by which) . . . nature and society are integrated."[22] Ancient Israel would regard such kingship as usurpation of divine authority, and idolatry. These distinctions therefore invalidated later charges against Jewish kingship as idolatrous, certainly in the primary sense of the term.

While in Israel judges, priests, and prophets were divinely instituted, kingship represented a later and (in Samuel) a disappointed concession. In theory, kingship did not have equal standing with divinely ordained institutions. Unlike other ancient views of divine initiation, in Israel kingship was initiated by the people.

Noting this cardinal difference, the borrowed aspects of kingship in Israel "are least significant."[23] The king functioned primarily, if not exclusively, in a profane realm. He did not integrate society and nature, even though he did perform limited sacred duties—Saul offering a sacrifice before his war with the Philistines, and David making offerings before the entry of the Ark into Jerusalem. But royal ministration in the Temple in Jerusalem was rare—Solomon at the dedication of the Temple, Ahaz after delivering treasures of the Temple to the king of Assyria.[24] The rare reference to the king as God's son (Psalms 2:7, 8) is nothing more than a metaphor. In such a system, the king was but a creature of flesh and blood who governed other creatures of flesh and blood, who led in war, and who always stood under divine judgment proclaimed by prophets. Certainly, Israel's king was not "like (among) all the nations."

Kingship in Israel did not emerge without a struggle; indications of a controversy over its merits are found in the Bible.

Although kingship came to be generally accepted, the incident in I Samuel 8 reflects more than a mere residue of opposition within ancient Israel. Gideon's rejection of rulership[25] is cited as a striking example of disapproval of kingship, perhaps reflecting nostalgia for the days of the judges. It has even been suggested that the final period of Saul's kingship shows a conflict between the king who had turned tyrannical and the earlier national leadership. "It may be that the slaying of the priests on Saul's orders (I Samuel 22:16–18) was part of (that) struggle."[26] Samuel's attack on kingship and its exploitative nature was drawn from existing conditions in the Near East. Parallels to *mishpat ha-melech* (the manner of the king), described in I Samuel 8:11ff., are to be found in Akkadian documents from the archives of Ugaritic kings dating from the fourteenth and thirteenth centuries B.C.E.[27]

Once monarchy was established in Israel, however, it became permanently entrenched and found popular acceptance. Samuel himself anointed Saul and proclaimed him a *mashiach adonay*. The king became the shepherd of God's flock.[28] He became God's servant.[29] Most symptomatic of the king's acceptance is the covenant into which he occasionally entered with the people, as in the cases of David and Joash.

Yet the older tradition of the "golden age" of premonarchical Israel did not perish. "In the words of Micah 5:1 concerning the dynasty of David, . . . the times of the wanderings of the tribes and the times of the conquest were the ideal era, the era of pure faith, the perfect society and the rule of God over His People through His servants Moses and Joshua. . . . The times of the judges were considered a continuation of the ideal age. . . . The judges . . . were chosen by God to rescue the People."[30] The ascendancy of kingship was irreversible, but the nostalgia for premonarchical times remained, and even the confrontations with it continued beyond biblical times.

The Book of Judges sounds the monitory note, "In those days there was no King in Israel," and three times adds, "and every man did what was right in his own eyes."[31] On this note, the Book of Judges draws to a close. The passage about prekingship times in Judges 10:6, "The Israelites . . . served the gods of Sidon . . . , Moab . . . the Ammonites. . . . They forsook the Lord and did not serve Him," seems to be a taunting response to antiroyalists who saw kingship as a rejection of God.

Notes

1. Josephus, *Antiquities of the Jews*, Book XIV, Chapter 3:2.
2. Salo,Baron, *A Social and Religious History of the Jews*, New York, 1937, Vol. I, p. 165.
3. *New York Times*, September 29, 1982, p. 15.

4. Avraham Shalit, *Hordos Ha-Melech*, Jerusalem, 1960, p. 254.
5. *Hilchot Chanukah* III:1.
6. *Hilchot Taaniyot* V:3.
7. *Hilchot Melachim U-Milchamot* I:8.
8. *Hordos Ha-Melech*, p. 258.
9. *Monde Juif*, p. 210.
10. Marcel Simon, *Verus Israel*, New York, 1986, p. 14.
11. Yaakov Liver, *Toldot Bet David*, Jerusalem, 1959, pp. 114–115.
12. Simon, pp. 12, 36.
13. Psalms of Solomon 17:21.
14. See J. H. Charlesworth, *The Old Testament Pseudepigrapha*, Vol. II, p. 642.
15. Josephus, *Wars*, Book II, Chapters 16, 17.
16. Daniel J. Elazar, "Some Preliminary Observations on the Jewish Political Tradition," in *Tradition*, Fall 1980, pp. 255, 256; also pp. 260, 262, 264.
17. Stuart Cohen, *The Concept of the Three Ketarim*, Ramat Gan, 1982, p. 15.
18. Ibid., p. 22.
19. Elazar, "Some Preliminary Observations," p. 256.
20. Henri Frankfort, *Kingship and the Gods*, Chicago, 1948, p. 23.
21. *Encyclopedia Mikrait*, Jerusalem, 1950, Vol. IV, p. 1081.
22. Frankfort, pp. 36, 60.
23. Ibid., p. 339.
24. II Kings 16:12.
25. Judges 8:22ff.
26. Ben Sasson, ed., *A History of the Jewish People*, Cambridge, 1976, p. 93.
27. Ibid.
28. Ezekiel 34:23; Micah 5:3; Psalms 78:71.
29. II Samuel 7:5; Psalms 89:4.
30. *Encyclopedia Mikrait*, Vol. IV, p. 1086.
31. Judges 17:6, 18:1, 21:25.

II

The Law of Kingship

Aside from biblical judgments on the virtues and vices of individual kings, we note significant division on the merits of kingship as an institution. There are specific references of approbation, as in various Psalms. There are also deprecations of kingship, as in Gideon's rejection of regal power, Jotham's derision of kingship,[1] and Hosea's rebuke, "I will give you a King in my wrath."[2]

Judges 19:1 regretfully recognizes an age of kinglessness. "In those days there was no king in Israel." The event that follows, concerning the Levite and his violated concubine, and the ensuing concerted act of vengeance by the united tribes upon the tribe of Benjamin, suggest two things: first, that for want of a king, there was violence and depravity in the land; second, that kingship is necessary to maintain order and internal peace.

Biblical scholars hold conflicting views on kingship. One school considers kingship "an accessory" and a comparatively short-lived element in Judaism. Thus, religion alone unified the people when the tribes settled in Canaan, and religion alone "preserved the unity of the nation under the monarchy."[3] According to a related view, religion alone preserved the people after the return from Babylon (Welhausen). Opposing these is the belief in Israel's earliest organization as a religiously informed but also politically unified entity under the rule of prophetic personalities, with Moses as the first "king" (Spinoza). All views agree on one principle, that Ammon, Moab, and Edom had been organized as kingdoms for generations before kingship was to come to Israel.

The "political" view is held by Ezekiel Kaufman in his *Toldot Ha-Emvitch ha-Yisreelit.*[4] It is predicated on the paradigm of the Israelite leader as a "prophetic messenger." "The messenger of God goes at the head of the tribes" who are brought together by him (or her).[5]

"Not a powerful magician, not a priest, not a military hero, but a messenger of God. . . . The account of Moses—that was the formative beginning of the Israelite faith."[6] "Moses created the covenant of the tribes of Israel. He was the leader of the tribes, the supreme shofet."[7] Out of the idea of the prophetic messenger emerged the ancient Israelite Kingdom of God, governed by the prophet . . . whose role was that of a king."[8]

Kaufman emphasizes two factors: first, that the tribes "were united from the beginning on the soil of Canaan in a unique political government"; and second, that "at their head stood prophets and judges."[9] The uniqueness of this system, a theocracy, rests in its nonpriestly leadership. When kingship was to emerge, it would be shaped (certainly in the reigns of Saul, David, and Solomon) by the prophetic, charismatic character that initially imbued Israelite leadership. However, "a consolidated and established political government cannot be born of this idea." The "kingdom" was God's alone and leadership was selected by Him alone with no process of succession or continuity. "From the beginning of this movement [of God's messengers] a dichotomy was revealed between its ethnic-economic goals and its religious-prophetic goals."[10] (This dichotomy will be reflected in later continuous ambivalence about the nature of kingship.)

The dichotomy became especially apparent during times of national danger when, in the absence of a more structured political system, the nation stood in jeopardy. This kind of "kingdom" could not endure during a time of crisis. In the time of the judges, Israel trusted in the God who had saved them from Egypt, and manifested little desire for monarchy. Nevertheless, as national peril increased, "opposition to kingship disappears with the disintegration of trust in the superiority of rule by the judges."[11] But when kingship arrived in Israel, the spiritual, prophetic stamp of primal leadership by God's messengers remained deeply imbedded in the new institution.

> The prophesier becomes a Judge-savior. . . . Samuel by his word causes the spirit of prophecy to descend on Saul, and with a cruse of oil he anoints him king. Prophecy seals the period of "the Kingdom of God" and establishes the Kingdom of God's anointed. It is not fortuitous that the first King prophecies and is a man of the spirit. . . . It is not fortuitous that all of the first three Kings in Israel were men of the spirit. Saul prophesied,

> David was a poet in whom "the spirit of God spoke." Solomon was wise in whom "the wisdom of God" abided. While we do not find such qualities in later kings, perhaps here is preserved a memory . . . from which was created the Kingdom of God.[12]

Kaufman raises two major elements. First is the uniqueness of Jewish theocracy in whose inception prophecy, beginning with Moses, dominated and continued to inform Jewish leadership into the period of the first three kings. The second is, accompanying Jewish theocracy from the beginning, the evolution of a political element into a well-organized system containing both ethnic and religious components. Kaufman also contends that as kingship began to emerge, it encountered a minimum of opposition. He dismisses the Gideon and Jotham events as inconsequential and Hosea's attack on kingship as an isolated expression. He presents two contrasting accounts in Samuel as expressions of a transitory period. It is obvious that prokingship sentiment abounds in the Bible. Even Jeremiah, whose tragic encounters with monarchy might have driven him to reject it outright, equates the permanence of the house of David with that of God's covenant with Israel.[13]

That kingship won out is self-evident. That is totally uprooted resistance is problematic. Our contention is that even with the establishment of kingship, the issue was not fully resolved; that ambivalence persisted, as reflected precisely in the prominent retention of two events in Samuel and in Deuteronomy 17:14ff. Kaufman's references to the "dichotomy" between the people's "ethnic-economic and its religious-prophetic goals" points to the ambivalence that would continue from biblical through rabbinic sources.

Of special interest to us are the passages in I Samuel 8, 9, 10, and 12. They are particularly important because, first, they concentrate on a single event (the selection of Saul), which represents the conflict within biblical thought over the desirability of kingship; and second, this conflict is reflected in Deuteronomy 17:14ff, the sole scriptural law dealing with the establishment of kingship. This law contains the ambiguities that characterize the Samuel-Saul incident, particularly as embodied in Chapter 8, and those ambiguities are carried over into subsequent Jewish legal literature. In I Samuel 8; 10:17–19; and 12:6–16, there is unequivocal opposition to kingship, accompanied by reluctant submission to it. In Chapters 9 and 10 (a later version), there is the willing selection and anointment of the king. The Samuel incident, like Deuteronomy 17:14ff; is believed to react adversely to the reign of Solomon, thus reflecting the continuity of antimonarchic thought into the time, at least, of the early kings.

In addressing the more definitive legal basis for kingship in Israel, we note that the sole scriptural passage confronting Jewish kingship from a legal perspective (Deuteronomy 17:14ff) is in turn historically related to I Samuel 8; 10:17–19; 12. These events and Deuteronomy 17:14–20 intersect. The Samuel event, built around public disaffection with Samuel's sons and a concern for Samuel's advancing age, describes public demand for a king.

Samuel's response is pained but he is reassured by God, who informs him that not Samuel but He is being rejected, and advises him to let the people have a king. Samuel then details the heavy disabilities that kingship will impose on the people—conscription, taxation, confiscation. In Chapter 12, Samuel reproves the people for its "evil" in requesting a king. "The day will come when you cry out because of the King whom you yourselves have chosen; and the Lord will not answer you."[14] These passages are clearly antimonarchical. Yet they permit monarchy because of popular duress. "The people would not listen to Samuel's warning. . . . The Lord said to Samuel, 'Heed their demands.' "[15]

After both God and Samuel had been "rejected" by the people in their request for a king,[16] God commands Samuel to "warn them and tell them the practice of the king *[mishpat ha-melech].* Samuel then proceeds to set forth the actions of the future king toward the people.[17] "*Mishpat ha-melech* is a summation of royal repression that involves confiscation and indenture; it is not a normative presentation of the king's prerogatives. What both precedes and follows is an obvious denunciation of the "*mishpat.*" The people are warned against it and are told that they will "cry out" to be rid of "the King whom *you* have chosen for yourselves and God will not answer you."[18]

Even if "*mishpat ha-melech*" stands alone as a possible prescription for the king's rightful prerogatives, we must contend with the contradictory and warning passages of Verses 9 and 18, assuming that they may be subsequent or prior insertions. Their inclusion, in the text interpolated or not, bespeaks a profound displeasure with royal authority, which is seen as repressive. Just as Deuteronomy 17;14ff. betrays ambiguity prompted by the "like all the nations" clause, so does the same clause in 1 Samuel 8 generate a vision of the repressive king.

In his *The Temple Scroll* of the Qumran community,[19] Yigael Yadin strongly suggests that the author of that scroll reveals a special "Torah" dealing with royal prerogatives. Yadin states that "there are clear hints in the Pentateuch that there had indeed once been a Torah on this theme." One of the prerogatives is the king's right to one tenth of the booty from war. "If they are victorious over their enemies . . . and carry away their booty, they shall give from it to the King his tenth, and to the priests one of a thousand. . . ."[20] "The main biblical source" for the statutes of the king is Deuteronomy 17:14–20, yet the significance of this "Torah" lies in the fact that already in *biblical* times kingship was invested with a legal authority that legitimized Samuel's *mishpat ha-melech*.

SPINOZA ON BIBLICAL POLITY

We digress to consider Spinoza, who perceived the political component in primordial Israel and thus helped Jewish modernity to reappropriate the full dimensions of its political character. Spinoza's contribution to our discussion lies in his contention that biblical Judaism represented a political-religious system, that its Torah was the legal formulation of that system, and that Moses was the people's ruler, governing by that system. Far more significant than his observation that a Jewish state might one day be reconstituted is Spinoza's assessment of the Mosaic system as a polity with a constitution.

Although Spinoza's place in this discussion is not directly relevant to the development of rabbinic thought on kingship, it does respond to it, and in a more modern setting carries on the same issue that concerned earlier scholars.

It is fallacious to credit Spinoza with pre-Zionist sentiments on the basis of his observation in *Tractatus Theologico Politicus*, Chapter III:

> Did not the principles of this religion make them effeminate, I should be quite convinced that some day when opportunity arises; so mutable are human affairs they will establish their state once more, and God will choose them afresh.[21]

Among those who saw a proto-Zionist sentiment in this passage was Nahum Sokolow, the Zionist intellectual and political leader.

Spinoza's observation is not to be construed in isolation. It is evident that he does not express a hope but rather raises the possibility of a future event that, as his argument proceeds, he does not view with equanimity; the state, were it to arise, would be priestly-theocratic. Responding rather directly to his own prior observation, Spinoza states in Chapter XVIII: "Although the Jewish State as conceived in the previous chapter could have lasted forever, it is neither advisable nor possible to copy it today." "For if men wished to transfer their right to God they would have to make an explicit covenant with God to that effect, just as the Jews did; and this would require God's willingness to receive their right as well as their own willingness to transfer it. God, however, has revealed through the Apostles that his covenant is no longer written with ink or graven on tablets of stone, but is imprinted by his spirit on men's hearts."[22] to Herman Cohen, "the center of the whole treatise" is the denigration of Moses and the laudation of Jesus. It also invidiously contrasts Jewish ceremonialism and Christian ethics, and the "Zionist" passage only serves to make the possibility of a future Jewish state vastly inferior to a universalistic Christianity. Leo Strauss, however, argues that he has indeed "suggested" a "Zionist" possibility.[23] But this possibility is inferior to the people's premonarchical condition.

In Chapter XVIII Spinoza contrasts the conditions when the people were sovereign with the times when kings reigned. Kingship incurred national tragedy. "It is noteworthy . . . that as long as the people held the Kingdom there was only one civil war, and it ended in the complete restoration of peace. . . . But after the people . . . changed into a monarchy, there was almost no end to civil wars."[24] "Before the monarchy they often lived at peace for forty years at a time, and once they had no foreign or civil war for the incredible period of eighty years. But after the Kings obtained sovereignty, the object of warfare ceased to be peace and freedom, and became glory instead.[25] Under kings, the laws became corrupted and abandoned, and prophets who were not required in premonarchic times proliferated in order to reprove the king.

Kingship is to be rejected, also, because it brings with it onerous power that the people cannot bear; not will the king be able to tolerate democratic laws and rights. In Israel, kingship came about through rebellion against God, resulting in the "decline of their country . . . until finally they broke the divine law completely and sought for a human King so that his court should replace the Temple as the seat of government, and the union of the tribes in one citizen body should no longer be based on the divine law and the Priesthood but on common allegiance to a King; [leading eventually] to the destruction of the whole State."[26]

Even Moses, under whom "their church began at the same time as their state," and who ruled as an "absolute monarch," did not adequately understand revelation.[27] He "merely saw how the people of Israel could be united in a particular strip of territory, could form an independent community, i.e., establish a State."[28] He did not see how it could receive "eternal truths," only laws commanded by a divine king whose highest reward to his people was national felicity in its land. "In the five books commonly attributed to Moses the only reward . . . is temporal well-being." The commands that are largely ceremonial apply to the Jewish people only and are "aimed at the welfare of their State only (Solius Hebraeae nationis maxime accomodata)."[29] "Sacred rites make no contribution to blessedness, and those prescribed in the Old Testament and indeed the whole law of Moses, were concerned only with the Hebrews' State (Hebraeorum imperium), and thus with temporal benefits alone."[30]

The statement about a future Jewish state must be understood in the context of a systematic attack on Judaism as a religion of statehood; as exclusive, particularistic, legalistic, contentious.

Thus, the "State that could have lasted forever" could have done so only if it had retained its original spiritual character, only if it had remained unencumbered with later debilitating accretions. Moses reigned over a primal state that he left neither a monarchy, nor an aristocracy, nor a democracy, but . . . a theocracy, which Spinoza so designated for the following reasons: First, the state palace was the Temple. Second, all the citizens had to swear allegiance to God, their supreme Judge, to whom alone they had promised absolute obedience. Finally, when a leader was needed he was appointed by God alone. All this is confirmed in Deuteronomy 18:15; Judges 6:11ff.; and I Samuel 3.[31] Such a "state" could have lasted forever if the righteous anger of the legislator had allowed it to remain in its original condition. (Spinoza uses "rempublica" and "imperium" for "state" in the same sentence.) All this applies to the first Jewish state, since the second was a vassal of the Persians, and the priests had usurped the powers of internal government, both civil and cultic. There is therefore "little need to say more of the second State."[32] In consequence of the priestly rule, as well as the ascendancy of kings in Israel, it is clearly disastrous to allow ministers of religion to "handle state affairs"; it is dangerous to "legislate concerning religious belief"; and how fatal it is "for a people unaccustomed to royal rule, and already possessed of established laws, to appoint a King."[33] The primal Jewish state, then became corrupted and perished.

For Spinoza, both Jewish kingship and priestly rule usurped the primal Jewish state, which can be restored only as a primal state; which was a theocracy, though not governed by the priests; in which God would be the supreme Judge to whom alone the people would be loyal; in which the symbol of the state would be the Temple; and in which God alone would designate the commander-in-chief. This contradicts the political principles of Maimonides, and thus rejects kingship as a political institution contrived to function within a historical situation.

In the absence of a state like the primal Israelite state created by Moses (before it deteriorated), an alternate kind (most suitable for base citizens) is one in which "divine law depends entirely on the will of the sovereign" who is also the interpreter of the divine law. Spinoza does not apply the term "king" to the earthly ruler, only "sovereign" (officium), who both decides matters of national welfare and security and also interprets religious matters. These religious matters concern the ethical principles upon which society is based. By interpreting them correctly, the sovereign fulfills God's commands and governs the state properly. In such a state there is no room for prophets who obstruct the necessary and tough-minded policies of the sovereign. "So no one can practice piety toward his neighbor as God commands unless he adapts his piety and religion to the public good. But a private individual can know what is good for the State only through the decrees of the sovereign . . . therefore nobody can practice piety or obey God properly unless he obeys all the sovereign's decrees."[34]

Spinoza invokes the precedent of Mosaic religion to place an imprimatur on his version of the state. In the early biblical state, Jews, though commanded to love their neighbor as themselves, were nevertheless required to report to the judges anyone who had acted illegally. This was to be done on the principle of adapting piety to the public good. In compliance with this principle, "Jews could preserve the freedom they had won, and maintain complete control over the territories they held, only by adapting religion to the needs of their own State alone, and making a clean break with the rest of the world."[35] Moses' state as a model for Spinoza's state, he presents a version of Jewish statehood on which is erected his own ideal state. Moreover, he uses Jewish statehood as a model for others.

Significantly, as we shall see, Spinoza is anticipated by scholars who pursue a vision of Jewish polity either with significantly limited kingship or, as in the case of Abravanel, even devoid of it, but a polity nevertheless.

KINGS AND IDOLS

According to Kaufman, Deuteronomy 17:14ff. follows I Samuel 8, which reflects a time when the principle of the "Kingdom of God" still prevailed and was applied through the institution of the judges. Samuel's resistance and reluctant acquiescence to popular demand

> was a passing shadow. From Samuel is heard the voice of a dying age. The iron pincers of conditions forced him to relinquish the "Kingdom of God" and to establish a King "like all the nations." The feeling [of guilt concerning kingship] existed only during the period of transition and then was hidden away forever, and was remembered only once, during the time of the Northern Kingdom's decline. The King is "God's anointed" and Samuel himself anoints him. Samuel himself ceases to oppose Kingship.[36]

Kaufman's position would appear to be validated by Genesis 17:6, 16, as well as Judges 19:1. To God, addressing the patriarchs, are ascribed promises of kings for Israel. Implicit in Judges is confidence in kings and their powers.

It is our contention, however, that Kaufman's argument is refuted by Deuteronomy 17;14ff., which follows, perhaps by many generations, the I Samuel 8 and 10 accounts. It is ambivalent, reflecting the divided position of an earlier period, and not as unilaterally committed to kingship as Kaufman contends. It is a juridical synthesis of the Samuel incidents, and it is as conflicted as the I Samuel 10 account.

Samuel's second speech of reproof (I Samuel 12), following the anointment of Saul, contains an additional element. It warns that the survival of kingship depends on national morality. While the element of warning concerning the king's excesses does not recur, a third component is repeated, linking the hankering for kingship to the national inclination toward idolatry. In I Samuel 8:8, the connection is strong: "from the day I brought them out of Egypt until this day they deserted Me and worshipped other gods; so they are doing also to you."

On one level, the analogy deals with the rebelliousness of the people. On a deeper level is a connection between the choice (or rejection) of a sovereign and the form of worship adopted by the people. In Verse 8 God is rejected from "being a King" over the people, and in the next verse they are accused of consequently seeking other gods. As the people's *shofet,* Samuel occupies a sacred place, as God's representative and also as ruler. While he is at first reassured that he is not being rejected (Verse 7), he then hears the very reverse—the people are "doing it to you" (Verse 8). Both God and he are being replaced by a king, and the worship of God as fostered by Samuel is also being replaced by "other gods." The identification of foreign kings with the worship of their nations' deities is well known. Thus, the desire to be "like other nations" masks a motive idolatry, beyond the wish for a king who will wage the people's wars.

This relationship between kings and deities is emphasized in I Samuel 12:10 and 21. In the context of Saul's enthronement, Samuel reminds the people of a succession of earlier and more recent events. They had worshiped the Baalim and the Ashtaroth and prayed, in their distress, for God's deliverance so that they might worship Him. Subsequently, when the King of Amon threatened them, they came to Samuel demanding a king, although "Jahweh your God is your King." The juxtaposition of God's rescue with national danger and the accompanying request for a king suggests that God no longer fights the people's wars and that they require a king like all the nations.

Not this alone but a change of deity "like all the nations" is also required. The proximity of king and other gods is stressed yet again in I Samuel 12:19, 20, 21. The people, following the reproof for having requested a king, say, "We have added evil to our sins by requesting for ourselves a King." Samuel responds, "You have done this evil, but do not turn away from God . . . do not turn to *tohu* (worthless things) that will not avail or save you, for they are *tohu.*" (Kimchi interprets *tohu* as "idols.") The dialectic of the themes of God, king, and idols represents Israel as openly requesting a king while secretly harboring the hope that kingship could lead not only to abandoning God but coming under the protection of other deities.

The connection between kings and idolatry is perceived as the danger that following "other nations" through adopting kingship not only leads to the adoption of idolatry but is identified with it. The threat that kingship could be short-lived reinforces Samuel's earlier warning. This is explicit, following a promise of the king's endurance if the people do not offend God, but predicting ruin for the people and the king if they rebel.[37] Reading Chapter 12 as a sequel to Chapter 8, one cannot construe *"mishpat ha-melech"* as anything but a condemnation of kingship. This is confirmed by, "your evil is great . . . that you have asked for a King."[38]

Confronting Kaufman's argument that antimonarchy was transient in the history of Israel, we must contend that it nevertheless did not vanish from biblical and rabbinic thought. Jewish history quite obviously adopted kingship (which proved to be conceptually *unlike* other nations), but Jewish religious thought continued to wrestle with the issue. This is manifest in the speeches by Samuel condemning kingship, which were not edited out of the Samuel and Saul sagas. While the nation turned toward kingship out of popular demand and national need, the retention in the Bible of Samuel's condemnations indicates a significant resistance to kingship. Even more, with the transition to monarchy, the inclusion of both the resistance and the ready acceptance of kingship indicates that, theologically, the issue had not been totally resolved and had been left ambivalent. This ambivalence is further reflected in Deuteronomy 17:14ff.

THE AMBIGUOUS LAW

Throughout postbiblical rabbinic literature, the issue of kingship revolves around Deuteronomy 17:14ff., since this is a legal passage. Our concern will be kingship as a legal problem to which Jewish thought and controversy continuously revert. The issue is whether the passage present kingship as a requirement or an option, a mitzvah or a free choice. To put the issue historically, the question is whether kingship was instituted out of theological conviction or whether Israel was compelled to adopt it out of historical exigency and then gave it a sacral justification. It has been assumed that a consistent chain of authority requires kingship. Yet the earlier literature is not so conclusive, and the text itself is ambiguous.

The ambivalence is also manifested in attempts to translate Deuteronomy 17:14. The Jewish Publication Society (1917) reads: "when (*Ki*) thous art come into the land which the Lord thy God giveth thee, and shalt possess it, and shall dwell therein; and shalt say: 'I will set a King over me, like all the nations that are round about me'; thou shalt in any wise set him King over thee, whom the Lord thy God shall choose; one from among thy brethren. . . ."

The 1962 New Translation of the JPS Torah reads: "If (*Ki*), after you have entered the land that the Lord our God has given you, and occupied it and settled in it, you decide, 'I will set a King over me, as do all the nations about me,' you shall be free to set a King over yourself, one chosen by the Lord your God. Be sure to set as King over yourself one of your own people. . . ."

The first rendition makes kingship a requirement ("thou shalt in any wise"), while the second makes it an option ("You shall be free"). Both reflect the controversy in rabbinic literature. Both are predicated on the word *ki,* which may mean either "when" of "if."

Targum Onkelos renders Deuteronomy 17:14 literally, while Targum Yonatan presents "Som tasim . . . asher yivchar Adonay" thus: "You shall seek instruction before God, and afterward appoint the King over you." The change suggests that not the demand by the people but submission of the matter to God's approval is a prerequisite for the selection of a king.

The intent of Deuteronomy 17:14 is anomalous in six ways. First, in a number of Deuteronomic regulations that begin with *ki tavo* or a similar introduction, the rule is straightforward and unqualified. The passage in Chapter 17 is the only exception. Second, other legal passages similarly constructed and centering around the term *ki,* if translated according to the principles identifying 17:14 as a law, would be patently absurd. Third, taking into account that the request for a king is accompanied by "like all the nations," if the passage were a commandment, it would be a commandment to transgress. Fourth, nowhere else in the Torah is there approval for the people to request the establishment of an institution. Fifth, all other institutions—judges, priests, prophets—are clearly and divinely ordained. Kingship is uncertain at best. Sixth, countering the ambiguity about the king is a series of limitations on his power that say in effect, "If you must have a king, he shall be subject to the following restrictions. . . ."

THE USE OF *KI TAVO*

Various passages in Deuteronomy, in addition to 17:14, use the formula *ki tavo* or something very similar. They contain no dubious phrases casting doubt on the passage's intent. Chapter 6:10–15, after beginning, "When the Lord your God brings you to the land," issues a stern warning against forsaking God and worshiping false gods. The introduction is the entrance to the land. The command that follows is "beware." Chapter 11:29 begins, "When the Lord your God brings you to the land," and then commands, "You shall pronounce the blessing on Mount Gerizim." This is preceded by references to the blessing and the curse incurred by "following other gods." Chapter 7:1 begins identically and commands, "You must doom them (the seven nations) to destruction." Chapter 26:1–12 begins with, "When you enter the land that the Lord your God is giving you as a heritage," and commands, "You shall take some of every first fruit of the soil." Chapter 18:9 begins, "When you enter the land which the Lord your God is giving you," and then commands, "You shall not learn to imitate the abhorrent practices of those nations."

Each of these commands, except Chapter 17:14, is clear-cut. The first three passages make entrance to the land antecedent to uprooting worship of false gods. The fourth accompanies entrance to the land with a rite of gratitude to God for His saving and protecting power. There is a unifying bond in the formula of entry and wholehearted devotion to God who alone is to be worshiped and whose worship is identified with hostility to the resident nations, notorious for their obnoxious idolatry. In all the passages cited, together with numerous others beginning with *ki,* the transition from *ki* to the command is succinct and direct. Only Chapter 17:14 differs from the other *ki tavo* references. It differs in the ambiguity of the text. Especially does it differ in what appears to be a summons to imitate the very nations who in other scriptural citations are rejected and loathed. The imitation is precisely in that institution, kingship, that in ancient cultures was intimately identified with the service of the resident gods, from whom kings were sometimes born and whose abominations they certainly practiced. This nuance was caught by Jewish commentary that asked in shock, "Like all the nations? Like their idolatry?" Thus a series of commandments contingent on entering the land demands total rejection of the ways of the nations and total commitment to God. Deuteronomy 17:14 is therefore most singular and most remote from the others.

While some (to be noted) commentators have established that Deuteronomy 17:14 is not to be translated as dogmatically as many passages similarly construed, and is therefore not a mitzvah, it does not necessarily follow that it falls into the category of other passages written in a similar style. The difference between Deuteronomy 17:14 and other similar passages is not so much in structure as in content. While other laws deal with specific cases such as the captive woman, or the hated wife, or the engaged virgin—civil and criminal laws—Deuteronomy 17:14 deals with a central national institution. Moreover, while the other laws present cases and their resolution in unambiguous fashion, the passage concerning the king is complex. It defies categorizing by analogy. It stands alone because it reflects a long and internal confrontation with an institution that could be neither rejected nor fully appropriated. That confrontation is embodied in the I Samuel 8 account, and Deuteronomy 17:14 recapitulates in legal form the earlier drama of Samuel and the people. Step by step it converts the encounter into a legislative structure, thus:

I Samuel 8:4–15	*Deuteronomy 17:14, 15*
"Appoint a King for us." *(Simah lanu melech)*	"I will set a King over me." *(Asimah alay melech)*
"Like all other nations" *(kechol ha-goyim)*	"As do all the nations." *(kechol ha-goyim)*
"Heed their demand"	"Set a King over yourself."
"The Lord said . . . appoint a King"	"Chosen by the Lord."
"He will seize etc."	"He shall not amass silver and gold."

(The usage *kechol ha-goyim* appears only one other time in Scripture. The threefold use of the term in both Samuel and Deuteronomy is not fortuitous.)

Deuteronomy 17:14, and particularly what follows, are more a reflection of internal tension over the issue of kingship than a clear biblical mandate or statement. It exposes the crisis of decision over the issue. It goes neither way, and as in I Samuel 8, represents not an affirmation of kingship but a submission to it. The passages following Verse 14 attest to this. As Samuel warned against royal excesses,

Verses 14–15ff. legislate against them. They say in effect, if you must have a king, he shall be limited in specific ways—he shall be chosen by God, he may not be a foreigner, he may not amass wealth or women, and he must be bound by the laws of the Torah, which shall always be at his side. (In other words, he shall not be in the manner of other nations.) This is a classic example of the irrepressible wish controlled by the inviolable law. Deuteronomy 17:14ff. stands alone as the expression of ambiguity concerning kingship. It represents an accommodation between submission to the pressure for a king and assertion of divine control over him.

If the people are insistent enough to demand a king (as with Samuel) who is displeasing to God (as in Samuel), they will not be refused (likewise as in Samuel), but will be required to accept certain conditions (or penalties, as in Samuel).

Thus, "*If* you say, I want to set over me a king, you must set (only) a king over you whom God selects." The imperative *som tasim* refers primarily not to the permitted act of setting up a king but to deferring to God in the selection.

I. THE CONSENT TO TRANSGRESS.

If the passage in question is indeed a divine command, it states in effect: When you come into the land, and you say, "I want to set over me a king like all the nations," you must then certainly set up a king. The improbability of this verse being a mitzvah is reinforced not only by its structure but by its content. This is the only "mitzvah" demanding that Israel commit an act that is diametrically opposed to the spirit of the Torah, to "be like all the nations," an obvious stumbling block for those who support the mitzvah theory and one that subsequent commentators unsuccessfully attempt to explain. With all that we know of the Deuteronomic resentment against Israel's idolatrous neighbors, this proposed rendition is unacceptable, both linguistically and theologically.

A more acceptable solution can be found by analogy in the Maimonidean approach to the ancient practice of sacrifice in Israel, where animal sacrifice is seen as a controlled and centralized deterrent to the people's idolatrous impulses.

> The first intention (of centralized and limited sacrifices) consists in your approaching Me and not worshiping someone other than Me. These laws concerning sacrifices and repairing to the Temple were given only for the sake of the realization of this fundamental

> principle. It is for the sake of that principle that I transferred these modes of worship to my name, so that the trace of idolatry be effaced.[39]

Likewise, I Samuel 8 and Deuteronomy 17:14 represent reluctant concessions, with safeguards, to the people's intractable desire for a king.

II. THE CONSENT TO REQUEST.

If Deuteronomy 17:14 were a mitzvah, it would be the only one that enables the people to demand a national institution. Indeed, it would be the only one tolerating such a request. Biblical commandments are for fulfilling God's will. Petitions are made at the initiative of the people, not God.

III. THE DIVINE SOURCE OF NATIONAL INSTITUTIONS.

By contrast with the reference to the king, Deuteronomy is very clear about the divine mandate for judges, priests, and prophets. The ambivalence concerning kingship deepens when we note that Parashat Shoftim, containing the seven verses concerning the king, is a compendium about various kinds of officials who are to govern the people. The first are judges and other officers, and the laws deal mainly with rules of justice.[40] Other categories are the priests,[41] prophets,[42] and "officials."[43] All of these categories predate kingship. They are designated by God and do not require the appeal by the people for their existence or validity. There is no suggestion of a controversial issue. Most suggestive is the absence of the king in Deuteronomy 20, dealing with rules of war, although priests and officials are prominent. Although we know that kings played vital as well as fateful roles in Israel's wars, the silence in this chapter points to indecisiveness about how prominent or significant the king should be, at least in law. The priests and the officials address the troops.

IV. THE KING'S LIMITATIONS.

The limiting clauses—against excessive multiplication of possessions—restrict royal power, suggesting that even if kingship is a mitzvah, or *because* kingship is a mitzvah, care must be taken to circumscribe it. Maimonides, however, is bold enough to turn Samuel's warning on its head and dogmatically declare that confiscation and expropriation are necessary prerogatives of the king. The greatest limitation on the king is his selection by God. "Set up a King whom God (not you) selects."

Equally significant is the decisive place of God "who is with you" in battles, representing God as the ultimate source of Israel's military power and victory. Thus, the king is limited in his own role by the law's restrictions, and he is further limited by a hierarchy of other authorities, designated by God regardless of the people's will and mandated by God to act independently of the king. The king must be an Israelite, which leads Pedersen to conclude that the passage was postmonarchic, since such a "demand could not possibly be made as long as the Davidic dynasty existed."[44] He must not amass horses, wives, and wealth, nor go down to Egypt, "like Solomon, to whom the writer clearly alludes."[45] (Ibid.). The king is not only limited but differentiated. The excesses against which he is warned refer to those of Solomon, but in turn his excesses emulated those of foreign monarchs. God's selection of the king precludes the king's assuming divine character, as among the Egyptians, Sumerians, and Akkadians.[46] Since he is bound by the regulations of the Torah, he is not the object of the cult nor a high priest, as among the Hittites.[47] While legitimized, he is not the natural son of God, as among the Egyptians.[48] Only in Israel are there clear references even to the rejection of kingship.[49] Again, we note the tension between demanding a king and permitting only one who is unlike kings among the nations.

> We find here [Deuteronomy 17:14ff.] an inclination to consider the King as an invader in the Israelite community. . . . Such presuppositions led to the forming of the Deuteronomic law relating to the King, no doubt during or after the Exile. . . . It is here indicated that the Kingship is un-Israelitish, introduced after the custom of other peoples, by the will of the people, not really by that of Yahweh.[50]

In sum, Deuteronomy 17:14ff. can be construed as follows: First, it is a juridical replication of the account in I Samuel 8. The request for a king, the justification for the request because of the desire to be like "all the nations," the consent by God, and the (subsequent selection of the king by God's agent are present in the Samuel incident and reproduced in Deuteronomy. Samuel's warning against royal excess is converted into a related legal idiom (though not as sweepingly) in Deuteronomy. Absent in Deuteronomy, however, is the sense of resistance to kingship (except in a subtle way), which appears in Samuel. This becomes submerged in Deuteronomy and assumes the form of a putative consent clause, *som tasim*. Thus, second, the

Deuteronomy passage stands as an after-the-fact statute, responding to the de facto condition of kingship, not entirely approving of it yet incapable of opposing it, offering approval yet striving to control it by retaining divine power of selection and setting limits to royal excesses. If Deuteronomy 17:14 is indeed a mitzvah it is a *mitzvah ha-baah b'averah* (a mitzvah achieved through transgression), compounded by suggesting that the first deed to be performed by God's people upon entering the land is to demand a king "like all the nations." Rabbinic literature does not fully confront the paradox of this "mitzvah," limiting itself only to those who made the request properly and those who did not, but the question of God permitting the improper request is hardly addressed.

We observe an organic relationship between the legal basis for kingship and the authority and limitations of the king. Both are logical components of kingship. Biblical law does not only establish kingship. It simultaneously attempts to define it. The definition of the king's role logically derives from the establishment of kingship, whether it is approved or not, whether the role is approved or not. Thus Deuteronomy 17, having accepted kingship, immediately decrees that the king must have a scroll of the law and that he must not multiply silver, horses, or wives. Samuel, having reluctantly acquiesced to kingship, tells the people what kingship entails *(mishpat ha-melech)*. The nature of the relationship depends, however, on the moral perception of kingship. Where kingship is perceived as mandated and desirable, *mishpat ha-melech* is viewed as normative. Where it is perceived as mandated and necessary, though not necessarily desirable, *mishpat ha-melech* becomes a necessary though burdensome consequence. Where it is perceived as unnecessary, *mishpat ha-melech* becomes tyrannical.

Notes

1. Judges 9:8, 15.
2. Hosea 13:11.
3. Roland de Vaux, *Ancient Israel*, New York, 1961, pp. 94–99.
4. Ezekiel Kaufman, *Toldot Ha-Emunah ha-Yisreelit*, Tel Aviv, 1952.
5. Ibid., Book IV, p. 72.
6. Ibid.
7. Ibid., p. 97.
8. Ibid., pp. 73, 74.
9. Ibid., p. 90.

10. Ibid., pp. 91–92.
11. Ibid., p. 103.
12. Ibid., p. 110.
13. Jeremiah 33:14–26; Yaakov Liver, *Toldot Bet David*, Jerusalem, 1959, p . 66.
14. I Samuel 8:18.
15. I Samuel 8:19, 22.
16. I Samuel 8:7.
17. I Samuel 8:11–17.
18. I Samuel 8:18.
19. Yigael Yadin, *The Temple Scroll*, New York, 1985.
20. Ibid., p. 77, col. 43:11–15.
21. Spinoza, *Tractatus Theologico Politicus*, translated by A. G. Wernham, New York, 1965, pp. 62, 63.
22. Spinoza, pp. 190, 191.
23. Leo Strauss, *Spinoza's Critique of Religion*, New York, 1965, p. 21.
24. Spinoza, p. 195.
25. Ibid., p. 197.
26. Ibid., p. 187.
27. Ibid., pp. 209, 223.
28. Ibid., p. 79.
29. Ibid., p. 190, 191.
30. Ibid., p. 79.
31. Ibid., pp. 169. 171.
32. Ibid., p. 189.
33. Ibid., p. 199.
34. Ibid., pp. 211–213.
35. Ibid., p. 213.
36. Ezekiel Kaufman, *Toldot Ha-Emunah Ha-Yisraelit*, Book IV, Tel Aviv, 1952, p. 160.
37. I Samuel 12:25.
38. I Samuel 12:17.
39. Moses Maimonides, *Guide of the Perplexed*, Chicago, 1963, Book III:32, p. 530.
40. Deuteronomy, 16:18.
41. Deuteronomy 18:1–8, 20–1–4.
42. Deuteronomy 18:15–22.
43. Deuteronomy 20:5–9.
44. Johannes Pedersen, *Israel, Its Life and Culture*, Copenhagen, 1940, Vol. III–IV, p. 96.
45. Ibid.
46. Georg Fohrer, *History of the Israelite Religion*, Abingdon Press, 1972, p. 143.
47. Ibid.
48. Ibid., p. 147.
49. Ibid., p. 150.
50. Pedersen, *Israel, Its Life and Culture*, Book III, pp. 95–96.

III

Theocracy and the Strategy of Josephus

The event in I Samuel 8 embodies the ancient-modern Jewish struggle over the Kingship of God and human kingship in its expanded incarnation through the nation. Despite assertions to the contrary, kingship did not eradicate the Jewish yearning for divine rule that transcended the rule of flesh and blood. The poignancy of God's declaration to Samuel that the people had rejected Him, and the insistence by the people on a human king, foreshadow the age-old conflict between these contrasting national impulses. Unlike among "all the nations," the tension was not resolved by allocating to each his own designated sphere of authority. In Christendom the "two swords," temporal and divine, attempted a neat separation, although it was not to work as a covenant of equals. In the Jewish tradition, the loyalty of the people to the transcendant King and the earthly king resulted in postexilic thought in a fusion of the kingships and of their governance. The kings would become both leaders of the people and delegates of God in their sacred tasks of governing under the authority of the Torah. The ideal king would be the King-Messiah. He would wage Israel's battles and lead it into a sacred era. He would be a political-spiritual being, ruling over what we would call a theocratic system. It is clearly not our purpose to commend such a system to a renewed Jewish or any other state, but rather to suggest that ancient Judaism rejected the total separation of the temporal and the sacred as inimical to its unitary vision. It is significant that two advocates of theocracy with whom we will deal, Ezra and Josephus, supported a narrow interpretation of theocracy—a limited ecclesiastical regime—only as a way of retaining Jewish existence under duress. Especially as Ezra understood it, pure theocracy was to be preferred to the total absence of autonomy; the crown of priesthood was better than no crown at all.

"Pure" theocracy, government by the direct rule of God who fights the people's battles and governs its society, is an ideal realized only in Israel's most nostalgic evocations of its earliest history. In its most purely theocratic time, God ruled through a designated instrument, Moses, whose governance was defined by divine law, but a divine law that required the administration of Moses. In its more normative sense, theocracy was a form of political government, distinguished by the fact that it was administered by a priestly class.

The focus of its rule was the Temple, but it had to be sustained by an administrative system that required taxation, legislation, judiciaries, public safety, and many other aspects of the social order. This could be achieved in one of two ways—either under conditions of national independence or under the domination of a foreign power. In the first instance, an attempt at "pure" theocracy came up against the reality of historical necessity and took on increasingly political form, as in the case of the Hasmonean priestly family that came to appropriate royal and political power. In the second case, the people could indulge, for a time, in the role of an ecclesiastical society, but under the necessity of abrogating its political life to a foreign power that maintained the social order, and at the cost of independence and the constriction of the national life. This prevailed during Persian rule following the return from Babylonia. In either case, this theocracy was priestly.

Welhausen makes the general statement that "in ancient Israel theocracy never existed in fact as a form of constitution. The rule of Jehovah is here an ideal representation; only after the exile was it attempted to realize it in the shape of a rule of the Holy with outward means."[1] He argues that a presupposition for a theocratic system must be a centralized state that is sufficiently well organized to support and administer such a system, and such a state did not exist in the time of the Judges. Yet the state was a "new creation" during the reigns of Saul and David, owing nothing to the "Mosaic theocracy," when "the relation of Jehovah to Israel was . . . a natural one (with) no interval between Him and His people to call for thought or question."[2] This suggests a form of "pure" theocracy by which God had once ruled Israel directly without benefit of human intermediaries or priestly institutions. Only after the exile did an institutionalized theocracy, governed by priests and obviating the need for kings, emerge. This had already been gestating during the decline of the monarchy. As monarchy weakened, the role of the Temple and the priesthood increased. With the return from exile, the reconstitution of the state was unthinkable, and an advanced form of theocracy emerged. Ezekiel Kaufman, however, perceives it as foisted upon the people by political exigencies that did not dull the popular yearning for royal restoration. The ideal "theocratic personae" for Welhausen are the priests ruling under the protection of foreign powers; for Kaufman this regime is inferior to an authentic theocratic government by prophetic leaders who precede the kings. When the reign of king's ends, the hopes engendered by the prophets live on. In this spiritual environment, argues Pedersen, the king of Deuteronomy 17 "is to submit to the priests from who he is to receive the Deuteronomic law."[3] Pedersen does not substantiate this conclusion, and in fact the primacy of the priesthood in Jewish theocracy is challenged by Kaufman.

Based on Welhausen, Gerson Weiler argues that theocratic government appears when national power declines, so that in losing sovereignty the Jewish people was compelled to reconcile its great memories of the past with a present in which the people had become only a religious community. In the process of national decline, new theocratic concepts penetrate the perceptions of the past, even as memories of national government grow dim. Yet not altogether, since messianic yearnings emerge, connected with the Davidic dynasty. During the Babylonian exile, Israel changed from nation to holy community, from political authority to the authority of the Torah, and later to the authority of the halachah.[4]

According to this concept, priestly theocracy did not take form until the Persian government brought the exile to an end and created the conditions for an artificial type of national existence. Under Ezra, the priestly theocratic idea became the central element in Jewish life. He had come to Jerusalem with a writ of authorization from the Persian king (Ezra 7:11ff.) enabling him to return to Jerusalem with fellow exiles, gather material help and funds, reestablish the Temple worship, and above all, enforce religious law.[5] He secured this authority, asserts Weiler, by convincing the Persian king that Jews were only one of a number of religious communities in his empire.[6] "He concealed those aspects of the Torah concerned with political independence, divine selection and a negative attitude toward other nations." The writ of authorization was therefore essential in this context. Without it Ezra could have achieved nothing. In the context of Ezra, he had the backing of Persian arms to enforce God's Torah.

Nehemiah pursued a similar strategy by referring to Jerusalem as "the place of my ancestors' graves."[7] Ezra was successful in "selling" his idea not only to the king but to the Jews. He was careful not to say that conditions were not yet ripe for national restoration, but rather that worship was the essence of the people's heritage and identity.

Thus he silenced any substantive nationalist speculations. In expelling foreign women who were married to Jews, he changed the national idea into a principle concerning "holy seed."[8] Nehemiah likewise enforced the Torah by rules against intermarriage and by securing the enforcement power of the Persian king. While Kaufman says that this was achieved because of the religious enthusiasm of the people, Weiler adds that the primary contributing factor was the king's support of Erza. "The ultimate victory of Ezra came with the destruction of the [second] Temple when the last pretense of national existence was wiped out. The program to convert the Hebrew nation was begun through the mediation of Ezra and Nehemiah by King Artachshasta, and was brought to a successful conclusion by Titus, the Roman general."[9]

The great theocratic institution arising during the period of Ezra-Nehemiah was the *Knesset ha-godolah.* It begins, asserts Weiler, in the assembly described by Nehemiah 8–10. It consists of a national gathering, a collective confession of sins, and a covenant to keep the Torah. Despite references to the national downfall due to the breach of the covenant, there is no mention of hope for the restoration of national sovereignty, even in messianic form. "The assembly secured the sanction of God, and [also] religious authorization for the final end through the loss of independence and the continuing subjugation to kings 'because of our sins.' " The covenant does not mention the hope for national sovereignty.[10] It limits itself to establishing the foundations of religious worship, Shabbat, festivals, sacrifices, sanctuary taxes, and religious purity through combatting intermarriages. The assembly evolves from a popular gathering into an organized, official body that comes to be recognized as part of the sacred chain of tradition from Moses, as Pirke Avot delineates. From this ultimately derives rabbinic, halachic authority that claims the Torah and the prophets as its sanction, but that eventually rabbinic law usurps. This is illustrated by a rabbinic dictum that the sage's word is superior to the prophet's. In the chain of tradition cited in Pirke Avot, the judges and especially kings are not mentioned. "In the transmission of authority, it is as though kingship never existed.[11] Bertinoro, supporting the rabbinical line of authority, says that while other nations devised their own scheme of ethics, even the Ethics of the Fathers came from Sinai, thereby establishing the all-encompassing authority of the rabbis.

Thus, the conviction was established that Judaism was based *initially* on religious law, that the Jews were a religious community, and that yearning for national identity was both an error and against God's will. "The halachah came into the world as a collection of anti-political laws and enactments.[12]

Weiler blames Ezra rather than Persian authorities for this "distortion" of Judaism. His notion is based upon Welhausen, who regards the destruction of the first Temple as the watershed between the Jewish people that was destroyed and the emergence of the Jewish ecclesia, and with it the theocratic system. As Welhausen put it, "[after the Exile,] the sole rule of Jehovah was to be carried out in earnest. . . . The reconstitution of an actual state was not to be thought of, the foreign rule would not admit of it." Welhausen asserts that the times were propitious for the priestly class that during the monarchy had attained to great power.

> So closely was the cultus of Jerusalem interwoven with the consciousness of the Jewish people, and so strongly had the priesthood established their order, that after the collapse of the kingdom the elements still survived here for the new formation of a 'congregation' answering to the circumstances and needs of the time. Around the ruined sanctuary the community once more lifted up its head. . . . If the divine rule was formerly a belief supporting the natural ordinances of human society, it was now set forth in visible form as a divine state. . . . The Mosaic theocracy, the residuum of a ruined state, in itself is not a state at all, but an unpolitical artificial product created in spite of unfavorable circumstances . . . and foreign rule is its necessary counterpart.[13]

Pfeiffer adds, "When the Persian Empire allowed the Jews every opportunity for religious development and organization but tolerated no attempts to regain political independence, the compilers [of the Priestly Code] set out to make a holy nation of the Jews, a church within the empire. . . . They succeeded in creating for the Jews the kind of theocratic state which could cause no uneasiness to foreign rulers."[14]

Kaufman contends, however, that the yearning for royal restoration was not stifled. Ezra, Nehemiah, and Ezekiel. The judges of the earlier biblical, variety serve as a basis for Kaufman's development of Jewish theocracy. Unlike Welhausen, he credits the prophets, not the priests, with establishing the religious foundations of the Jewish polity. Relating the concept of "Kingdom of God" to the unique phenomenon of Israel's prophet-messengers, he writes:

> Before Israel's entrance into the land a prophetic-messenger was sent, who united them through the word of God, freed them from oppression, and established among them the belief in the saving God and His messengers. He did not give them political government, but provided a paradigm for the rule of God through His prophetic-messengers. The unique political government of the period of the judges serves as a monumental historical testimony pointing to a great religious-national event in the lives of the tribes of Israel before their entrance into the land, at whose center stood the . . . first prophetic-messenger.[15]

Welhausen's analysis of Israelite theocracy differs perceptibly from Kaufman's, but nowhere more markedly than in the precondition they assume. For Welhausen, national statelessness and subservience to foreign domination is a precondition for priestly theocracy that, he acknowledges, is a mere shadow of prior political independence. Abolition of the state, subordination to an occupying power—these alone allow for theocracy, and its administrators are the priests. In contrast, Kaufman's prophetic theocracy involves the redemption of the people and its restoration. This has been and is recurrently brought about by God's prophet-messenger whose task is to reconstitute the nation in the spirit of the God who sends.

The implications of Kaufman's theocracy are far reaching. He rejects the brand of theocracy that is dependent on national disaster in favor of one whose criterion is national renewal. But even more, he restores the synthesis of Jewish politics and Jewish religion through the action of the divinely commissioned messenger. He is not a political agent alone. He is a person of prophetic and spiritual power. As a consequence, his mission, unlike those of political heroes alone, is to transform the inner life of the people as part of its redemption within history. Redemption becomes a noneschatological act, and the prophetic messenger brings his message to a living people whose spiritual experience takes place within a free society, not a conquered land. It is not living, as Pfeiffer describes postexilic Judaism, as "a sort of monastic order, living in the world but apart from outsiders . . . theoretically impervious to political vicissitudes."[16]

Kaufman rejects the notion that centralized theocracy came to Israel as a new concept, replacing kingship. "Judaism never knew a theocratic-priestly ideal. It did not deprecate kingship during the time of the second temple. . . . The rule of priests is not an ideal in the Bible."[17] He challenges the Welhausen theory that the destruction of the first Temple represented the watershed dividing Jewish history, separating the record of the Jewish people as a national entity from that of the "Jewish church." The post-Babylonian theocratic system did not emerge from the people's will. It considered theocracy as a form of servitude and sought its abolition. The rule of postexilic priests was imposed on the people who, although they could not restore the state, yearned for the restoration of the Davidic dynasty. The rule of the priests was not considered an extension of the earlier Kingdom of God. Kaufman contends that the true theocracy, which has deep pre-monarchic roots, does not abide in priests, priest-kings, or king-deities as may be found among ancient people, but in the rule of prophet-judges. Even during the time of Ezra the longings for the restoration of monarchy did not subside in the minds of people. It was, he declares hyperbolically, "an expectation which [the people] did not forget for a single hour."[18]

The accounts of the earliest heroes—Moses, Miriam, Joshua, Deborah, Gideon, Samuel—testify that the first theocratic leaders were charismatic people of spirit, prophetic personalities addressed by God.[19] Israelite theocracy does not impute special sanctity to its theocratic leaders but rather the gift to lead and to rule. "The people believes that God will raise up prophetic leaders and people of spirit, and it awaits their appearance. The basis for this is explained in Gideon's words, "Where are all His wonders of which our ancestors told us, saying, did not God bring us up from Egypt?" The Exodus is the paradigm and the beginning of this kind of theocracy. The tentative rulership of the seer was converted into a political government."[20] In this context, it is *not* the priest but the prophet who is God's messenger, who anoints the king. "He is no longer sent to judge and save, but to anoint the king, to reprove him or to rise up against him. Thus ends the early prophetic theocracy."[21] In this context, the early "Kingdom of God" as rooted in the expectation of deliverance is not a prelude to the later priestly theocracy, as perceived by Welhausen.

Kaufman contends that the prophet, "the messenger of God," preceded kings, heroes, or priests in Israel.[22] "He is a charismatic personality in a special context: God chose him and sent him."[23] His rule is the paradigm of God's governance of Israel, which has its origins at Sinai and to which the people yearningly look back. This prepares a "Kingdom of God" to be led by a prophetic figure, not by a priestly class. The theocracy identified by Kaufman is unrelated to priesthood. Instead of a priestly theocracy, he advances the concept of a prophetic theocracy. "Amos refers to this kind of theocracy. In the period of the Exodus and the conquest of the land, God raised up prophets and Nazirites (Amos 2:9–11). Governance in the time of the judges was in the hands of people of spirit whom God stirred up to perform great deeds, to save the people and judge them. This was not a hereditary rule but dependent on spiritual selection."[24] Thus, while kings were to emerge, prophetic theocracy came first.

> Kingship contains . . . the continuous hope for the emergence of God's [prophetic] messengers. This kingship was born through the appearance of the first prophet-messenger-savior, sent for the covenant of the tribes [in the time of the judges]. Since every savior has a [prior] model . . . (Jewish) government was born with the appearance of the first "model." When there appeared, not a priest-seer, but a prophet-messenger in the name of a ruling God, kingship came into the world. [Kingship] was based on the expectation of a prophet-messenger, on the renewal of this appearance in every generation. Moreover . . . the theocracy [of the time of the Judges] is not original. It is sustained by the past. The people await a savior, because its eyes are turned to . . . the age of heroism, [and] preceding that period, . . . to Sinai from which God's help will be manifested.[25]

For Kaufman, then, prophecy is not only the antecedent to kingship but the precondition and the ultimate goal of kingship.

Within the texts of Ezra and Nehemiah themselves, there are occasional hints that the authors did not abandon their political hopes. The weight of evidence points to a priestly theocratic orientation, but only as a temporary strategy. This need not be regarded as

Ezra's outright deception of the King, or most certainly of the people. While it may represent his conviction that priestly theocracy was the best that he could achieve at the time, it did not signify a turning away from the eventual goal of kingship. There is the apt analogy in modern Jewish history when pre-Israel Zionism cited the Balfour Declaration's commitment to the establishment of a "Jewish national home in Palestine," which it eagerly embraced while not abandoning the idea of a Jewish state. The Persian writ authorizes Ezra to "appoint magistrates who may judge all the people . . . and whoever will not do the law of your God and the law of the [Persian] king, let judgment be executed on him." While this is not a grant of political independence, neither is it a strict limitation of the restored people to a cultic system in which civil law is to be administered by the Persian government. A significant measure of autonomy inevitably leads to a people's growing political aspirations, an awareness that might not have escaped the Persian king.

Nehemiah 11:1 speaks of *sarei ha'am,* princes of the people who dwell in Jerusalem. But even more, the memory of Israel's greatest royal glory is kept alive in Nehemiah 12:45. "They kept the word of their God . . . according to the commandments of David and of Solomon his son." The explicit recollection of these two kings in a book presumably committed to transforming the consciousness of the people is not fortuitous. This, together with the ever-present prophecies of Ezekiel about future kingly restoration, hardly corroborates the argument about the repression of the national impulse that somehow erupted despite the repression. It rather illustrates the conscious preservation of national longing that increasing theocratic stress could not and did not choose to obliterate.

Additional clues to attitudes toward kingship can be found in Ezekiel. An analysis of Ezekiel seems to indicate that the prophet had expectations for a future Jewish polity and also that it provided for the rule of the people by a king. Ezra's views prevailed, but the promulgation of Ezekiel's beliefs indicates that the ambivalence over kingship was not eliminated but rather continued to agitate the spiritual and intellectual life of Israel. Ezekiel sought not to annual kingship but to reform it. On one hand, he condemned the excesses and repressions of former kings. "My princes shall no longer defraud My people. . . . Enough, princes of Israel. Make an end of lawlessness. . . . Put a stop to your evictions of My people.[26] His references to the king as *nasi* rather than *melech* does not signify that Ezekiel envisioned a future leader other than a king, because he equated *nasi* with kingship.[27] This applies especially to a future in which rulers will no longer oppress their people and will apportion the land more equitably.[28] Kimchi interprets this to mean that future kings will no longer expropriate land as Ahab did, and will lift the heavy burden of taxation. Kimchi, commenting on "they shall not oppress" (45:7–10), recognizes the political nature of the state when he argues that kings must not again oppress when kingship is restored. In addition, Ezekiel foresees the restoration and the everlasting rule of the house of David, the *nasi*![29]

Another reference by Ezekiel is noteworthy. His use of the term *kechol ha-goyim* (25:8) is the only one used in Scripture other than in Deuteronomy 17 and I Samuel 8. This is not fortuitous, and suggests that the people's similarity to the other (idolatrous) nations is confined to sharing their calamitous fates.

Perhaps the most striking example and the first outright advocate of priestly theocracy under foreign domination is Josephus. When he stood beneath the walls of beseiged Jerusalem and made his plea for national surrender, he qualified as Judaism's first ideologue of priestly theocracy in a society devoid of its own political sovereignty. Political power had been torn from Israel before, but Josephus converted that condition into a principle. It was the priesthood that was indispensable. By his total commitment to a "kingdom of priests," Josephus not only affirmed its centrality within the Jewish experience, not only regarded it as divinely mandated, but dismissed Jewish political sovereignty as unsupported by religious law. He openly renounced sovereignty and unconditionally (by inference) accepted the terms of the Persian empire whose requirements Ezra and Nehemiah had attempted to evade. This represented a moral break with his nation, as serious a break as his political defection. As he advocated it, political sovereignty was not only not required by the Torah, it was rejected. It came close to a subsequent stand by Abravanel.

We can learn much from Josephus's appeal to the inhabitants of Jerusalem to surrender to the Romans. Whether he spoke as a traitor or as one concerned with saving his people from destruction, his words impinge strongly on his theocratic position. Certainly, the argument for religious security under political domination is explicit in his speech. After making the curious statement that "God, when He had gone round the nations with his domain, is now settled in Italy . . . God is fled out of this sanctuary and stands on the side of those against whom you fight,"[30] he states, "Our forefathers who were far superior to them [the Romans] . . . did yet submit to the Romans, which they would not have suffered had they not known that God was with them."[31] This strongly suggests that the loss or serious diminution of political autonomy is acceptable as long as the religious modes of Jewish life are unimpaired. Josephus then proceeds to argue that again and again a strong Jewish faith obviated the necessity for political or military recourse in time of danger. When Abraham's wife Sarah was taken captive, when Israel was redeemed from Egyptian slavery, when the holy Ark was rescued by the Philistines, when Israel was miraculously rescued from the Assyrians, "it was God who then became our general, and accomplished these great things for our fathers, and this because they did not meddle with war and fighting, but committed it to him to judge concerning our affairs. . . . We can produce no example wherein our fathers got any success in war, or failed of success when without war they committed themselves to God."[32] By recourse to politics, the tragedy of the siege of Jerusalem was ultimately brought about. "Where did our servitude commence? Was it not derived from the seditions that were among our forefathers, when the madness of Aristobulus and Hyrcanus, and our mutual quarrels, brought Pompey upon this city and when God reduced those under subjection to the Romans who were unworthy of the liberty they had enjoyed?" He suggests that the Jews were never intended for military prowess but rather to obey Moses, "our legislator." By violating his laws, the essence of which is submission to God, the people has suffered disaster. Josephus draws his plea to a close with the assurance that surrender would at last gain the people the opportunity of pursuing their religion in peace under a benevolent occupying power. "[The Romans] neither aim to destroy this city nor to touch this sanctuary; nay, they will grant you besides, that your posterity shall be free, and your possessions secured to you, and will preserve your holy laws inviolate to you.[33] The essence of the people's life—the sanctuary and the holy laws—warrants the abandonment of political independence and subjection to any occupying power.

For Josephus, the guarantee of Roman protection (which he considers credible) is worth the price of national independence as long as the people's religion, centering around the Temple, can be preserved intact. He quickly shifts his illustrations of past divine intervention in behalf of a nonresistant Israel, and at the expense of its enemies, to an argument for surrender to the adversary, because God (and the adversary) will protect Israel even in defeat. Josephus' theocracy thus emerges out of a reconciliation with the realities of Jewish experience—the people was not intended nor does it have the resources to be warlike. By responding appropriately to this awareness, the people can attain to a higher kind of collective existence— a sacred community, unburdened by the customary impediments of nationhood, and sheltered by a benevolent power. His theocracy has its origins in his own personal confrontation with Rome and Jerusalem, and years later becomes refined in a utopiana, unhistorical perspective in "Against Apion." His address to the besieged people of Jerusalem and his apologetic work reflect not a historical but a theological attempt at interpreting Judaism. The illustrations he brings to bear sidestep numerous other, and more historically valid, examples of Jewish military exploits resulting in the people's rescue. Moreover, even from a theological perspective, he avoids the admonitions of the people by Moses himself to fight the wars of conquest and defense. Nor does Josephus explain, except by pointing to national sinfulness, how the God who fought for Israel in the past (despite its patent sinfulness, as attested by prophets and chronicles) has chosen to go over to the other side in the war against Rome. As has been suggested, Josephus swings between contradictory theologies, from a position where the people does not have to fight because God is its warrior, to a position where the people should not fight because what is most precious to it, the cult, can be preserved without war. A "pure" theocracy where God alone fights (and rules) is really not what Josephus has in mind in "Against Apion." There his delineation of a priestly government and "constitution" is precise. "The people's conduct was committed to them."

Josephus was the first to use the term "theocracy," and he applied it to Judaism. Even more, he advanced it as a preferred alternative to political independence, and with some specificity. "Against Apion" was written c. 94–100. It was composed about sixty years after Philo had been delegated to Rome by Alexandrian Jewry concerning attacks by Apion, a spokesman for an anti-Jewish Greek mission to Caius Caligula. Thus Josephus' "response" really addressed the Roman public of his own time, barely thirty years after the destruction of the Temple.

In "Against Apion," he writes:

> Some legislators have permitted their governments to be under monarchies, others put them under oligarchies, and others under a republican form; but our legislator (Moses) had no regard to any of these forms, but he ordained our government to be what, by a strained expression, may be termed a theocracy, by ascribing the authority and the power to God, and by persuading all the people to have a regard to him. The reason the constitution of this legislation was ever better directed to the utility of all than other legislations was, in this, that Moses did not make religion a part of virtue, but he saw and he ordained other virtues to be part of religion. . . . He left nothing of the very smallest consequences to be done at the pleasure and disposal of the person himself. . . . And where shall we find a better or more righteous constitution than ours, while this makes us esteem God to be the Governor of the Universe, and permits the priests in general to be the administrators of the principal affairs, and withal entrusts the government over the other priests to the chief high priest himself? . . . These men had the main care of the law and of the other parts of the people's conduct committed to them; for they were the priests who were ordained to be the inspectors of all, and the judges in doubtful cases, and the punishers of those that were condemned to suffer punishment. What form of government can be more holy than this? What more worthy kind of worship can be paid to God than we pay, where the entire body of the people are prepared for religion . . . where the whole polity is so ordered as if it were a certain religious solemnity? . . . Though the Lacedemonians seemed to observe their laws exactly while they enjoyed their liberty, yet when they underwent a change of their fortune, they forgot almost all those laws; while we, having been under ten thousand changes in our fortune . . . have never betrayed our laws under the most pressing distresses we have been in.[34]

In his digest of Jewish theocracy, Josephus presents the Torah as Israel's constitution, which Moses devised. While God is the source of authority and power, Moses is the founder of the unique system and even initiates the "regard" for God as well as "persuades" the people to be obedient. Thus, the dominant factor in the organization of the theocracy is Moses.

God is the integrating symbol, but the organizer is Moses and the priests are the managers. Despite their depolitization, the priests are "inspectors" and "punishers."

Nevertheless, such a theocracy is invoked from a remote past, not operative in the people's present. Moreover, Josephus' theocracy is an extended congregation whose central concerns are ecclesiastical and personal status matters, "What sorts of food they should abstain from . . . what communion they should have with others, what great diligence they should use in their occupations, what times of rest should be interposed, [that] we might be guilty of no sin . . . forbids women to cause abortion . . . if any one proceeds to such fornication or murder, he cannot be clean . . .[35] All this is reinforced by the reference to the "polity" as having "a certain religious solemnity." Josephus describes not only an idealized society but one that could have come about, if indeed it ever did, only when Jewish life had been stripped of most if not all of its political powers. The kind of society described by Josephus was, either unwillingly or else in the utopian vision of Josephus, confined (or self-limited) to an exclusively sacerdotal community whose political and civic needs are handled by the occupying authorities. This is the paradigm for the exilic community under optimum conditions. Nowhere in rabbinic literature is this separation between sacramental and political life presented so radically.

Josephus makes his position explicit when he compares the lapse by the Lacedemonians from their laws with the devotion of the Jews to their laws in their respective changes of fortune. Theocratic government, argues Josephus, enables the people to survive and to remain true to its laws despite its loss of power because it is not based on a system of power. God will abandon the people unless it confines itself to its cult. Because of such a system, the only hierarchy that need exist is the priesthood. Kings are not referred to, despite the fact that during the best days of the sacerdotal system, kings and priests coexisted. Nor are acholars mentioned, although Josephus does refer to judges. Josephus does nothing less than renounce not only kingship but any form of political system. For Josephus, the destruction of the Jewish state presented an opportunity for the emergence of the preferable theocracy that, we must however add, could not exist independent of a dominant and hostile foreign political system. The necessity of theocracy linked to subjugation is apparent. By Josephus' definition, the priesthood cannot coexist with Jewish power, only with foreign power. Yet it would be a mistake to identify Josephus with the school of thought initiated by Ezra, as Weiler suggests. As indicated above, Ezra and Nehemiah did not abjure kingship and the political system linked to it. They subdued it but still significantly to it. Unlike them, Josephus rejected it.

The theocracy of Josephus never existed, except as an ideal. Neither biblical thought nor rabbinic Judaism was prepared to dispense with some form of political system. The very "legislator," Moses, to whom Josephus defers, was credited with establishing a structure of laws and institutions that transcended a depoliticized theocratic system.

While Jews have considered Josephus a traitor, pre-Josephus Pharisaic elements were also vehemently opposed to the Maccabean state and accepted only the kingship of God. The fact that rabbinic Judaism, argues Weiler, demonstrated its compatibility with his views. He adds, "both [Josephus] and Yochanan ben Zakkai chose and knew what they were doing."[36] To equate these figures, however, fails to take into account the clearly political preferences as expressed in much of rabbinic literature, to which we have referred and with which we shall deal more extensively.

Josephus renounced further political aspirations for the Jewish people and, at the same time, raised the hope of the possible restoration of priestly rule. J. G. Mueller indicates, "Jewish theocracy can co-exist with all forms of Jewish government—judges, kings, priests, prophets, even *external* rule and also without any of these"[37] Yet it is vital to note that by stressing priestly rule, Josephus thereby did not renounce Jewish life in the land of Israel. Thus, whatever one may think about Josephus, he was not an advocate of Jewish exile as an intrinsic value. His theocracy did not contain external rule devoid of any form of internal human authority. What can be said is that by renouncing a political state as no longer realistic he embraced a rule of God that was just as unrealistic. Some kind of government was inescapable for the survival of a Jewish theocracy, and Josephus was willing to place its destiny in the hands of a Roman regime in the Jewish striving for moral and spiritual purity. This was in the spirit of those (invoked by Josephus) who, in the time of Pompey, preferred a Roman king granting religious freedom to a Jewish king treating the religion of the Jewish people lightly. Yet a distinction must be made between a short range strategy devised by Pharisaic leaders (whose objection was not to a Davidic king but to a non-Davidic king) and an absolute rejection of any kind of Jewish political system by Josephus.

Various rabbis who express some measure of belief in kingship reflect an essential difference between themselves and Josephus.

Josephus expressly rejected any form of rule except his own version of theocracy.

The silence of rabbinic Judaism concerning Josephus is not acquiescence to his theocracy. The rabbis could hardly have subscribed to a system in which the rabbinical role is so absolutely excluded as in Josephus' scheme. They could hardly have subscribed to the assertion, "where shall we find a better constitution than ours . . . [which] permits our priests to be the administrators of the principal affairs? . . . These men had the main care of the law and of the other parts of the people's conduct entrusted to them . . . who were ordained to be the inspectors of all, and the judges in doubtful cases, and the punishers."[38] This applies not only to priestly governance but to priestly interpretation of Torah, suggesting that Josephus was reaching back to a pristine period that preceded and precluded rabbinic authority.

Philo's is a different theocracy insofar as it is more political than Josephus'. A product of the Diaspora, he chafed under Rome's repression and wrote obliquely about wanting to see it defeated, and the Jewish people restored to its land. He recognized the validity of Jewish kingship, and in his ideal theocracy governed by the Torah as the constitution, the king and not the priest would be paramount. His theocracy was not a product of exile but of redemption, and indeed, the sacred polity he envisioned would govern the world.

Yet Philo's concept of kingship saturated with Pythagorean thought. Also intermingled with his politics is a large measure of messianic mysticism that interchangeably speaks of a "Man" and a divine being. The biblical theme of redemption informs his Jewish politics, and the models of Joseph and Moses serve to shape his perception of the king as sage and deliverer.

God is the ideal King but the title belongs also to a deeply devout sage. He is the people's father, caring for widows and orphans, but he also has a divine nature, meaning not that he is a deity but that he possesses more of "that divine part" than is given to others. Philo's conception of the king has its source in the Bible, Joseph being the archetype of the ideal king.[39] Of special significance is that in Philo's theocracy, kingship is "the prescribed form of government."

For Philo, the concept of a Jewish king as redeemer is cardinal. He conceived of a messianic king, an ideal warrior who would "subdue great and populous nations." Writing obscurely in order to avoid Roman wrath, he wrote in his allegory about Joseph as "the true herdsman who was to lay the axe at the very roots."[40] Elsewhere, in his *Life of Moses*, Philo defined him as a king and also endowed him with priestly qualities.[41] (The priestly element is Pythagorean rather than Jewish.) But his chief duty was to administer justice.[42]

In describing a future Golden Age, a promised Man would appear.[43] Jews in exile would be allowed to go free and gather from all over the earth in Palestine.[44]

Yet Philo's Jewish state was a "holy polity, the ecclesia or church of the Lord." By this he meant that Scripture "called them no longer multitude or nation or people but ecclesia," because they were united not only "in body but in mind." This ecclesia was established on earth because "God wished to send down from heaven to earth an image of His divine virtue . . ."[45] The Philonic state fused polity and ecclesia, with the Torah as its constitution and kings as its rulers.

Notes

1. Julius Welhausen, Prolegomenon to the *History of Israel*, Edinburgh, 1885, p. 411.
2. Ibid., p. 417.
3. Pedersen, *Israel, Its Life and Culture*, London, 1926, Vol. III–IV, p. 96.
4. Gerson Weiler, *Teokratiya Yehudit*, Tel Aviv, 1976, p. 304.
5. Ezra 7:26.
6. Weiler, pp. 113–114.
7. Nehemiah 2:3.
8. Weiler, pp. 115, 116.
9. Ibid., p. 118.
10. Ibid., p. 122.
11. Ibid., p. 124.
12. Ibid., p. 125.
13. Welhausen, pp. 420–422.
14. Robert Pfeiffer, *Introduction to the Old Testament*, New York, 1941, p. 190.
15. Ezekiel Kaufman, *Toldot Ha-Emunah ha-Yisreelit*, Vol. 3, p. 708.
16. Pfeiffer, p. 191.
17. Kaufman, Vol. 3, p. 688.
18. Ibid., Vol. 1, p. 694.
19. Ibid., Vol. 3, p. 699.
20. Ibid., p. 701.
21. Ibid., p. 707.
22. Ibid., p. 686.

23. Ibid.
24. Ibid., p. 698.
25. Ibid., p. 707–708.
26. Ezekiel 45:8–9.
27. Ezekiel 7:27, 12:12, 19:1, 21:17, 22:6, 7.
28. Ezekiel 45:7–10.
29. Ezekiel 37:25ff.
30. Josephus, *Wars*, Book V, Chapter 9:2.
31. Ibid.
32. Ibid.
33. Ibid.
34. *Life and Work of Josephus*, Whiston translation, Philadelphia, 1957, pp. 891–895.
35. Ibid., 891, 893.
36. Weiler, *Teokratiya Yehudit*, p. 32.
37. Joseph Mueller, *Des Flavius Joseph Schrift gegen den Apion*, Basel, 1877, pp. 296, 297.
38. Josephus, "Against Apion," 2:21.
39. Erwin Goodenough, *The Politics of Philo Judaeus*, New Haven, 1938, p. 111.
40. Ibid., p. 115.
41. Ibid., p. 97.
42. Harry Wolfson, *Philo*, Cambridge, 1947, Vol. II, p. 336.
43. Ibid., p. 115.
44. Ibid., p. 117.
45. Ibid., p. 395.

IV

Shiloh and the Awaited One

By contrast with Josephus, a countercurrent in Jewish thought sought to preserve the spirit if not the content of kingship in times of its disappearance from Jewish history. This ardently held belief found its support in the vaguely and variously interpreted passage in Jacob's blessing: "The scepter (*shevet*) shall not depart from Judah, nor a staff from between his feet, until Shiloh comes and the homage of peoples be his."[1] In contrast to Josephus, something more than pure theocracy has been deduced by subsequent commentators from this verse. That "more" is kingship, and if other components also intervene, the persistent commitment to kingship is particularly noteworthy. Thus, both pure theocracy and renewed kingship claimed biblical authority in the perceptions of Josephus and the king-affirmers.

Genesis 49:10 can be construed as the obverse side of Deuteronomy 17:14. The latter presumably legislated rulership. The former foresees it, and in the light of commentaries, defines its future manifestation. The latter is legalistic and its implications are debated in rabbinic literature in that context. The Shiloh passage is theological-historical, and the literature searches out its meaning in that obscure context. There is another set of factors. The legal issue over rulership is discussed as a component of the internal life of the Jewish world. The Shiloh issue, however, reflects not only internal questions but also a confrontation with Christian theology and with Christendom. In that sector of Jewish life that lived under Christian rule, the implications of the Shiloh passage impinged forcefully on Jewish existence. Christian claims had to be faced, and Jewish responses had to be forthcoming. Thus the rendition of "Shiloh" gave primacy to the conflicting claims of Judaism and Christianity and transferred the legal question of Deuteronomy to an urgent issue of immediate confrontation with Christianity and the compelling future expectations of Israel.

The earliest attempt to identify the "Shiloh" passage is related to kingship in Ezekiel 21:30–32. "And to you, O dishonored wicked prince of Israel, whose day has come—the time set for your punishment—thus says the Lord God: Remove the turban and lift off the crown. . . . It shall be no more until he comes to whom it rightfully belongs (*ad bo asher lo hamishpat*) and I will give it to him." Ezekiel speaks of King Joachim, one of the last monarchs of Judah, or perhaps of Zedekiah. He predicts the king's downfall due to his evil reign, just as he denounces other rapacious kings of the people. Yet he predicts the coming of a future successor who will reassume the monarchy. He fully expects the restoration of the monarchy (unlike perhaps Ezra), and employs a variant of the Genesis statement as the basis for his prophecy.

The speculation around the Shiloh passage took on more urgent meaning because it became a basis for Christian messianic speculation. Thus Jerome (340–420) concluded that Ezekiel's reference to the turban and crown applied to the emblems of the high priest and the king whose offices would cease until the advent of the Christ to whom these symbols belong, as stated in Jacob's blessing, "till he come to whom the kingdom belongs." Salvagus Porchetus (beginning of fourteenth century), in his "Victoria adversus impios Hebraeos," agrees that the reference to Shiloh applies to the Christian messiah. Martin Luther, in "Von den Juden und iren Lügen," agrees and dismisses the notion that Ezekiel refers to a future Jewish king, since the Jewish kingdom had been destroyed.

Jewish thought was thus confronted both by the problem of the destiny and identity of the people and by the challenge of Christianity, which rejected such a future in its claim of the transference of rulership from Israel to Christendom. In fact, even before the Christian challenge, Judaism was confronted from within by Josephus who wrote,

> What elevated them the most in undertaking this war [against Rome] was an ambiguous oracle that was found in their sacred writings, how, "about that time, one from their country should become governor of the habitable earth." The Jews took this prediction to belong to themselves in particular, and many of their wise men were thereby deceived. . . . Now this oracle certainly denoted the government of Vespasian, who was appointed emperor of Judea. . . . But these men interpreted some

> of these signals according to their own pleasure . . . until their madness was demonstrated, both by the taking of their city and their own destruction.[2]

This statement was taken over by the Roman Tacitus: "Most [Jews] were convinced . . . that one out of Judea would take over the rulership. This oracle predicted Vespasian and Titus but the people . . . could not be drawn to the truth."[3] Seutonius makes a similar statement.[4] From these we learn how Josephus' rendition of the "ambiguous oracle," distorted as it is and torn out of its Genesis 49 context, penetrated Roman belief. At the very time when Josephus was proclaiming the principle of priestly theocracy as the authentic expression of the Jewish people's life, he (or someone else) was acknowledging that "the Jews" and "many of their wise men" were impelled by a different idea. At the very least, this passage, whether it came from Josephus or not, indicates that the idea of national redemption remained firmly rooted as a biblically validated principle, among both the people and many of their leaders.

A major departure from the rendition of *shevet* as king comes in the application of the term to the newly created institution of the exilarchs. It came to be accepted that authority over the people in the Babylonian dispersion had been transferred to the exilarch. This transference kept alive both the memory and the authority of the kingship, at least partially. In pseudo-Jonathan (c. 780), the following passage occurs: "Rabbi [Yehudah ha-nasi] once asked Rabbi Chiya whether he would offer the sacrifice prescribed for the prince. R. Chiya replied, 'Your rival (the Exilarch Huna I, 150–190) is enthroned in Babylon.' " The patriarch replied, "But the kings of Israel and the kings of the house of David offered it, too, each group independently of one another." R. Chiya responded, "They were independent of one another, but we are subject to them," (i.e. to the princes of Babylon).[5] This exchange derives from B. Sanhedrin 5a, which states "The scepter. . . . These are the exilarchs in Babylon, and lawgiver . . . these are the descendants of Hillel who proclaim the law." Maimonides comments, "The Babylonian exilarchs take the place of a king; they may govern and sit in judgment over Israel anywhere . . . as it is written, the scepter shall not depart from Judah" [who are members of the tribe of Judah].[6]

It would at first appear that these passages reflect a final transition in Jewish thought in which the kingship would be sublimated into other categories—exilarchs and teachers. To be sure, exilarchs did exert a kind of royal authority that could, in a limited context, be viewed as a continuation of kingship, especially since exilarchs claimed direct descent from David. Ibn Ezra, commenting on Zechariah 12:7, states, "Until this day, the house of David is in Baghdad and they are the exilarchs. They are a large and great family and they possess a genealogical book." Benjamin of Tudela wrote, "In Baghdad lives Daniel ben Chasdai, called Rosh Galut, and they have a genealogical document [going back] to King David.[7] But given this assumption, rabbinic sources do not abrogate hope in a future political restoration in the land of Israel. The exilarchs were caretakers of power, pending the return of authentic kingship. The exilic "scepter" is to be held until Shiloh comes. Genesis Rabbah renders "Shiloh" as "he to whom kingship belongs." Some commentators were less sanguine about the royal role of exilarchs. Rashi recognizes their dependency despite their descent from David. Nachmanides, noting God's displeasure over Saul's kingship, stresses that while authority will come out of Judah, it will not be from kings. Overwhelmingly, however, rabbinic opinion defines "the scepter" as a (caretaker) exilarch, a king of undefined role, or as Messiah (undifferentiated from the king, and frequently referred to as "King-Messiah"). "Shiloh" is overwhelmingly defined as "Messiah" or more specifically as "King-Messiah."

Monarchy, which is identified with messiahship, bears strong political characteristics. Thus pseudo-Jonathan, which acknowledges the authority of the exilarch, makes the following comment: "Kings and rulers will not cease from the house of Judah, nor those knowing Scripture and teachers of the law. From his descendants—until the time when King Messiah, the youngest of his sons, comes." Aggadat Bereshit (thirteenth century) is most explicit in identifying *shevet* as the original kingdom of Judah, "lawmaker" as sovereignty, and "Shiloh" as the time when the kingship of David is restored, after Ezekiel 37:25, "They shall dwell in the land . . . forever . . . and David My servant shall be their prince forever."[8]

Targum Yerushalmi (eighth century) states, "Until the time when the messiah comes who has the rulership and to him all the governments of the world will be subject." Tanchuma (ninth century) states, "The scepter designates king messiah and the throne of his kingdom," after Psalm 45:7, "Your throne is everlasting, and a scepter of equity is your scepter." Genesis Rabbah (as does Moshe ha-darshan) interprets "scepter" as Messiah, son of David who will rule, after Psalm 2:9, "with an iron rod." But Midrash Ha-Gadol (thirteenth century) indicates that "scepter" is the ruler, king of Judah, and "Shiloh" is the Messiah. Targum Onkelos (published 1482) renders the passage, "until the Messiah comes to whom kingshp belongs and nations will heed him."

While for many the Jewish Messiah appears to act within history, he does so not on his own initiative, but God's. There are differing opinions as to whether supernatural events will accompany his advent (Abravanel) or whether he will govern without recourse to divine, wondrous events (Maimonides). But whatever the identity of the Messiah and his role, he supersedes the exilarchs who may enjoy kingly status but only limited autonomy. In addition, the only true king waits to be disclosed to Israel. Although a flesh and blood being, he rises to a special character, eminence, and power beyond comparison with former kings. Thus, both the natures of the contemporary "kings" (the exilarchs) and the future king (Messiah) are altered. The former are limited. The latter is expanded so that in his end-of-days role he acts within a universal setting, and even in his historic role he assumes the role of a super-king. Thus *shevet* becomes subordinate to "Shiloh." "Shiloh" relinquishes none of the political attributes normally ascribed to the king. There occurs a fusion of the political and the sacred. The king and the Messiah become one. The ambiguity induced by Deuteronomy 17:14ff. and the prophecy of Genesis 49:10 become transmuted from a problematic commandment to a central principle.

In *ha-melech ha-mashiach* (King-Messiah), each component becomes linked to the other. Even more, the term expresses belief that the Messiah is a flesh and blood king, a view that differs from other, supernatural perceptions of the Messiah. Thus, "whoever omits mentioning . . . the kingdom of the house of David referring to the 'throne' of David (in the fourteenth prayer in the Amidah) has not performed his duty."[9] Solomon Schechter, quoting from a text of the Amidah, found in a genizah, quotes, "Have mercy on the *kingdom* of the house of David, Your righteous *messiah*."[10] So, too, does the following passage ascribed to Yochanan ben Zakkai link the king to the Messiah: "Make ready a throne for Hezekiah, King of Judah, who is coming."[11]

The confrontation with Christianity, which proclaimed the "Shiloh" passage as proof of its messianic-kingly claim, prompted Jewish thought to defend its own position with special zeal. Sovereignty would yet return to Israel. The king/King-Messiah would reign. According to Christian doctrine, the rule departed from Judah when Jesus appeared. Yet, argues Ibn Ezra (1092–1167), a reference to Judah's loss of power could hardly be appropriate in a blessing by Jacob that had just bestowed power on Judah. The term *"ad"* in the Hebrew text does not suggest temporary loss but rather progressive possession. Those who see in the passage a forecast of the loss of ruling power disregard the state of mind of he who bestows the blessing.

Joseph Kimchi of Narbonne (1100–1175) takes a historical approach. Using the Christian argument that Jesus will inherit the scepter from the line of David, he points out that in fact the non-Davidic Hasmoneans and Herodians took over long before Jesus. The second Temple stood for 420 years[12] and continued beyond Jesus. How then can it be said that the scepter will not depart from Judah until Jesus comes?[13]

Moshe ben Shlomo of Salerno (c. 1240), who debated with Nicolo de Paglia of Giovenazza (1197–1265), offers the following refutations to Christian claims: Jesus was never king in the land; the argument for Jesus' supernatural birth invalidates the claim of descent from Judah; Jeremiah (presumably speaking of the Messiah) says, "in his days Judah will have rescue and Israel will live in peace." But ever since Jesus, Jewish lives are more disturbed than ever.

In his disputation with Pablo Christiani in Barcelona in 1236, Moshe ben Nachman (Nachmanides) (1194–1268) denied that the "scepter" refers to kingship, but rather to the exilarchs who had lived in Babylon for generations after Jesus. Thus, the scepter did not pass to him but to them.'[14] Elsewhere a different strategy is employed,[15] asserting that even though kingship has been temporarily lost in Israel, it will be restored, since David himself predicted it: "The God of Israel has chosen me . . . that I should be king over Israel forever."[16] As for the Hasmoneans, they were usurpers and consequently became subservient to their slaves.[17] No, says Nachmanides, the scepter has not been taken away but has only been sequestered, as during the time of the Babylonian exile.

The Shiloh trail in Jewish thought kept alive not only the belief in the legitimacy of kingship, not only its temporary transference to exilarchy (however dependent on external power), but most of all in its future restoration. This belief, even in its confined form of exilarchic power, was to burst out of its theological and time-bound restraints. By contrast, Josephus' doctrine stood discredited. Yet it, too, a deformed derivative of Ezra's tactic, was to be transmuted into the thoroughly theocratic thesis of anti-Zionist orthodoxy and the moderating religious factors seeking to contain uninhibited nationalism.

Notes

1. Genesis 49:10.
2. Josephus, *Wars*, Book VI, 5,4.
3. Tacitus, *Historiae*, Vol. 13.
4. Suetonius, *Vespasian*, Chapter IV.
5. B. Horayot 11b.
6. *Mishneh Torah, Hilchot Sanhedrin* IV, 13.
7. Benjamin of Tudela, *Masaot*, ed. London, 1841, I, p. 52.
8. *Beit Ha-midrash*, Vol. IV, p. 113.
9. Berachot 49a.
10. Joseph Klausner, *The Messianic Idea in Israel*, London, 1956, p. 460.
11. Berachot 28b.
12. B. Avoda Zara 9a.
13. Joseph Kimchi, *Sefer Ha-Brit*.
14. *Sefer Vikuach Ha-ramban im Frey Paoli, New York, 1975.*
15. Ernst Sellin, *Shiloh-Weissagung*, Leipzig, 1908, p. 172.
16. I. Chronicles 28:4.
17. B. Kiddushin 70b.

V

From Disgrace to Divine Selection (Kingship in Sifre and Talmud)

From the Deuteronomic law and the Samuel event emerges an extensive body of rabbinic literature ranging over the legal, theological, and moral convictions about the king in Jewish thought. While the Jewish literature predominates, Christian concern with the same area is significant. In 1674 Wilhelm Schickardi, a Christian scholar at Tübingen, composed "Ius Regium Hebraeorum," with an accompanying commentary by Jo. Benedictus Carpzov of Leipzig. The Hebrew *Mishpat Ha-Melech* in Hebrew characters over the Latin title, and the vast number of rabbinic references, reflect the direct derivation of the material from the Samuel and Deuteronomy.

Rabbinic tradition, as well as Deuteronomy 17:14, is deeply conflicted over the issue of kingship. While the biblical law seems clear enough, it reflects considerable internal ambiguity. While rabbinic law leans toward recognizing Jewish kingship as required, there are significant shadings of conviction concerning this. Even more, an important body of opinion is torn over this issue and even rejects kingship outright. Then there is the issue of the role of the king—what are the limits of his authority; what degree of autonomy, if any, can he exercise? We confine ourselves to the theoretical and legal aspects of the problem, not to the historical fact that in biblical times Jewish kings functioned in more authoritarian and political fashion than the law may either have allowed or contemplated. Postbiblical Jewish thought could only approach the issue theoretically, but this was often done against the background of history, or else of eschatological speculation. There were occasional allusions to kings of Israel, illustrating rabbinic misgivings and even censure. The speculation was rooted, especially in Maimonides, in a firm conviction about a

Jewish role in history through a flesh and blood King-Messiah whose claim to authenticity would rest on his political and military prowess.

The basis for the debate over kingship in Sanhedrin and in subsequent rabbinic literature is found in Sifre to Deuteronomy 17, Piska 156. The passage opens with the declaration, "Perform the mitzvah (of setting up a king) by whose *secharah* (anticipation) you will enter the land." This "mitzvah" is not attributed to anyone. Then follows, "Rabbi Nehorai says concerning 'you will say, I will set a king over myself,' this is shameful *(genai)* for Israel, since [I Samuel 8:7] says, 'They have not rejected you but Me from ruling over them.' " This clearly rejects the concept of kingship as divinely ordained. But Rabbi Judah (bar Ilai) says, "But is this not a mitzvah from the Torah to request a King, since it says, 'You shall surely set a King over you.'?" Then Judah is asked why they were punished in the days of Samuel. "Because they were premature" (in their request, since the time for a king was not yet ripe). But Nehorai retorts, "They requested a king only so they could be subjected idolatry, as it says (I Samuel 8:20) 'So that we can be like all the nations, so that our king might judge us and go forth before us and wage our wars.' " The inclusion of this verse suggests that by becoming like all the nations and submitting to kingship, the people become susceptible to idolatry. In Midrash Tannaim, referring to the opening phrase in Deuteronomy 17:14, "When you come into the land," we find that "Moses notifies Israel what they are destined to do." (That is, it is only a prediction that they will ask for a king, but not by divine command.) The editor adds, "It seems to me that this Tanna agrees with Rabbi Nehorai that there is no commandment to ask for a king."[1]

There follow limitations on the king, including the interpretation of "whom the Lord your God shall choose," meaning "by a prophet."

The phrase *som tasim alecha melech* is designated as a positive command (Piska 157). It is also explained, "so tht the fear of him (the king) shall be upon you." Nehorai's argument is thus dismissed and kingship becomes divinely required. Also, kingship is defined as an awesome institution, created primarily to control through fear.

Other restrictions (as listed in Sifre and drawn from Deuteronomy 17) disqualify women and foreigners as monarchs; prohibit the proliferation of horses with which the people could return to Egypt; prohibit the increase of wives who could corrupt the king, and the amassing of wealth for personal purposes. The king must also have a scroll of the Torah at hand at all times, even during battle, so that he might be always observant of the law.

Significant for our study is the emphasis and the reiteration that demanding a king is a mitzvah, although a new component informs this mitzvah: the people are meant to be intimidated by a king. Nevertheless, the tradition that the opinion of R. Judah supercedes that of Nehorai reinforces the dictum that kingship is a mitzvah. Equally significant, however, are the extensive expressions of support for Nehorai's position in subsequent rabbinic literature (although usually he is not named). These reject kingship outright or else reduce its role so that the mitzvah becomes virtually inoperative. No other biblical institution—the Temple, the cult, judges, biblical prophecy—is subject to such intensive debate and reduction through attenuation of its role, because all these, except kingship, are unequivocally ordained in the Torah.

Using both biblical texts (Samuel and Deuteronomy), B. Sanhedrin 20b becomes a central and primary source for rabbinic discussion about kingship. Rather than clear up the biblical ambiguity, it generates a debate: whether the powers of which I Samuel 8 warns are really operative.

The talmudic debate concerning kingship is conducted against the background of the Mishneh of Sanhedrin 20b. Its "cast of characters" increases from the two in Sifre to five. It declares that a *milchemet reshut* (an "optional" war of conquest that the Torah does not require) must be approved by a Sanhedrin of seventy-one men. This Mishneh contains two components. The first presents kingship as a given in the polity of Israel, and does not (yet) concern itself with the legitimacy of kingship. It deals with a new rabbinic issue—what is *mishpat ha-melech,* the role of the king? What are his powers? What are his powers? What are the limitations on him? The Mishneh leads into an ensuing discussion in the Gemara on the role of the king and also the legitimacy of kingship. Both the role and the question of legitimacy will intersect. What follows are, first, a sequential presentation and clarification of the discussion as set forth in Sanhedrin 20b; second, a summary of the various themes according to differing arguments; finally, an analysis of the arguments.

THE DISCUSSION.

What is the scope of *mishpat ha-melech,* and what is the basis of his legitimacy? The term *mishpat ha-melech* comes from I Samuel 8:11

where Samuel warns (or describes, according to various rabbinical views) the actions of a future king in relation to his subjects.

1. The discussion opens with the requirement that the king must get permission from the Sanhedrin for a war of conquest. This is an obvious restriction on royal power, reminding us of prior restrictions in Deuteronomy 17:15 ff. (Other restrictions will appear later.) The debate begins with an exposition of what the king may not do. It then advances to a discussion of what he *may* do. The operative term is *mutar*—it is permissible.
2. R. Judah, citing R. Shmuel, states that *mishpat ha-melech* is permissible *(mutar)*. He is already on record in Sifre and later in the discussion in the Gemara as stating that kingship is a mitzvah. On the strength of this, it may be assumed that *mishpat ha-melech* is normative, that is, that the litany in I Samuel 8 is not to be regarded as opposed to kingship, but is rather a legitimate function of kingship.
3. Rav says that *mishpat ha-melech* is invoked *only (ellah)* to intimidate the people (and thus keep them obedient.) Following directly upon Judah's statement, and also noting the term "only," this may be considered a caveat suggesting tht *mishpat ha-melech* is not generally applicable, but is primarily a deterrent to national disobedience. Nevertheless, silence about kingship itself reflects acceptance of Judah's position that it is a mitzvah.
4. Jose says, "all the (powers described in) *mishpat ha-melech* are permitted," in agreement with Judah.
5. (a) Judah asserts tht *mishpat ha-melech* was invoked to intimidate the people. Rav's previous words are repeated verbatim. Does this mean that Judah agrees with Rav? This possibility cannot be overlooked. Yet Judah then continues, (b) "By three commandments was Israel commanded [after they were to] enter the land—to select a king, to destroy Amalek, to build the Temple." This clear-cut statement, exactly as in Sifre, seems to stress both the divine mandate for kingship and the total applicability of *mishpat ha-melech*. Since Judah is emphatic in his rigorous reading of Deuteronomy 17:14, it is also possible that he stands by his view of the king's role as normative at all times, *as well as* intimidating. Thus, he may be saying, "Despite the more lenient view (represented later by Rav), be mindful that kingship is commanded and that Samuel's litany is not merely provisional."
6. Nehorai: *Mishpat ha-melech* was invoked (not as a normative

royal prerogative but as a penalty by Samuel when he submitted to the people) "because people's of the *taromet*, since they said in Deuteronomy, "I will place a King over me (like all the nations)." The word *taromet* means complaint. It also means "sedition" (see Berachot 12a). As used by Nehorai, who in Sifre referred to kingship as "disgraceful," the second rendition is appropriate, since I Samuel 8 refers to the people's demand as a rejection of God and also a lusting after foreign practices. Nehorai does not discuss whether *mishpat ha-melech* is permissible, and since he denies the legitimacy of kingship it may be assumed that the denial applies to *mishpat ha-melech* as well. It can only be a penalty.

Eliezer: The elders properly requested a king by saying, "Give us a king to govern us," but the rabble spoiled things by demanding a king "like all the nations." By asserting that the people spoiled matters, i.e., by their unworthy motives, Eliezer may have expressed doubt about the king's legitimacy, and perhaps for this reason . . .

7. Jose wraps up the discussion by repeating verbatim Judah's dictum, "Three commandments was Israel commanded etc."

OPPOSING THEMES

1. Status of kingship
   a. It is a mitzvah—Judah, Rav, Jose
   b. It is dubious—Eliezer
   c. It is not a mitzvah—Nehorai
2. *Mishpar ha-melech*
   a. It empowers the king and is probably a normative, ongoing practice—Judah, Jose
   b. It empowers the king, but only as an intimidation—Rav
   c. It is a punishment for sedition—Nehorai
3. "Like all the nations"
   Among those who defend kingship as a "mitzvah," no one defends the principle of "like all the nations," and as the debate expands beyond the Talmud, a number of kingship's defenders even find the principle repugnant.

I. THE SIGNIFICANCE OF *MUTAR* (PERMITTED).

Judah, Jose, and Rav declare that *mishpat ha-melech* (as defined in I Samuel 8) is *mutar*. Judah and Jose also declare kingship in Israel to be a mitzvah. They do not, however, define what mutar means. To understand the term we must bear in mind that the discussion in

Sanhedrin begins with a passage restricting the king. In contrast to this discussion, there ensure a debate on what is "permitted" *(mutar)*, that is, what the king is *empowered* to do. "Permitted" in this context means something stronger than approval; it signifies authorization. Were it to mean anything less, there would be no point in references by Judah and Rav to the king's intimidating power. It can be assumed to mean that the king is permitted by law to carry out the list of powers described by Samuel. This basis for this assumption derives from the fact that since kingship is (presumably) mandated, the essence of kingship is the exercise of power. But under what conditions is this power permissible? Under all conditions or only under extraordinary circumstances, as in time of war or national emergency? Is the king required or enabled to exercise power? (Not until Maimonides do we have explicit answers.) Nothing is said about this, so the problem is whether royal power is to be limited only to crisis conditions. Maimonides was one who believed that it was available to the king at all times, and he explicitly defined it as a normative day-to-day prerogative.[2]

In contrast, Rashi, citing views not his own, declares that the king's power is *lo mutar*, which we construe to mean that it is not permissible as a day-to-day prerogative but is limited to extraordinary conditions. With Maimonides explicitly defining royal power as not limited in time, we may now ask: Would Judah and Jose have declared that the king's power is *mutar* if they had been considering extraordinary conditions alone? Would they not have taken that as an accepted fact? Only by way of stressing those powers as constant did they lay down their definition. Judah not only said *mutar* but included by way of emphasis that "fear of the King *(eimah)*" shall be over the people (at all times). By contrast, Rav reflects a different perception of the role of the king. Rav employs the term *eimah* but not mutar by way of suggesting that the king's power should be kept in check, but that the threat of his exercising it would keep the people obedient.

II. SIGNIFICANCE OF EIMAH.

Rashi notes that R. Judah alludes to the I Samuel 8 incident and concludes that by reciting the litany of the king's severe powers, the prophet Samuel was trying to put the people in terror of the king, although these powers were the king's rightful prerogatives *(mutar lo)*. (Certainly, the author of I Samuel 8 would not agree with this last observation.) Also, Rav as well as Judah argue that *mishpat ha-melech* was proclaimed as a warning to the people, "so that the fear *(eimah)* of him might be over you." Concurring with this opinion are passages in Yevamot 45b and 102b; Ketubot 17a, Sotah 41b and Kidushin 32b. They reiterate that the authority or fear of the king shall be over the people. The last two references state, "The honor of the king is not subject to renunciation by the sovereign, for it is said *Som Tasim alecha melech,* teaching that his authority shall be over you." These passages affirm not only the legitimacy of the king but also his authority, as cited in Sanhedrin by Judah, Rav, and Jose. Rashi later interpolates, "But it is not permissible to do this," (to exercise repressive power). Thus, Judah interprets *mishpat ha-melech* as an inherent function of kingship, while Rav sees it as an intimidating deterrent, only a warning. Against what? Presumably the king's exercise of his intimidating power, even provisionally.

The term *eimah* means more than awe or reverence as some translations suggest. While Maimonides[3] stresses the importance of treating the king reverently, the basic intent is to call attention to *mishpat ha-melech* (I Samuel 8), which presents a frightening litany of the boundless and burdensome power of the king.[4] The mere list of royal powers suffices to keep the people in fear of the king, so that the powers need not be used.

In sharp contrast, as has been indicated, Nehorai does not deal with the issue of *mutar* or *eimah* altogether, because he considers kingship "shameful." While this latter reflection, found in Sifre, is absent from the Gemara, Nehorai's reference to the sedition of the people is amply clear.

Despite their differences, Judah and Jose agree that the reference to the king's authority is a warning. They disagree over the legitimacy of the authority. Jose and Judah assert the inherent right of the king to exercise his power. Nehorai does not. Wherein is the difference? In one case, the king may draw upon his legitimate, Torah-sanctioned authority. In the other, it can be assumed that the king will, only if provoked, act repressively. This is what Rashi cites when he refers to *mishpat ha-melech* not as a legal sanction (Maimonides) but as a prediction of things to come. It is a cause and effect situation, not necessarily a juridical one.

III. A CASE OF SEDITION.

The discussion around the people's demand for a king places kingship under a cloud because of the people's manner of intervention. R. Nehorai presents a conflicting opinion to Judah and Samuel, predicated primarily on the people's nature. The king's authority stems only indirectly from God, not from the merits of the situation, but because of the people's sinfulness. R. Nehorai declares that Deuteronomy 17:14 was a response only to the *taromet* (complaint) of the people, which is the context of Sifre means nothing less than an urge for idolatry, hence their sedition. R. Eliezer qualifies this by station that the elders (in I Samuel 8) had made a proper request, because they wanted a king to act as judge over them, but the rabble (*amei ha-aretz*) ruined things by requesting a king in order to be like all the nations, and for the king to lead them into battle.

What is the nature of the *taromet?* The first meaning is applicable to the people's blunt words to Samuel, "You have grown old."[5] The word suggests both incivility and sedition. But was this the sole cause for provoking not only Samuel but God? It is rather the peremptory (and in Samuel's eyes, seditious) request, "Appoint a king for us," that is, "We want to replace you and institute a new form of government." It is this that displeased Samuel the most and prompted God to state, "It is me that they have rejected." Thus, it is obvious not only that the people, not Samuel or God, initiate the demand for a King but also that they do it for the wrong reasons—"like the nations," and "worship other gods." Therefore, this *taromet* leads not to the emergence of a mitzvah but rather to a punishment. Had the people not wanted to be like all the nations, they would not have incurred royal repression.

R. Judah and R. Jose pronounced kingship a mitzvah, together with the destruction of Amalek and the building of the Temple. But Rashi's citation (reflecting early opinions), "It was revealed that they [the people] would be seditious by saying in the future, 'so that we might be like all the nations,' " raises the vexing question whether the mitzvah or the brusque demand by the people was primarily responsible for the selection of a king. It is noteworthy that Rashi ascribes the *taromet* to the people's desire for a military leader. He also comments, "som tasim was said not because it is a mitzvah, but in regard to their *taromet* it was apparent to Him that they would complain because of this and say, 'so that we too can be like all the nations.' " That is not to say, you are commanded, but rather, in the future you will say this.

Yet, both sides in the controversy have an important element in common—royal power is not inherently desirable but it is a necessary response to the people's character. It is not an intrinsic good, only an inevitable, possible deterrent. Even where *mishpat ha-melech* is accepted as divinely commanded, it is essentially a curb on unruly human impulses. Under the very best construction of the issue, the people's request for a king was rewarded with a series of threats. I Samuel 8 accurately portrays the emergency of kingship from the historical-social conditions and Samuel's response as a reluctant concession. Both sides in the talmudic debate accurately recognize its significance.

Nevertheless, R. Judah declares that kingship is one of the three mitzvot incumbent on Israel upon entering the land. Thus, we encounter disagreement, not consensus, neither clear commitment to theocracy as an alternative to kingship nor kingship as a dominant requisite.

IV. Ambiguity Concerning Kingship.

The merging of kingship, the building of the Temple, and destruction of Amalek raises special questions. The only place in the Torah where kingship is even putatively required is in Deuteronomy. But the destruction of Amalek and the building of the Temple are demanded unambiguously elsewhere, in Deuteronomy 25:19 and in Deuteronomy 12:5. The commandments in both cases are not susceptible to doubt or special interpretation. Only the establishment of the monarchy is ambiguous as a mitzvah, and it attains authenticity by linking it with the other two. In fact, the mitzvot about Amalek and the Temple become subject to the establishment of the monarchy upon which the other two actions come to depend.

Because of the objectionable motives of the people in selecting a king, restraints upon the king's authority were imposed, beginning both with Samuel's speech (an attempt at moral restraint) and the laws of Deuteronomy 17. Sanhedrin 21b adds restrictions to Deuteronomy by stressing the requirement of the Bet Din's consent for waging an optional war. It expands the biblical restrictions against multiplying wives and horses, in order to curb the King's impulses, drawing him from his national duties in one instance and distinguishing between personal restraint and military need in the other.

Or Chayim adds the following reasons for restraining the king. First, he may not wage war for personal aggrandizement and thus turn the people's heart from God. Second, he may fight only for Israel's honor so that God, indeed, can save Israel through its king whose designation by the Bet Din is unlike that by the nations. The return to Egypt (presumably under the leadership of the king) is proscribed so that

"Israel might not learn from their ways since the Egyptians are renowned and notorious for every abomination."[6]

Schickardi sums up the limitations of the Jewish king: "The status of a Jewish king was not that of an absolute monarch, but a mixture with aristocracy. Along with the king there was a great senate of seventy-one men without whose consent the king, in the gravest circumstances, could make no decisions."[7]

The differences over kingship, as reflected in rabbinic debate, are not resolved simply by the dictum in Sanhedrin that it is a mitzvah. That dictum is, first of all, that of two scholars (appearing also in Pesikta Rabbati 13). Second, and of greater significance, the king is so enveloped by restraints that his role becomes far less than absolute. These restraints are already evident in Deuteronomy. Rabbinic law denies the king a seat in the Sanhedrin, lest its members suppress their true opinions out of deference to him. Nor may he (or the High Priest) be members of the body for the intercalation of the year, since it would be in his interest to intercalate or not, since payment of his armed forces could be by the year or by the month.[8] The king's power is further limited by requiring the consent of a court of seventy-one for waging a war of aggression or to expand the nation's borders.[9]

Not only may a non-Davidic king not sit in judgment, but he may not be judged. As the discussion unfolds, it becomes evident that this is not a matter of immunity but of moral disqualification, and also that this does not apply to kings of the Davidic dynasty. This ruling is based in Josephus and in Sanhedrin.

When Herod, during the rule of Hyrcanus, was summoned before the Sanhedrin on charges of murder, King Hyrcanus, attempting to get him off, allowed him to appear in fine apparel and with an armed guard, intimidating the court. According to Josephus, a certain Sameas (probably Simeon ben Shatach of whom a similar account is given in Sanhedrin) arose and said, "I do not make this complaint against Herod himself . . . but against yourselves and your king who gave him a license to do so." Hyrcanus, seeing that Herod was going to be condemned, arranged to have the trial delayed and arranged for Herod to flee Jerusalem.[10]

Similarly, in Sanhedrin, in a murder involving a slave of King Jannai, who was summoned in accordance with Jewish law to testify concerning the slave, the king came but refused to testify, defying the request of Simeon ben Shetach.

> [Simeon] then turned first to the right and then to the left, but they all [for fear of the king] looked down at the ground. Then Simeon b. Shetach said to them: Are you wrapped in thoughts? Let the Master of thoughts [God] come and call you to account. Instantly, Gabriel came and smote them to the ground. It was there and then enacted: a King [not of the house of David] may neither judge nor be judged; testify, nor be testified against[11]

In this manner, the talmudic text retroactively disqualified the Maccabean dynasty and its successors who ruled the land of Israel for two centuries. It also ruled out the possibility of any king of Israel, except one from the house of David, enjoying the prerogatives of respected citizenship. By definition, anyone who could not conclusively prove Davidic descent would, by ineligibility to appear before a Jewish court of law, govern under a moral cloud.

All this was a speculative exercise lacking all but theoretical validity. As the condition of Jewish statelessness intensified, discourse about kingship lost all connection with prevailing reality. Weiler makes much of this fact and cites it to prove his thesis that rabbinic scholarship had lost touch with the realities of the Jewish past, that it had no awareness nor interest in political problems, and hence carried on its discussions in an unrealistic vacuum. He seems to disregard the rabbis' conviction in ultimate restoration for which Jewish law must be ready. While admittedly that law was not adequate to the demands that might be made upon it, this did not concern the rabbis as much as the premises that they sought to establish. Those premises were that kingship in Judaism, unlike among other nations, is by legal definition limited; that unlike in other places, kings are subservient to the Torah; that kingship is an inherently dangerous enterprise that demands constant vigilance and control.

The talmudic requirement that kings of the Davidic dynasty may both judge and be judged (must be subject to the courts) represents a limitation on royal power. They were unlike the kings of Israel "who were violent men and unsubmissive to the judges,"[12] and "who were arrogant."[13] Their refusal to recognize the Torah's authority disqualified them for human judgment. Unlike tyrants among other nations, the Davidic kings knew the Torah, submitted to it, and acted humbly.

In Deuteronomy Rabbah (Seder Reeh, Perasha 5), R. yirmiyahu differs over the requirement for judging a Davidic king, and comments on Psalm 17 ("a prayer of David"), "let my judgment come from before Your presence" (and not that of an earthly judge). The midrash states, concerning David himself, "no one may judge the king except God Himself." Here, David is disqualified (not exempt) from human judgment instead of being subject to it. Thus, the rationale for excluding even Israelite kings from judgment appears to apply even to David.

One critical issue remains unresolved, as indicated by Rashi's citation that royal confiscation is *eino mutar laasot* (is not permitted), suggesting that it is better not to exercise it, except in special circumstances. But this begs the question. What kind of power can a king wield if he cannot use it at will? The very declaration in Sanhedrin that the *mishpat ha-melech* is *mutar* could reflect at the very least a difference about its permissibility. This conjecture is validated by the surprising comment by R. Nehorai that the "mitzvah" of kingship derives from the people's *taromet*. Here is a mitzvah predicated not only on the basis that the request was seditious but that it derived from the demand of the people. There is only one related example in scripture, the demand for fashioning the golden calf, which of course was no mitzvah. The remark by Nehorai prompts a defensive response by Eliezer but his assertion of improper motivation by most of the people taints the "mitzvah" that is based on "like all the nations." Only the elders were properly motivated, but the masses had ulterior purposes. On the strength of this, a mitzvah was established. We must conclude that the internal dialectic of this text that is central to the rabbinic views of kingship reveals strong tension and conflict over the receptivity to kingship in Israel. At best it is reluctant, acknowledging an unprecedented, human, rather than divine origin, and predicated in large measure on unworthy motives. In addition, it reflects serious misgivings about acknowledging the moral legitimacy of what is elsewhere regarded as proper royal confiscatory rights.

A review of talmudic material demonstrates the ambivalence of rabbinic thought on this matter. Although it determines, arbitrarily and unconvincingly, that kingship is a mitzvah, it finds itself in conflict with a concept that smacks of *chukot ha-goyim* (practices of the heathens). For good or ill, or both, kingship as a historical reality in Judaism and as enshrined by the Davidic mystique was a given. Yet it presented serious historical and theological problems. It therefore became necessary to come to terms with the concept through compromise and restraint.

Some comment about Judah bar Ilai is in order because of his authoritative position on Jewish kingship as a mitzvah. We know little concerning Rabbi Judah's motivations or rationale for his position. In addition to the passage already cited we may refer to a few from the many hundreds of his comments in talmudic and midrashic literature that have a bearing on this issue:

a. Unlike in some wars from which bridegrooms as well as brides are exempt, "In a *milchemet chova* (a required war) all go forth, even a bridegroom from his chamber and a bride from her chamber."[14] The same citation adds, "that which is optional for the Rabbis is a mitzvah for R. Judah; what is a Mitzvah for the Rabbis is mandatory for Rabbi Judah."

b. "From the anointing oil that Moses made in the wilderness . . . were anointed high priests and kings."[15]

c. Referring to the law in Deuteronomy 17:17 against excessive wives, "they must not distract him."[16] "They must be worthy of him and be from a royal house."[17]

d. "Rabbi Bar Chanah says that Yochanan in the name of Judah bar Ilai says, Rome will be defeated by Persia (by the following reasoning): the first Temple was destroyed by the Chaldeans and they were defeated by the Persians; since the second Temple, built by the Persians was destroyed by the Romans, doesn't it then follow that the Romans will be defeated by the Persians?"[18]

e. In a gathering of Rabbi Judah, Rabbi Jose, and Shimon bar Yochai, Rabbi Judah said, "How excellent are the works of this (Roman) nation. They maintain market places, bridges and houses." Rabbi Jose was silent. Rabbi Shimon bar Yochai said, "Everything that they maintain is for themselves alone." (Another) Rabbi Judah, son of converts reported the conversation about which the authorities heard. They said, "Let Judah (bar Ilai) who praised (the government) be elevated (to high station); (to become rosh hamedabrim, chief spokesman, according to Rashi); let Jose who was silent be exiled to Sepphoris; let Shimon who criticized be executed."[19]

Passage "a" reflects a firm commitment to undeviating obedience to government, presumably the king, in time of war; "b" suggests Judah's belief in the Torah's commitment to monarchy in premonarchical times, thus supporting Deuteronomy 17:14. Together, these passages represent a predilection for kingship. But "e" is the most impressive, for two reasons. First, here is a clear predisposition to the allure of the Roman imperium. In a political discussion, Judah spoke admiringly of Rome and its administrative effectiveness. Obviously, this does not by itself identify him with a commitment to Jewish kingship. Yet it was Judah bar Ilai, the admirer of kingship and of Rome, who construed the passage "I will place over me a King *like all the nations*" to be a mitzvah.

The second point is intriguing. According to passage "e," it is Rome that elevates Judah bar Ilai to high station and, according to Rashi, to rosh hamedabrim, the first speaker at rabbinical assemblies. Thus, he is perceived as a Roman instrument, and yet he champions Jewish kingship. It is possibly with this latter title that he issues his pronouncement on kingship as a mitzvah. Whether that was indeed his title at the time of the pronouncement or whether that reference was a later addition, or whether the incident concerning Rome is itself a late account, it appears that Judah's approbation of Rome and his favorable construction of Deuteronomy 17:14 are related. What are we to make of his declaration about the Jewish king? Did he carry the day because he was Judah bar Ilai or because he had won Roman favor? Was he rosh hamedabrim because of his own great authority or because of Roman support? Is this compatible with Rome's objectives? More, was this compatible with the role of a Roman instrument? Did he nourish his own inner, Jewish agenda, based on the transitory nature of empire and his perception of the Torah's demand? There are no conclusive answers.

If "d" is correctly attributed to Judah bar Ilai, it presents not a condemnation of Rome but a realistic appraisal of the rise and decline of empires with Israel at the center of their rise and fall. Yet the passage does not suggest that national power per se will pass. Rome will descend, but while it endures, it achieves mightily. And, if indeed this is Judah's position, nations rise and fall, but the requirement of a Jewish king is constant. And the unspoken inference is that as before, the Temple would be rebuilt.

Notes

1. Midrash Tannaim, ed. Hoffman, Berlin, 1880.
2. *Hilchot Melachim* IV, especially latter part of paragraph 1.

3. Ibid., II:1.
4. Ibid., IV, especially paragraph 1.
5. Berachot 12a.
6. Wilhelmus Schickardi, *Ius Regium,* p. 196, 198.
7. Ibid., p. 9.
8. Sanhedrin 18b.
9. Sanhedrin 20b.
10. Josephus, *Antiquities,* Book XIV, Chapter 9:4.
11. Sanhedrin 19a, b.
12. *Hilchot Edut* XI:9.
13. *Hilchot Melachim* III:7.
14. Mishneh Sotah 8:4; Sifre Shoftim.
15. Sifra, Vayikra, 8.
16. Sanhedrin 21a.
17. Ibid., 19b.
18. Yoma 10a.
19. Shabbat 33b.

VI

"We do not want a King"—The Ruler in Midrash

Talmudic opinion supports the legal claims of Jewish kingship, but one aspect of midrashic literature is exceedingly harsh on it. We confine ourselves here as in our Talmud study, to the linkage to Deuteronomy 17:14ff.

Midrash Rabbah to Deuteronomy (Seder Shoftim) contains a bitter diatribe against kingship and rather than dwell on the mandatory nature of kingship, denounces the people for demanding a king. The proem begins with the halachah that kings may neither judge nor be judged. R. Yirmiyahu adds that this applies even to King David, who is to be judged only by God. This would appear to suggest that David had been too virtuous to be judged by flesh and blood, and we have noted that the kings of Israel were excluded from being judged only because of moral defects. Now David, the paragon of kingship in Judah, is excluded in the opinion of R. Yirmiyahu. Could this be by reason of moral defect? Two texts that follow would appear to suggest this, one of them explicitly. "God said to Israel, my children, I thought that you might be free of Kingship . . . Just as a wild ass that grows up in the wilderness does not experience fear of man, so I thought that the fear of Kingship would not be over you; but you did not seek it that way but 'snuff the wind in its eagerness,' and 'wind' (*ruach*) connotes Kingship." The attack continues. "You might think that I don't know that at the end you will desert me? I had already warned Moses and told him that ultimately they will seek a King of flesh and blood, and some of them will enthrone for themselves a foreign King." How do we know this? From what we read: "You shall say, I will set over myself a King. To this Job[1] refers when he says: 'that the godless man reign not, that there be none to ensnare the people.' R. Yochanan says, 'If you see hypocrites and a tyrant leading a generation, it would be better for that generation to float in the air rather than have him.' " The Rabbis say, "When Kings arose over Israel and began to enslave them, God said, 'Do you not desert me and seek Kings for yourselves (by saying) I will set a King over me? This is the significance of the verse [Psalm 146:3], 'Put not your trust in princes.' R. Simeon in the name of R. Joshua Levi says, 'Whoever trusts in God becomes worthy of being like Him . . . but he who trusts idolatry *(avodah zarah)* becomes obliged to be like it, as the verse says Psalm 115:8: those who make them [the idols] will become like them." The Rabbis say: "Whoever depends on flesh and blood departs, even the promise of reward departs . . . God says: 'Don't they know that flesh and blood are nothing, yet they set aside My glory and say, set a King over us. Why do you seek a King? By your lives, at the end you will feel what is destined to befall you under your King" . . . [However], concerning 'You shall say, I will set a King over me,' R. Judah b. Ilai says, 'Israel was commanded concerning three things upon entering the land, to wipe out the memory of Amalek, to select a King and to build the Temple. They designated a King and wiped out the memory of Amalek. Why did they not build the Temple (sooner)? Because their sons were informers.' "

We note that this midrashic passage closely relates Jewish kingship to idolatry. Also, the reference to "trust in princes" applies specifically to Jewish princes. R. Judah b. Ilai is cited, presumably, to modify the preceding diatribes, and to suggest that, after all, kingship is a mitzvah. The Judah b. Ilai passage could also be a later interpolation. But more significant, while the midrashic passage cites Judah, its virulent antimonarchic passages are dominant, as the attack continues.

The same midrash, rejects kingship outright and specifically refers to David as morally unworthy. Concerning "I will place over myself a king", the Rabbis state that God said, you sought kings in this world and the kings rose up and cast you down by the sword. Saul cast them down at Mount Gilboa . . . David brought on a plague . . . Ahab was [responsible for] restraining the rain . . . Zedekiah destroyed the Temple. When they saw what happened at the hands of the kings, they all began to scream "We do not want a human King, we want our First King." God responded, "by your lives, this (retribution) is what I will do." In this especially radical passage, even David is held accountable for the people's downfall. The usually careful distinction between other kings and the house of David, and even the unique position of David as the consummate king, are obliterated. By its very nature kingship, even that of David, is evil, bringing on national disaster. Most radical of all (one could almost say heretical), is the disavowal by the people themselves of the biblical command to demand a king.

These are clearly antimonarchical, even to the extent of speaking sardonically of the "I will set up a king" passage. The attempt to put a positive face on it toward the end of the first pericope does not mitigate the powerful negative tone that repeatedly cites Deuteronomy 17:14 in a derisive fashion. The elusive aspect in the theocratic stress is whether its advocates believed that government must be directly under divine control in some supernatural manner, or whether an earthly representative of God could reign under divine guidance as prescribed by the Torah. The text does not specify, but its antipathy to kingship is clear. From the perception of the midrashic material we have examined, there appears to be a radical rejection of kingship altogether, as illustrated by the repeated ironical references to the "mitzvah" of kingship.

The entire passage is irrevocably opposed to kingship, except for the statement by Judah bar Ilai which could serve as an apologetic reminder that kingship does have redeeming value and is required. But the rest is "anarchistic," stressing even the absence of government rather than the tyranny of a Jewish monarch. Likewise, kingship is related to idolatry, since the reference to idolatry is not only made in the context of the discussion on kingship, but immediately follows the reference, "Put not your trust in princes." The intensity of this passage is perhaps the strongest indication that, if kingship were indeed a mitzvah, it would not have been so furiously attacked. A question occurs: does the attack refer only to non-Davidic kings, to whom the people were subject in the latter part of Israel's independence? If so, then the attack could have been more explicit, ruling out the line of David. But instead, the attack sounds like a litany with its mocking, repeated references to *"asimah alay melech."* Above all else, a specific condemnatory attack on David himself convincingly categorizes *all* forms of Jewish kingship.

Does the passage present any alternatives to kingship? Is it, as Weiler attempts to demonstrate with all rabbinic literature, concerned with establishing theocratic government in place of monarchy? There is no indication as to how the rejectionist Rabbis expected the day-today challenges to their people to be met. Did they count on divine intervention in time of stress? Or did they more pragmatically divest their leadership of such responsibilities and assign those responsibilities to foreign rule under whose dominion they were content to live as long as their religious existence was not infringed upon, (thus invoking the plea of Josephus)? Is it, perhaps, an expression of rage against a discredited institution?

Against what historical background does this passage occur? It is difficult to date it accurately, but its protagonists could be Tannaim of the early post-Bar Kochba period, reacting to the disastrous consequences of an attempt at reconstituting the Jewish commonwealth. This may be confirmed by our knowledge that Judah bar Ilai lived during that period. Complicating the problem, we have thus far found not merely some clear-cut rabbinic predilection for divine rule (either in place of monarchy or as a corrective to it), but a conflict within rabbinic Judaism over the role of kingship.

We note the controversy between Akiba and some of his colleagues over the messianic authenticity of Bar Kochba, who may have been regarded as a king. Akiba saw Bar Kochba as a restorer of the people's national fortunes. His conception of the Messiah as national deliverer was compatible with that aspect of Jewish thought that saw the Messiah in strictly historical and human terms, as Maimonides would later define him.

R. Yochanan ben Torta's response to Akiba, that grass would grow from his cheeks before the Messiah would come, reflected the depth of rejection of an imminent national deliverer.[2]

Midrash Pitron Torah,[3] commenting on the passage, "A king was in Jeshurun," states, "God did not require them to have kings, officials and leaders, because His Shechina (presence) was in their midst, aiding them in all matters."

Nevertheless, other midrashic material strongly affirms kingship, especially that of the Davidic line. "R. Azariah, quoting R. Judah bar Simeon says (referring to Sheva ben Bichri's insult to David), whoever defies the King is as though he defied a scholar. . . . R. Yudan says . . . as though he defied the divine Presence. . . . R. Simeon said, whoever rebels against the house of David deserves to die."[4]

Commenting on "Shiloh" (Genesis 49:10), one passage says, "This is *melech ha-mashiach* (the King-Messiah)," while another adds, "This is he to whom kingship belongs . . . who will set on edge the teeth of all the nations."[5]

The difficulty in dating the material before us obstructs an effort to relate the relevant passages to historical events. Midrashic material, like that which preceded, is by no means monolithic on this subject. It can also be said that until we encounter Abravanel, the antikingship material in the Midrash is the most radical. Its retention testifies to the existence of this rejectionist position and, even more, its claim on Jewish thought of its time.

An intriguing hypothesis is proposed by Professor Lou Silberman, who suggests that such references to kings may have been veiled attacks on the reigning patriarchs in Palestine who ruled autocratically and considered themselves in the Davidic lineage. Their special relationship with the Roman government, their exemption from taxes and their lording it over the people could have prompted some preachers, not in the conventional strata, to lash out at these "kings." Yet even if the allusion were to the patriarchs, the references to the ancient kings in the harshest terms could not be confined only to contemporaries. If we call a modern tyrant "a Nero," we pass judgment not only on the tyrant but on Nero.

The primary passages we have cited are, of course, extreme examples negating Jewish kingship. Most of all, they illustrate the persistence of the rejectionist impulse in rabbinic thought. Even more, they present intense opposition to the concept of kingship as a mitzvah.

Just as rabbinic Judaism was not monolithic in its attitudes toward Jewish kingship, it also held diversified positions toward non-Jewish rule. The affirmation of foreign rule sometimes verged on the excessive. Defiance of a foreign king matched in principle the defiance of Jewish kingship. Affirmation was predicated on the following premises: First, there was a natural order that required government as the regulator of human destructive impulses. This premise was defined by Hanina, the perfect of the priesthood, in the classical declaration: "Pray for the welfare of the government. If it were not for the fear of it, men would swallow one another alive." This might have been said when the revolt against Rome was in its incipient stages. Later, a scholar said, "As with fish of the sea, the bigger swallowing the other, so with mankind; if not for the fear of government everyone greater than his fellow would swallow him up[6]. These passages reflect the influence of Jeremiah 29:7, "Seek the welfare of the city where I have caused you to be carried away captive, and pray to the Lord for it; for in its welfare shall you have welfare." These passages invoke the principle that government is indispensable to an orderly society and that rather than leading to cooperation and peace, anarchy leads to destruction. Government is necessary even when it is not Jewish, both for the preservation of the social order and for the kind of structure with which the requirements of the Torah can be observed.

Not only is government necessary, it is divinely ordained. Kings govern by divine designation.[7] (Berachot 58a). At times, extreme justification is offered for foreign rule. After the uprising against Rome had been crushed, R. Simeon ben Lakish went so far as to suggest that Rome served a beneficial purpose. " 'Behold it was very good.' This is the earthly kingdom. Is then the earthly kingdom very good? Yes, for it exacts justice of mankind, as it is said, 'I made the earth and created man [Adam] upon it.' "[8] The author changed the vowels in "Adam" to read "Edom" (a synonym for Rome), thus rendering, I created Rome over it." Another scholar prayed, "Blessed is the All-Merciful who has invested you (Rome) with dominion."[9]

The second premise was that of *"dina d'malkhuta dina"* (the law of the kingdom is the law, for Jews). While this formula has been assumed to be binding and immutable, it was challenged by some rabbinic authorities. It certainly did not apply to instances of coercion to commit idolatry or incest or murder, although there were exceptions in the first two offenses where Jewish law provided certain loopholes. But generally, Jews were counselled to defy edicts forcing them to idolatry. Thus, "[Meshach, Shadrach and Abednigo] said to King Nebuchadnezaar, 'If you impose a town security tax or poll tax or crop tax on us, we will call you king, but if you impose idolatry on us, you and a dog are the same' "[10]

Dina d'malkhuta would appear to support the idea that foreign domination is not only conceptually but legally binding. Yet, in keeping with some of the more invidious judgments on foreign kings that we have cited, the principle of *dina d'malkhuta* argues that kings are principally civil authorities, not divine representatives. Stated differently, the king may be sent by God to protect or chastise Israel, and he may rule by divine consent, but the law that he administers is not sacred. Divine law has been conferred on Israel alone. Yet even under this limitation, the king's administration of law is not absolute. If it is applied unjustly, it ceases to be law and becomes its violation. Unjust taxation becomes extortion. Eventually, the principle of *dina d'malkhuta* is refined in order to substantiate the position that kings are principally civil authorities and not divine representatives. Their laws are to be obeyed, not because they represent God, but because the exigencies of life demand obedience. But even in purely secular matters like taxation, if the law is applied unconscionably, it ceases to be law and becomes extortion. (If a King breaches the accepted laws of the land in which he rules), "he is regarded as a robber who uses force . . . whose laws are not binding. Such a king and all his servants are deemed robbers in every respect."

Moses ben Nachman (Nachmanides 1195–1270), takes a similar position (although he is erroneously credited by Yitzhak Baer as the first to do so). In one instance, he wrote,

> It appears to me that when we say that "the law of the realm is law,[11] we mean the royal legislation in effect throughout the realm which the king or his royal predecessors have enacted and which are inscribed in the chronicles and legal codes of the kingdom; but any temporary measure or new law for which there is no precedent and which is instituted for the purpose of mulcting the people is but royal robbery, and we cannot regard that as law.[13]

Rabbi Solomon ben Abraham ibn Adret (c. 1233–1310) likewise opposed facile subservience to the *"dina d'malkhuta"* formula. In Perpignan, a father requested that his deceased daughter's dowry be returned to him in accordance with the king's law. The case was referred to Ibn Adret who ruled as follows:

> To adopt this as a practice simply because the Gentile law so provides, seems to me to be forbidden beyond doubt, for it means imitating the Gentiles. . . . Our people, which is the estate of the Lord, is prohibited by the Torah from showing a preference for the law of the Gentiles and their ordinances. What is more, it is forbidden to carry litigation into their courts even in matters in which their law is identical with the Jewish law. We here are, therefore, amazed how the seat of justice in your city, endowed as it is with learning and perspicacity, could be a party to actions which our Torah forbids.[13]

A similar position was taken by Meir of Rothenburg (1220–1293) who unequivocally rejected the absolute rule of the king as *"dina d'malkhuta."* It was limited only to his legitimate functions, which, when overreached, were not to be regarded as the law of the land. Obviously, the victims of tyranny had to submit, but it is significant that Meir drew a moral distinction between obedience to legitimate rule and to usurpation. In one responsum dealing with a case involving the king's expropriation of a Jew, he writes, "It is theft and violence, and has no relevance to the principle of *dina d'malkhuta*." In another responsum, he writes, "This is not *dina d'malkhuta* but theft by government, and it is no law."

The less than enthusiastic response to the principle of *dina d'malkhuta* suggests that rabbinic thought did not consider itself as bound to royal authority as might appear. Even in matters not affecting Jewish religious law, there were (in theory) clashes between rabbinic opinion and civil authority, thus reducing considerably the abstract principle of submission to foreign authority. All this supports the argument that for rabbinic Judaism, submission to the state was neither a permanent nor absolute condition for Jews. As long as external conditions required, the most satisfactory accommodation was worked out with the state, but this condition was never regarded as adequate for living a Torah existence, as Gershon Weiler contends, nor was the state's authority even in secular matters considered absolutely binding. Equally significant, as a responsum of Solomon ben Abraham ibn Adret indicates, even where Jewish law and the law of the land appear to be compatible, clashes nevertheless can take place. While in theory, a protected Jewish community can observe its laws in isolation under a benevolent king, the fact of its existence outside its own land is in itself a contradiction and a deterrent to a full religious life. The effort to demonstrate the possibility of such an arrangement is not supported and thus undermines any claim that rabbinic thought was so apolitical that it could readily make its peace with foreign rule.

A spirit of resistance, directed outwardly as well as inwardly, asserted itself from the beginning of Jewish subjugation. Simeon bar Yochai made an open and highly disparaging remark about Rome, was informed against, and had to go into hiding. He had said, "They build forums in order to house harlots, baths to refresh themselves in, bridges to collect tolls from them." Also, the Midrash to Psalm 14 asks, "Why is Edom called a villain?" "Because it has filled the world with villainy." And, "The kings of the heavens are like wild beasts trampling about in the woods in the middle of the night."

Notes

1. Job 34:30.
2. Echah Rabbah 2:2.

3. Midrash Pitron Torah, Jerusalem, 1978.
4. Bereshit Rabbah, Vayigash, Parasha 94.
5. Bereshit Rabbah, Vayechi, Parasha 98.
6. Avoda Zara 4a.
7. Berachot 58a.
8. Isaiah 45:12.
9. Berachot 58a.
10. Midrash to Psalm 28, Vilna, 1891.
11. *Hilchot Gezelot* V:13.
12. Baer, *A History of the Jews in Christian Spain*, Philadelphia, 1966, Vol. I, pp. 286–287.
13. Ibid.

VII

Awaited and Rejected—The King in Commentaries

A perusal of the commentaries on Deuteronomy 17:14ff and I Samuel 8 reveals conclusions different from those adduced from opposing ends of the spectrum by Gershom Weiler and Leo Strauss. Weiler, without citing the commentators, contends that rabbinic literature is monolithically opposed to kingship. Strauss asserts that except for Abravanel and Ibn Ezra the commentators were uniformly prokingship. An examination of the commentators will, however, reveal both variety and also great subtlety in treating with the problem, so that advocacy of monarchy is accompanied by restrictions and also theological misgivings. Because of the special significance of Abravanel's opinions on this matter, we shall deal with Abravanel later. Here we shall discuss medieval and modern commentaries under three rubrics.

I. KINGSHIP IS AN UNQUALIFIED MITZVAH.

This category cannot be sharply differentiated from others because even where kingship is categorically asserted, it is by its biblical definition limited, and in the spirit of a good part of prophetic literature, subject to sanctioned criticism. Even as a mitzvah, the selection of the king is not an absolute good.

In fact, this category falls into two distinct subdivisions. The first perceives kingship as an intrinsic positive value. While the second accepts it as a mitzvah, it nevertheless perceives it as an anticipatory concession to national weakness.

Nachmanides (1194–1276) states that "in the opinion of our rabbis,"[1] the verse, "You shall say, I will set a king over me," has the commanding force of "You shall surely say, I will set a king over me." He adds, "This is a positive commandment," referring to Maimonides.[2] "He has obligated us to say so (i.e., as the verse states, 'You shall say.') after conquering and settling (in the land). The expression is similar to [Deuteronomy 22:8]. "When you build a new house, you shall make a parapet for your roof . . . (required, not optional) . . ." The words, "You shall say" are included because the people are commanded to appear before the priests and judges and say, "It is our wish to set a King over us."[3] Nachmanides relates the request for a king to the fact that God makes the ultimate choice, through His prophets. God selects the kings of nations, and *"som tasim"* means that the choice, decreed from heaven, comes in the form of a response to a request, likewise divinely ordained. "Even the superintendent over a well is designated from heaven."[4] As Nachmanides indicates in the same explanation, "it is a positive commandment to say it *("asimah alai melech")*. Yet, as we will note, he contradicts himself.

However, while Nachmanides cites "the opinion of our Rabbis" and accedes to it, the only legal basis he has for considering kingship a commandment is the authority of Maimonides in *Sefer Ha-Mitzvot* and in *Hilchot Melachim Umilchamot*. Prior to Maimonides, only R. Judah had asserted the existence of this "mitzvah," and not without opposition. Maimonides codified that determination. In the same commentary to Deuteronomy 17:14, however, Nachmanides proceeds to qualify the nature of the mitzvah by adding that "it is my further opinion that this is one of his (Moses') allusions to future events . . . when the people [said] to Samuel 'Make us a King to judge us like all nations' (I Samuel 8:5) . . . and 'that we may also be like all the nations.' For what reason is there that the Torah should say [I will set a King over me] like all the nations . . . when it is not proper for Israel to learn their ways. . . . This is [rather] an allusion to what will be." Nachmanides' projection of the Deuteronomy passage into a futuristic event in Samuel's time poses a problem. How can he categorically identify that passage both as a command and also as a future event? In either case, he recognizes the difficulties he tries to extricate himself. If it is a command, then the wish to be "like all the nations" reduces the command to a sinful act. If it is a prediction of an inglorious event, it is not a command. Nachmanides thus accepts a halachic decision by Maimonides, and proceeds to circumvent it. As will be noted in a later category, this is done so extensively that the initial reference to kingship as mandatory is vitiated.

Kli Yakar (Ephraim Solomon ben Chayim of Luntshitz, 1550–1619) advances a similar argument against popular government. "There are those who say that this passage is not a commandment but rather a foretelling of future events." But, he says,

> it was God's will that the king should rule justly in order to impose his fear over all of them, as our Rabbis said, "Pray for the peace of the government, for without the fear thereof people would swallow each other alive." [Kingship was established] not for the purpose of [issuing] laws, since there were law courts in every city, but only for the purpose of maintaining government. . . . They [the rabble] [sinfully] said "Give *to* us a king," not "give *over* us a king," because they did not want his mastery; rather, they wanted him to be placed in their hands.[5]

Kli Yakar argues for an authoritarian kingship, as among other nations. He asserts that in Samuel's time Israel rejected this form of monarchy.

Although *Kli Yakar* draws a bleak conclusion from the Samuel incident, he concedes that the original divine intent was that the kings of Israel might rule their people in justice. A king was required so "that the awe of kingship might be over them . . . because after the inheritance of the land . . . everyone did what was right in his own eyes in the absence of a king. . . ." However, in Samuel's time, the people sought a king not to govern them but to control them. Therefore, their request was not in accord with the Torah's intent and in the end it became necessary for God to rule over them in wrath.

Kli Yakar adds a powerful psychological motive for the people's desire for a king: "I shall place a king over me so that his awe may be upon me . . . so that he might master me with a mighty hand like all the nations round about me, and that I may do as the most advanced among them who do not rebel against their kings and accept their authority."[6]

II. Kingship as Required, yet Problematic.

Or Ha-Chayim (Chayim Ibn Attar, 1696–1743) confronts the possible alternative that the selection of a king might be optional. Yet he concludes that the emphatic phrase, *"som tasim"* proves that it is a commandment by God to establish a King. He states that Jewish kings fight for the honor and the glory of Israel; they are God's chosen instruments to save Israel.

Malbim (Meir Leib ben Yechiel Michael, 1809–1879) *(Ha-Torah v'ha-mitzvah)* states, "Israel must perform this deed by all means." His commentary, mindful of the "when" and "if" controversy, amplifies: R. Judah says, "this is a command. I command you to say to the Prophet and the Sanhedrin, "I will set a king over me," and one does not construe *'v'amarta'* to mean 'if you should say.' They are commanded to set up a king and they are also commanded to say, 'I shall set up, *asimah.*' The reason they were punished in the days of Samuel is that . . . the command concerning the King is only that they should conduct themselves according to the way of the world and of nature by which they would need one man to lead them, to fight their wars and to govern them." Instead they wanted a king whom they could control.

Further stressing the mandatory character of kingship, Malbim declares that "they were not commanded concerning this until after [they were to gain] possession and settle [in the land].[7] The importance of this mitzvah is so great that the reward for it preceded the time requiring the mitzvah, and [its merit] helped them to come into the land. . . . The words, *som tasim* were repeated in order to teach that it is not [merely] optional to set up [a king] but required."

Still, the comment by Malbim reflects an inner ambiguity. Kingship is required, but only because the "miraculous condition" prevalent until Samuel's death came to an end. The "miraculous condition" precluded the need for kings. Should it return, kingship will again become unnecessary. Thus kings are not in themselves important to Israel, but are rather a necessary replacement for an ideal, lost condition.

It is apparent that even among the endorsements of kingship as mitzvah, there are instances where the mitzvah is not inherently desirable but chiefly a deterrent against rebelliousness toward God.

Baal Ha-Turim (Jacob ben Asher, 1270–1340) astutely renders "like all the nations around me" to refer to the institution of kingship in place of overlords among the Philistines. He strongly suggests that had kingship been a mitzvah, it would have been fulfilled upon the entry to the land. Instead, it was postponed until Samuel's time in imitation of the Philistines. Thus the institution of kings represents political, not religious, motivation; the will of men, not the will of God.

III. Reservations and Qualifications.

Moshe Chayim Alsheich (second half of sixteenth century) offers a curious justification for the mandatory character of Deuteronomy 17:14–15. "One way or another you will do this [establish kingship];

therefore it is good that My commandment should be fulfilled. . . . Therefore you shall . . . perform the mitzvah." This unusual concept of a mitzvah as a means of anticipating and validating a popular but unworthy impulse suggests that kingship, though commanded, reflects God's will less than the national desire to which God acquiesces. The people's sin is cancelled in advance. A more strained rationalization for mandatory kingship is hard to find.

In Mar'ot T'zvaot, Alsheich interprets the text concerning Samuel's corrupt sons, homiletically in order to prove that they were upright. "Their only sin was that they did not go from city to city" to sit in judgment as their father did. Therefore, the request by the people for a king was odious to Samuel because his sons were qualified to succeed him. Thus, there must be a better reason for the selection of a king before it is permitted.

Alsheich agrees with Abravanel, who denies that kingship is a mitavah, insisting that the text should be understood in the manner of the case of the beautiful captive (whom the warrior is *not* commanded to capture but to respect *if* he captures her). If the people had not demanded a king, there would have been no king. But "the scholars [not identified by Alsheich] do not agree and declare that setting up a king is one of the positive commandments. . . . The writings of the scholars teach that the monarchy is destined to be in Israel" (indicating that it *was* perceived in futuristic terms) "through God's choosing," and the Torah spoke truly, "kings shall issue from your loins." . . . If Israel had not requested a king, would they not have been obliged to set up a king? We know that there is free will and it is possible that they might not have asked. . . . The scholars, speaking of the seven sheep of Abraham, say that seven kings among other nations preceded the [first] king in Israel. [They say] it was a punishment that kings in Israel did not precede other kings. . . ." But Alsheich refutes this by saying that while God appoints rulers for other nations to look after them, yet "out of His love for us, he has provided directly for our needs *without* any ruler." "He has sustained us and brought us across the Jordan and has given us the lands of [other] nations."

But Israel refused to recognize God's providence and hankered after kings as among the nations. "What did God do? He prepared the cure before the sickness and commanded us, upon entering the land to set up a king even if Israel should not request one. . . . Although you see God's providence fighting and conquering without your having to fight . . . I, [God] know that you will not recognize My providence and you will say 'I will set a king over me like all the nations'; I therefore anticipate you and I say, 'You shall surely set a king over you. '. . . Even if you don't ask, you shall set a king over you . . . *God anticipated them before they could sin and say this evil thing* [Author's emphasis]. . . . [The people could then say) 'It is the holy King's [God's] command and we are not guilty for the request.' " Thus, despite the qualifications of Samuel's sons on one hand and God's kingly role on the other, Israel was commanded to request a king, thereby avoiding sinning because of such an otherwise heinous offense.

This convoluted thinking might be superficially perceived as a recognition of kingship as a mitzvah. Indeed, Strauss erroneously cites Alsheich as a salient example of those who so perceive it. Yet the purpose of the mitzvah as interpreted by Alsheich, is not to give Israel a king but to give Israel advance absolution for this sinful request and "evil thing."

Alsheich matches the labored explanation of Samuel Raphael Hirsch (1808–1888) that kingship is "not for conquering the land and not for safeguarding its possession, altogether not for developing forces to be used externally."[9] This interpretation is justified by the Deuteronomic verse that indicates that kingship is to come after the possession of the land. Even more, the Hirsch interpretation manifests the judgment that God alone wins victories for Israel. "For that, Israel required no king." Then what role was the king to perform? "A Head of State will shine forth as an example as the first faithful dutiful Jew . . . who will be filled with the spirit of your calling as Jews." Hirsch in effect annuls or circumvents the law by creating a "head of state" who is in no way a king. He compounds this invention (thoroughly bypassing Maimonides) by explaining "like all the nations" thus: all the nations subordinate themselves to "one unifying head of state," and so does Israel, except for one detail—other heads of state pursue "the greatest possible power" while Israel's head of state "will oppose with all the might of his word . . . everything which is in opposition of this spirit [and] . . . the internal protection of your national calling."[11]

The commentators follow Deuteronomy 17:14ff in establishing limits to the king's power. This is done especially in response to the reference, "like all the nations."

Nachmanides states explicitly that the selection of a king is a command syntactically similar to Deuteronomy 22:8, which reads, "When you build a house, you shall make a parapet," and stresses the constraints in the selection process. Citing Ibn Ezra, he states that this must be done by a prophet or by the divination of Urim and Tumin. God, not the people or any unauthorized individual, will choose. By a pun on *Som tasim,* he adds that whoever is ordained by (Shamayim) (Heaven) shall rule. Thus, if the people are commanded to request a king, this becomes a ritualistic formality predetermined by God's choice. If, as is more plausible (as in the Samuel event), the demand and its "like all the nations" motivation represents a retrograde act, it is offset by God's final decision. Nachmanides seems to lean toward the second alternative, since his preference is for the interpretation of Deuteronmy 17:14 as prophetic. In that context, it is "my opinion . . . that every ruler over people receives his position from God."

Nachmanides asserts that Israel must "not learn from them nor envy evil doers," and that this passage admonishes against the events concerning Samuel. He connects this reference to the following by stressing the word *rak* in Deuteronomy 17:16 thus: "Though you place a King over you, like all the nations, nevertheless *(rak)* he must be unlike their Kings, not increasing horses as they do, because their sole desire is to increase horses and horsemen." The restriction against returning to Egypt is construed in this spirit: "Because the Egyptians and the Canaanites are wicked and sinful against God . . . and God did not want them (the Israelites) to learn from their deeds." The restriction against superfluous horses distinguishes Israel from other nations because, says Nachmanides, "his trust must be in God." Here we have an allusion to the subordinance of the king to God who is the ultimate source of power in Israel.

Yet this is far from suggesting, as others may argue, that the king is expendable, since God fights Israel's battles. As will be seen, the king must wage Israel's battles even in situations where God is the true ruler. The intent of Nachmanides' statement is a warning against monarchical self-sufficiency and arrogance, not in behalf of military defenselessness. Confirming this is the comment by Malbim, who stresses that "horses which are required for the chariots of the king and his horsemen for the purpose of war are not forbidden." Likewise, the warning by Nachmanides against royal arrogance (Verse 20) is a reminder that greatness and loftiness are God's, intended to make the king aware of his limitations, not of his dispensability.

The commandment for the king to have a scroll of the Torah with him at all times (Deuteronomy 17:18, 19) also represents a restriction, "lest he sin and lord it over a people who are his brothers and the sons of kings."[12]

Abraham Ibn Ezra (1092–1167) puts the stress not on the desirability or undesirability of kingship but, rather, on the method of selection—not by the people but by a prophet or by the divination of a prophet or the Urim. He uses the term *reshut* (permission) in reference to *som tasim* to indicate that God consents to monarchy, but does not command it.

> The idea of the king being like the kings of other nations, retaining his kingship for himself and his dynasty is loathsome to God, but He commanded this when they stiffened their necks for the purpose of establishing a king for themselves. However, they may not choose any but a worthy person whom God would select so as not to cause Israel to violate its religion. He might not be a foreigner, even though such a person may be a worthy person and even though he may be a mighty man of war. When they (Israel) sinned in requesting a king who should rule (and establish a dynasty) like all the nations, (they were punished) . . . (as it is stated), "You shall cry out that day before your king whom you have chosen and God will not respond to you on that day"; and as it says, "I will give you a king by my wrath."

According to Chayim Ibn Attar, the selection of a king is based on two antithetical motives. The first is that, like among other nations, the king wages the nation's wars. This is "hateful to God" because among other nations, the king goes forth to battle for base purposes and not for good cause, thereby turning aside from God. The second motive is to establish the king as God's instrument for fulfilling His redemptive purposes as "through the judges and the worthy kings of Israel." When the people of Israel demanded a king "like all the nations," they were motivated by the first criterion, which was objectionable. The passage *som tasim* in Deuteronomy 17:15 suggests "that this evil thing shall not come about, but you shall set up only such a king whom God will choose" by means of a court of seventy and by a prophet, unlike the manner of the nations. "It is forbidden to set up a king like all the nations . . . Had they asked (Samuel) for a king to fulfill God's will and not for power, in the way of the nations, then they would have fulfilled a positive mitzvah." Ibn Attar thus argues that the "like all the nations" phrase in both Samuel and Deuteronomy invalidates the mandatory character of Deuteronomy 17. If the intent of the verse "is to permit rather than to command, consent is given."[13]

Or Ha-Chayim then suggests a radical interpretation of Sanhedrin 20. He acknowledges that the law is according to R. Judah and that this is confirmed by Maimonides.[14] "Nevertheless, the passage should be interpreted according to R. Nehorai, who stated explicitly that the request for a King is disgraceful. It is possible to say that if Israel will be worthy they will not demand a king and [yet] God will be their king . . . but if Israel will . . . desire a king, then the command concerning a king will apply to them. . . ."[15] Thus kingship will be commanded as a punitive alternative.

Commentaries on I Samuel 8 do not deal with the sanction for kingship but, rather, with the basis for the king's authority. Believing as they did that the law of Deuteronomy 17 preceded the events of I Samuel, the divine mandate for kingship was already established in their minds. Thus Kimchi (c. 1160–c. 1235) repeats the fundamental triple principle of Sanhedrin as axiomatic—that three commandments concerning kingship, the Temple, and Amalek were given in the wilderness. He then proceeds to deprecate the manner of the request by the people who, instead of asking for a king who would rule in justice and in faith, demanded a king in a rude manner and a king like among all the nations. Besides, they demanded a king who would wage their wars instead of their depending on God for victory. In addition, according to some, says Kimchi (repeating Sanhedrin 20b), the elders made a proper request while the ordinary people wanted to be "like all the nations." However, commenting on I Samuel 12:20, "You have done this evil," he explains, "by asking for a king for yourselves." "In the days of Samuel they were led because of Samuel's merit by the miraculous divine providence and God was the King who went before them to fight their wars. . . . They had no need for a king. . . . Only after Samuel's death the miraculous condition ceased—and leadership conformed to nature; then they were commanded to seek a king. . . . [Thus], why were they punished in Samuel's days? Because they made the request before it was necessary." By way of confirming this, Malbim's commentary *Ha-Torah v'Ha-mitzvah* to Deuteronomy 17:14 adds, "In Sanhedrin 20b, R. Nehorai says, this passage [in I Samuel 8] was stated only because of the people's complaints."

DEPRECATION BUT RELUCTANT ACCEPTANCE OF KINGSHIP.
Nachmanides is not content to limit kingship but clearly deprecates it. In his comment on Jacob's approaching encounter with Esau at "Seir, in the fields of Edom," and referring to Edom, which comes eventually to be identified with Rome, he writes, "This indicates that we began our fall into the hands of Edom when the kings, during the Second Temple, entered into covenant with the Romans . . . and this is mentioned in the words of our Rabbis and is recounted in books." Nachmanides cites Deuteronomy 4:25, 26 as proof that Deuteronomy 17:14 is not a command. The passage reads, "*Ki tolid banim*—When you have begotten children and children's children—should you act wickedly—you shall perish from the land." Nachmanides states that this portion is stated as a warning. . . . The text serves to give a double message—a warning . . . and a prediction of things to come. Nachmanides seeks to equate the structure of verses 4:25, 26 with 17;15ff., suggesting an implied warning in reference to "like all the nations," and a prediction (rather than a command) of future kingship. The analogy, however, is not apt, since in 4:25 there is no putative mandate as there is in 17:15. Deuteronomy 4:25, 26 is a simple statement of cause and effect—should you act wickedly after you have begotten descendants, then you will be punished.

David Kimchi (c. 1160–c. 1235) asserts that had the people possessed greater faith in God's power to fight their battles, their request for a king would not have been shocking. Instead, their reference to "all the nations" betrayed a predilection for idolatry. (I Samuel 8:5) Commenting on I Samuel 8, Kimchi takes note of the discussion in Sanḥedrin whether the king's functions are permissible or mandatory, and he cites R. Judah who states that they are intended only to warn the people. He does not note, however, that Judah endorsed kingship as a mitzvah.

Referring to the Samuel event, Kimchi states, "There was a controversy among the scholars. Some asked, why were they punished? Because they preceded their request with 'like all the nations' and some of them made the request for a king only so that he might be able to lead them to idolatry; while others said that the elders among them made a proper request by saying 'place a king over us.' "

Levi ben Gershom (Gersonides, 1288–1344) explicitly declares that Israel would have been better off without a king. Repeating Deuteronomy Rabbah, he states approvingly: "God said to Israel, 'I thought that you would be free of Kingship (*malchuyot*).' What is the basis for this? [Citing Deuteronomy Rabbah] It refers to A wild ass used to the wilderness (Jeremiah 2:24). Just as the ass grows up in the wilderness without the fear of man, so I thought that the fear of kingship would not be upon you, but you did not seek this [course], instead you lusted after it." Gersonides adds: "God wanted to withdraw them from this [kingship] because of the evil future that would derive from it, and He commanded Samuel to tell Israel the consequences so that they would withdraw from it . . . since the king would rule over them until they would become his slaves."

Gersonides cites Samuel's speech as a warning against the evils of kingship "like all the nations," where kings impose arbitrary laws on the people, but Israel must be governed in accordance with the Torah. The people's intent was to depart from the authority of the Torah. Hence, the requirements in Deuteronomy 17:18 (that the king write a scroll of the Law to guide him). Commenting on I Samuel 8, he adds, "Their kings became the cause of leading Israel astray and removing them from God until they were exiled from their land. They cast off the yoke of the kingdom of heaven and this is what they meant when they said 'to judge us like all the nations,' since among the nations the ruler is both king and judge."[15]

Gersonides also expresses reservations about the institution of kingship, which even if permitted was not requested by the Torah but instituted in order to imitate the nations. He stresses that since Israel was enjoined from having a king not of their own brethren, as other nations do, it was clearly not the intent of the Torah that Israel select a king "like all the nations." Therefore, at best, the mandatory character of Deuteronomy 17 is restricted. The purpose of the demand that the king write a special Torah for himself was twofold—to remind him that he is governed by it, and to remind him, as Samuel told the people, that there is no king but God. God told Samuel that their request was for the purpose of departing from the ways of the Torah.

> The end of the matter is that their kings became the cause of making Israel go astray and to remove them from God until they brought about exile from their own land. . . . All these things were mentioned as reminders that the king would rule over them until they became his slave. . . . Samuel wanted to frighten them and told them what the king would do when he would rule over them, that he would deal harshly with them which is impossible

> to do [when that are] in compliance with the laws of the Torah—God would not be able to help you because the spirit of your decision would have brought you all this. . . .

The only reason God complied with the people's request was that without a king they were at the mercy of their enemies. Nevertheless, they were warned that disobedience to the Torah would bring destruction upon them and their king.

In his commentary on I Samuel 8, Gersonides writes, "The end of the matter is that their kings were the reason for Israel going astray and departing from God so that they were exiled from their land." (Bachya ben Asher, too, voices this theme and cites the midrash from Deuteronomy Rabbah in which the kings are accused of bringing about Israel's misfortunes.)

Gersonides adds, "The God of Israel is their king and He will save them when they return to him just as he did in the days of the judges . . . and if they turn aside from the paths of the Torah, a king will not avail them, and God's hand will [then] be in their behalf as it was in behalf of their ancestors who had no king."

In his comment on I Samuel 21:25, Gersonides attacks kingship. "God was their king and He raised up judges when (the people) returned to Him, saving them from their enemies. So their request for a king did not apply to this but to evil."

Much more explicitly, Gersonides raises two questions: Why are judges preferable to kings, and what is more objectionable even than asking for a king? First, from the commentators we have cited, it would appear that the judges were selected by God in direct response to the people's suffering and their penitence. The book of Judges resorts to a formula for divine intervention and selection of judges: "God raised up a savior."

God's direct and supernatural involvement is articulated in other ways, indicating the judge's role as God's instrument. In the case of the kings, however, their rise to power or their usurpation of it is more the product of historical circumstances than God's intercession, and the absence of the formula in the Book of Kings reflects that. Second, while the "evil" to which Samuel 12 refers is the request for a king, Gersonides sees a deeper evil, idolatry, to which he refers enigmatically, limiting himself to the comment that Israel should abstain from it.

Ovadia Sforno (1470–1550) manifested a negative view of kingship, as evidenced in his comment on Psalm 69:22,23. In his comments on Deuteronomy 17:14ff., he states

> For the King to be like the Kings of the nations, holding rule for himself and his descendants, is contemptible to God. [Therefore] He commanded that when they obstinately establish for themselves a king in this manner, they may select only such a man whom God selects, neither causing Israel to transgress its religion, nor being a stranger (however qualified and heroic in war). When they sinned in requesting a king (and his descendants) like all the nations, the penalty came in ensuing events. ("On that day you shall cry out before the king whom you have chosen and God will not respond.") The selection of a king was [therefore only] optional, as in the case of the beautiful [captive] where the passage suggests that [the captor] will subsequently come to hate her, [thus] siring a rebellious son, as in thecase of Absalom, [son of David, the King].

Just as David's lust for Uriah's wife led to the birth of an evil son, so Israel's request for a king would lead to national disaster.

David and Yechiel Altschuler, eighteenth century states in *(Metzodat David)* "When [our] ancestors [in Egypt] cried out to God . . . He sent Moses, and they did not have a King." After their subjugation to the Philistines and Moabites,

> they cried out to God but did not ask for a king to fight their battle. [God] sent Jerubaal and Bedan. Although there were no kings in Israel, God saved you through them [Jerubaal and Bedan]. . . . But when you saw that war came upon you, you said to Me, 'We will not be like our ancestors before whom the judge went forth to war, but a king will rule over us, and he will wage our war.' . . . But God is your King and He will wage your war together with the judge. You have done foolishly in the request for a king . . . since you see that there is no deterrent for God to save by means of a Judge and without a king. . . . If you will fear God then all of you will follow God who will go to war before you. . . . Should you say that if the request for a king was a evil in God's eyes, why did He agree to our request? . . . You must understand the ways of God who fulfills the request of the petitioner even if it is evil in God's eyes, and even if it is not considered good by the petitioner.

Saadia (882–942), in his translation of the Torah, is of the opinion, as is Abraham ibn Ezra, that the selection of a king is optional, not a mitzvah.[17]

Rabbi Samuel ben Chofni (d. 1034) wrote, "[Kingship] was established only when waging war was necessary and in the time of Samuel was not required" (since Samuel could lead the people in war).

Most recent and most forceful not only in deprecating kingship but in denying it as a mitzvah is Naftali Tzvi Yehudah Berlin (1817–1893). Commenting on Deuteronomy 17:14, he states categorically, "It is not an absolute mitzvah to select a king, only permissible, as in 'if you say, I will eat some meat, for you have the urge to eat it, you may eat meat.' " (Deuteronomy 12:20)

"It is not possible to command the selection of a king as long as the people does not agree to suffer the burden of a king . . . [even] the Sanhedrin is not commanded unless the people say that they want the leadership of a king. For three hundred years the chosen Sanctuary was in Shiloh [thereby fulfilling a prerequiste for kingship]. But there was no king because the people did not consent."[18] Berlin emphatically declares that kingship is permissible only because the people, not God, demand it. It is an irresistible impulse. As for the phrase *kechol ha-goyim,* this cannot apply to the king's establishing laws like those of the other nations, as suggested by I Samuel 8:5, since "it is forbidden to depart from the laws of the Torah"; nor does this apply to warmaking, since "throughout the time of the judges there was no one in charge of . . . warfare unless the word of God reached the judge. [The people] want a king to be in charge of this, but God was incensed over this." The phrase *"kechol ha-goyim"* therefore applies only to the organization of the internal affairs of government, and there are differing opinions as to which form of government is preferable. It is only this aspect of kingship that the people could properly request.[19] Berlin assumes that the laws of the Torah suffice to govern the Jewish people, and that generals will always be found to wage their wars. If the people insist on having a king, he would clearly serve in a limited capacity, with judges legislating and warriors conducting the nation's military affairs.

In summation: First, in some instances there is unambiguous rabbinic support for kingship. Second, by this stringent attitude toward kingship, Nachmanides virtually invalidates his assertion of kingship's divine requirement. In his comments on I Samuel 8, he refers to the judgment of "the commentators," referring most probably to "my judgment," which considerably and even radically modifies the earlier position. Third, kingship is not an ideal or a desideratum but an unfortunate necessity. Before Samuel's advanced age, it was not required. In addition, it must be restrained in order to curb royal rapacity. Also, the naturally rapacious kings are needed to keep the people intimidated. Thus, at best, kingship is not to be equated with priesthood or judgeship as a morally justified or divinely ratified office. In fact, according to Nachmanides, it is the judges and priests before whom the people must come to request a king. Fourth, the issue of kingship as mandated becomes subordinated to the question of restraints upon the king. Ibn Ezra illustrates this in concentrating on the method of selection, which by its very mature is intended to place restraints on the king. Stress is placed on the limits, not on the prerogatives of the king, as in *mishpat ha-melech.* Virtually the only role assigned to him is to be the nation's leader in war, and the restrictions are designed to prevent him from both exceeding and abusing his role. Fifth, some of the very commentators who do not deny the "mitzvah" of kingship virtually invalidate it by their recriminations against it. They are not inconsistent. They are instead caught up in the dilemma of a law they cannot repudiate and an institution some of them abominate at worst, and wish to hedge around at best. They clearly distinguish between undesired kings and the yearned-for Messiah. It is obvious that they do not identify the king with the Messiah, else they would not have been so harsh toward the king. An attempt at synthesizing both is made when they are merged into "King-Messiah." Sixth, despite Maimonides, who, as we shall learn, codifies kingship as a mitzvah, other later authorities such as Berlin (and Abravanel) unambiguously deny that kingship is a mitzvah based on the Torah.

Notes

1. Sanhedrin 20b.
2. *Sefer Ha-Mitzvot,* on Deuteronomy 17:14, number 173.
3. Commentary to Deuteronomy 17:14.
4. Commentary to Deuteronomy 17:15, 15.
5. Commentary to Deuteronomy 17:14–15.
6. Deuteronomy 17:14.

7. Kiddushin 37a.
8. Alsheich, *Mar'ot T'zvaot*, Offenbach, 1719.
9. Hirsch, *The Pentateuch*, New York, 1971, p. 332.
10. Ibid.
11. Ibid., p. 333.
12. Schickardi, *Ius Regium*, p. 129.
13. Chayim Ibn Attar, *Or Ha-Chayim*, Venice, 1742.
14. *Hilchot Melachim* I.
15. Ibid.
16. I Samuel 8.
17. M. Zucker, *Al Targum R. Saadia Gaon LaTorah*, New York, 1959, pp. 423.
18. *Haamek Davar*, Deuteronomy 17:19.
19. Ibid.

VIII

Forerunner of Jewish Nationalism Moses Maimonides (1135–1204)

Maimonides' political system is a significant element in his philosophy. In the fourteenth chapter of *Millot ha-higayon (Tractate on Logic)* Maimonides "implies that the function of the Torah is emphatically political." This interpretation is confirmed by the *Guide of the Perplexed,* where "regarding the governance of the city, everything has been done to make it precise in all its details."[1] Maimonides "suggests that the function of revealed religion is emphatically political."[2] The importance of *Millot ha-higayon* derives from its objective, which was not the dissemination of Aristotelianism, as is supposed, but rather "the strengthening of faith in the doctrine of Judaism. His book . . . is a kind of preface to "The Guide of the Perplexed" to which it is organically bound."[3] Maimonides adds that the Torah's laws for governance of a city are sufficient "for these times" and that since they precede philosophic thought on politics by centuries, it (political thought) is superfluous for Jews. He suggests, says Strauss, that the "Jews in exile, the Jews who lack a political existence, do not need the books of the philosophers," but that under changed circumstances the Torah would not be sufficient for the guidance of a political community.[4] This would imply that "the political books of the philosophers will again be needed after the coming of the Messiah, as they were needed prior to the exile."[5] Nevertheless, says Strauss, following Maimonides, since "the function of revealed religion is emphatically political, political philosophy is as necessary 'in these times' as in all other times for the theoretical understanding of revealed religion."[6]

A central component in Maimonides' system is *nomos,* significantly a Greek term (the "governance by human beings in divine matters").

In the *Guide* he suggests that the *nomos,* in contradistinction to the divinely revealed law, is directed only toward the well-being of the body and is unconcerned with divine things.[7] The *nomos* is, to use Wolfson's expression, essentially the order of a "civil state" as distinguished from a "religious state."[8]

In his one-page statement, alluding to the political nature of revealed religion (which Strauss construes from the term "great nation," meaning any of the three revealed religions), Maimonides establishes the extension of politics from sacred into civil categories. In so doing, he opens the possibility that while philosophy has nothing to contribute "in these times" to the civil arena of Jewish politics, this may be possible at a future time. For Maimonides, divinely revealed law is paramount precisely because it is a branch of political philosophy. "It is necessarily free from the relativity of the nomos . . . a much loftier social order than the nomos."[9] But it is a category that does not exclude the *nomos.* The latter is left open, not only by the reference to the superfluity of the philosophers "in these times" but also to some clues in *Hilchot Melachim* to kingly conduct that encroaches on what we know as the civil realm. The response to *nomos* is developed further in the *Guide,* which ascribes to the king powers that expand his divinely ordained prerogatives. He speaks of

> a ruler who gauges the actions of the individuals, perfecting that which is deficient and reducing that which is excessive, and who prescribes actions and moral habits that all of them must always practice in the same way, so that the natural diversity is hidden through the multiple points of conventional accord and so that the community becomes well ordered. Therefore I say that the law, although it is not natural, enters into what is natural.[10]

The distinction between *nomos* and divine law is significant both because Maimonides employs a Greek philosophical term to characterize the former, and because, within the context of the *Guide* he recognizes it validity thus:

> Accordingly if you find a Law the whole end of which and the whole purpose of the chief thereof, who determined the actions required by it, are directed exclusively toward the ordering of the city and of its circumstances and the abolition in it of injustice and oppression; and if in that Law attention is not at all directed toward speculative matters, no heed is given to the perfecting of

> the rational faculty, and no regard is accorded to opinions being correct or faulty—the whole purpose of that Law being, on the contrary, the arrangement, in whatever way this may be brought about, of the circumstances of people in their relations with one another and provision for their obtaining, in accordance with the opinion of that chief, a certain something deemed to be happiness—you must know that that Law is a nomos and that the man who laid it down belongs, as we have mentioned, to the third class, I mean to say to those who are perfect only in their imaginative faculty.[11]

Maimonides lays down a basic principle—that government, while subordinate in value to the perfection of moral values, is indispensable to it. "The welfare of the soul . . . can only be achieved after achieving the governance of the city and the well-being of the states of all its people."[12] The objective of the Law is twofold: The welfare of the soul and the welfare of the body, which in the context of Maimonides' discussion is the body politic. Even the welfare of the soul is socially oriented—"the acquisition by every human individual of moral qualities for life in society so that the affairs of the city may be ordered. . . . This [the perfection of the individual] cannot be achieved in any way by one isolated individual. For an individual can only attain all this through a political association, it being already known that man is political by nature."[13] The last passage is a reference to Aristotle and clearly establishes Maimonides' commitment to the political foundations of Jewish law. This is explicated in what follows:

> The true Law . . . of Moses our Master has come to bring us both perfections, I mean the welfare of people in their relations with one another through the abolition of reciprocal wrong doing and through the acquisition of a noble and excellent character. In this way, the preservation of the population of the country and their permanent existence in the same order became possible. . . . The letter of the Torah speaks of both perfections and informs us that the end of the Law in its entirety is the achievement of these two perfections.[14]

Ultimate perfection can be attained by having correct opinions, but in addition, "The Law also makes a call to adopt certain beliefs, belief in which is necessary for the sake of political welfare. Such, for instance, is our belief that He . . . is violently angry with those who disobey Him."[15] The commandments of the Torah are to be understood as applying "either to the welfare of a belief or to the welfare of the conditions of the city."[16] Thus, the Torah "in its entirety" is concerned with both the spiritual-ethical and political-social existence of the people. There is a strong similarity to this in the commentary to the passage in Pirke Avot, "Pray for the welfare of the government," in which Maimonides succinctly integrates the political and religious aspects of Jewish law into an organic unity: "All [the commandments] are bound up with three things: opinions, moral qualities, and political civic actions."[17] When Spinoza was to speak of the Torah as the law of a state, he was recognizing Maimonides' perception and at the same time was rejecting it as unworthy of the true aims of religion.

In *Sefer Ha-Mitzvot,* which preceded the *Mishneh Torah* by about two years, Maimonides defines the selection of a king as a positive commandment. "We are commanded to appoint a king over ourselves . . . who will bring together our whole nation and act as our leader."[18] By this statement, in the context of his definition of the King-Messiah as a human figure functioning within the natural limits of history, Maimonides presents a major, one might say revolutionary, political concept. Explaining his dictum, Maimonides says:

> "[the Sifre states that] he must be held in awe and that our unique respect for him and estimation of his greatness and preeminence must be such as to place him on a higher level of honor than any of the prophets of his generation. The Talmud says explicitly: The king takes precedence over the prophet (Horayot 13a) and when this king gives an order which is not in conflict with a commandment of the Torah, we must obey his behest, and he has the right to put to death by the sword anyone who disobeys them. The life of anyone who rebels against the kingly authority, be he who he may, is forfeit to the king duly appointed in accordance with the Torah."[19]

The provisions of this commandment are explained in the second chapter of Sanhedrin, at the beginning of Keritoth, and in the seventh chapter of Sotah. Here Maimonides applies the principle of the rule of *nomos,* extending beyond revealed law.

While it is the rabbinic tendency generally to restrict the role of the king, this passage appears to expand it. Placing the king on a higher level than the prophet is a departure from one line of thought that makes the king subordinate. Here the prophet who is responsible for selecting the king concludes his task and steps aside in his favor, thus leaving the king a greater degree of latitude. Of course, the king is still under God's and the Torah's control, but the direct surveillance by the prophet has been set aside. Second, provision is made for the king to act and to be obeyed on such matters as are not under the Torah's jurisdiction, and disobedience may be punished by execution. Maimonides justifies this by citing Joshua 1:18, "Whoever shall rebel against your command and shall not hearken to your words in all that you command him, shall be put to death." This would appear to open a vast area of nonsacred legislation in which the authority of the king is paramount. We have already alluded to Maimonides' references to the *nomos,* and the citation from *Sefer Ha-Mitzvot* suggests the expanding development of civil authority in Maimonides' thought.

Finally, the extensive power of the king to suppress rebellion by anyone manifests a vast dimension of authority, even if Maimonides adds the qualifier that the king must be "appointed in accordance with the Torah."

For Maimonides, the legitimacy and authenticity of kingship resided firmly in Deuteronomy 17:14 ff., and in I Samuel Chapter 8. There is no ambivalence in his striking opening of *Hilchot Melachim u'milchamot* with the dogmatic assertion that among the three commandments enjoined upon Israel when entering the land was the selection of a king. Maimonides was aware of the strong negative comment on kingship by Nehorai in Sifre, yet he posited his affirmation unilaterally. Intimately connected to this assertion is his selection of the I Samuel 8 incident as the primary paradigm both for kingship and for the authoritative role of the king. Just as he rejects Nehorai's position on kingship, he transmutes the Samuel incident in which kingship is clearly regarded as offensive both to Samuel and to God, and he lays down the demand of the people "to judge us and wage our wars" as a primary imperative for kingship.

Other biblical justifications for kingship might have been selected, but it is a sign of Maimonides' particular commitment to the principle and to the functions of kingship that he selected as his model a text in which kingship was considered most odious and in which the role of the king was presented as most oppressive. In doing so, Maimonides sides with the people against Samuel. He also allows the people to define the functions of the king. Finally, he employs Samuel's warning as a legitimate definition of the rights and prerogatives of the king. By deliberately selecting an event that from the perspective of God and Samuel represented a rejection of their authority, and of divine kingship, Maimonides seems to have justified his unqualified commitment to kingship as embedded in Jewish law. Even more, he transforms the litany about the king's repression into a constitutional prescription for the king's rights and powers. All this serves to reinforce his convicition that *keter malchut* was given to the people as "the first of the commandments" when, upon the people's creation, it prepared to enter the land. Thus it is a primordial institution no less that *keter Torah* and *keter kehunah*.

Even more, kingship predates the anointment of Saul and in a very real sense is continuous beyond the termination of the institution in the land of Israel. "Moses our master was a king."[20] From "king" Moses to the Judges there is a direct transition of royal authority that continues until the command to select a king. In addition, Moses, who is called a king, is also the paradigm for the nonhereditary *nasi* of the Sanhedrin who is preeminent intellectually.[21] Kingship reaches out particularly into the rule of the exilarchs whose political dominance is an extension and a continuation of kingship. The exilarchs in Babylon stand in place of the kings; they may rule over Israel in all places and judge them, whether or not they wish.[22] On the strength of this passage Maimonides adds, "The rule of the exilarchs is like that of the king . . . against their (the people's) will and by compulsion."[23] Here there is more than a hint that in the Maimonidean system kingship incorporates not only the war-waging power but involvement in shaping the law.

Maimonides' concept of the king's role is compatible with the biblical image of the judge fulfilling the functions of the king—like a king he rescues the people and rules over them. Hence Gideon's rejection of the people's request is couched as a rejection of kingship. The act of anointing the king symbolizes the organic transition from the institution of judgeship to monarchy, but the essential nature of the new institution has not changed, according to Maimonides.

How far-reaching or how limited was the authority of the Jewish king as conceived by Maimonides? In addition to his perceptions of Deuteronomy 17 and I Samuel 8, other clues point toward a "political" as well as authoritarian ruler. The very title of the last book in

Mishneh Torah, which in itself is climactic, is *Sefer melachim u'milchamot* (the Book of Kings and Wars), clearly designating the king primarily as waging the people's wars.

We have observed the theoretical principle of the three crowns that presumably stand in equilibrium but that we have already observed are not only in tension but also in conflict in much of biblical history. Nevertheless, the principle of their autonomy and their "check and balance" relationship represents the intention, albeit theoretical, of the three crown system. From one perspective, the Maimonidean principle seems to be committed to this, but from another perspective the commitment is more to a concept of the king as first among equals, with the authority to impinge actively on the domain of *keter Torah*.

In its earliest formulation, kingship was established according to Maimonides as an instrument for destroying Amalek and building the Temple. As the institution unfolds, however, it assumes in the Maimonidean system an expanding and increasingly dynamic life. Yet Maimonides recognizes that upon the destruction of Amalek and the building of the Temple additional functions lie in store for kingship, and that an indeterminate historical role lies ahead beyond the building of the Temple. "Thus, all of his deeds must be for the sake of heaven and his thoughts and purposes must be to raise up the true religion [*dat*] to fulfill righteousness, to break the power of the evildoers and to wage the wars of God." Kings must first be enthroned in order to do justice and to wage war, as it is said, "so that our king may judge us and go before us and fight our wars."[24] Clearly the task of "lifting up the true *dat*" is a prolonged one, and waging the "wars of God" is not limited to the destruction of Amalek.

An illustation of this may be found in the way in which Maimonides deals with the question of the rights and the restrictions of kings in matters of judging and being judged. On the basis of Sanhedrin II:5, which denies the right of the non-Davidic kings to judge or to be judged on the grounds of their moral defects that could "bring damage to the *dat* of Israel, Maimonides adds, "because they do not submit to the discipline of Torah." If indeed, as Maimonides affirms, non-Davidic kings are ab initio condemned as undermining the foundations of justice and the Torah, why does he recognize the legitimacy of such a king, especially since he does not accept the authority of the Torah? Why is royal power granted to such a king? On one hand, Maimonides denies non-Davidic kings the right of judging and being judged "because their rule is evil,"[25] which the rule of Davidic kings is legitimate. On the other hand he acknowledges with more than equanimity the legitimacy of the rule of the Hasmoneans, including Herod. Blidstein suggests that the main purpose of Maimonides is "to isolate the religious institutions from the bad influence of the king."[26] This argument raises fundamental questions, inasmuch as the ruling by Maimonides does not apply merely to individual kings who may be evil but to all non-Davidic kings of Israel, virtuous or corrupt.

There is more than a blurring between *keter malchut* and *keter Torah*. There is a crossing over from the latter into the former and an appropriation of some of its prerogatives. One might go further and say that in the Maimonidean system the prerogatives of *keter Torah* are organically part of *keter Malchut*. It is the king who is responsible for "*haramat dat ha-emet*" (exalting the true religion) and "*chizuk mitzvoteha*" (strengthening its commandments). "The spiritual-social-territorial are bound closely" in the teaching of Maimonides,[27] since the "heart of the king" is the heart of the entire community of Israel.[28] The ambiguity between the lines of kingship and the Torah is recognized by Blidstein, who on one hand observes that "there is no doubt that Maimonides aspired to an institutional separation" between the two.[29] Yet on the other hand he adds, "There are areas where the division is not clear . . . there is no escaping the moral-paternalistic atmosphere" emanating from kingship. "The entire image of the people is fixed by the king, since he is the 'heart of the people. . . . He bears their burden . . . like a nurse bearing an infant.' "[30]

Ultimately, Maimonides concludes his study of kingship by proclaiming the king a symbol of the social-political relationship destined to directly serve the spiritual-religious component.[31] It has already been observed that the Davidic king may serve as judge. Maimonides elaborates his system on the strength of Sanhedrin 14b, which states, "Your elders, this refers to the Sanhedrin; your judges, this refers to the king and the high priest," signifying of course that the king plays a central role in *keter Torah*. Maimonides adds, "Even if the Davidic kings are not seated in the Sanhedrin [nevertheless they judge the people and may be judged].[32]

Maimonides augments the power of the king by consistently enabling national institutions to go beyond the prescribed limits of the halachah. Thus, a court may punish extralegally so that "one Shabbat may be violated in order that many Sabbaths may be observed," as "a limb may be amputated so that the patient may live." "From this Maimonides understood that he was stressing and laying bare the authority working beneath the Talmudic terrain."[33] Maimonides expanded on the principle that nonlegal measures could be taken in accord with the needs of the time, and based this on the principle that "the Bet Din may beat and punish not in accord with the law."[34] It is clear who would determine the "needs of the time," especially when we see that the lines between religious and civil law were indeterminate, even if different officials presided in each. Even taking into account that it is the Bet Din of seventy-one that presumably appoints the king, and the king does not appoint the members of the Bet Din, the king apparently has the power to determine the nature of the times in which great latitude is given to him. This becomes clearer still in the declaration by Maimonides that the king (and "the exilarch who stands in the place of the king") is authorized to appoint judges for the people. In so doing, he accords to the king a preeminent role in the judicial system. He not only judges the people but delegates his authority to his appointees. The king, being responsible for upholding the law that derives its legitimacy from the Torah and its enforcement from *malchut,* assumes power far beyond the formal definition of his role.

The king may execute miscreants for purposes of *tikun olam* (improving the social order). This is explained as designed "to establish an order which will restrain even those shedders of blood with whom the courts cannot deal with the desired severity."[35] It would appear that this special prerogative of the king represents an appropriation of power that the courts for whatever reason may have abrogated. The king expands his authority at the expense of the court.

The king may also execute by the testimony of a single witness, which is contrary to the requirements of the Torah, but which Maimonides says may be necessary for "*tikun hamedinah*" (improvement of the state). Continuing to expand the king's power, Maimonides proclaims that the king may punish offenders who are not subject to execution by the court but who nevertheless deserve execution by divine intervention.[36] The basis of this is the Noahide declaration that God would demand the blood that is shed. Maimonides places the unexecuted offender in this category and permits the king to carry out God's sentence, thereby not only expanding the law but placing the king in the category of God's agent.

Thus, the preeminent place of the king in the hierarchy of Jewish public figures is established by Maimonides. He is careful to place *keter Torah* above *keter malchut*,[37] but in his commentary to the Mishneh, he writes, "The reason for giving the scholar precedence is only theoretical . . . but in practice it is inappropriate to give anyone precedence over the honor of the king, even if [the king] is an *am ha-aretz*, since it is stated, "You shall certainly set a king over you." Likewise, a prophet is subordinate to the king and must prostrate himself to him.[38] Even if the king is required to heed the words of the prophet, "the stature (of the king) is greater than that of the (greatest) prophet in his generation."[39]

All this results from the expression by Maimonides of the principle that "*Mishpat ha-melech mutar*" that is, that the actions of the king based on Samuel's litany are constitutional royal prerogatives, as among all kingships. The right of the king to circumvent the law because of the political order flows directly from *mishpat ha-melech. Mishpat ha-melech* is regarded as normative, and Maimonides derives it from Tosefta Sanhedrin 4:5 and Sanhedrin 20b. In essence, *mishpat ha-melech* is necessary for carrying out royal duties, and derived from a perception of the realistic needs of the state.[40] As we have indicated, this in turn is based on the principle of *dina d'malkhuta*, which applies to the Jewish kingdom as well as all others. On the strength of this, Maimonides permits the king to transfer confiscated wealth to his servants. He declares, "Every law which the king decrees is not theft . . . all the laws of the king concerning money are judged in accordance with this."[41] When a king acts contrary to the laws of the Talmud, such as forcing the sale of land in order to raise money for the payment of taxes, "if it was the decree of the King," it is valid.[42]

Against this background, we may perceive that Maimonidean thought recognizes the king in civil terms, even though he is still confined to a (more expanded) theocratic system. It appears that according to Maimonides there is both a requirement for a king, as prescribed by the Torah, and an expanded role as well. Knowing rabbinic ambivalence concerning the selection of a king, he issues the verdict in favor of the dominant opinion. He is mindful of the dissatisfaction with the people's request in I Samuel but judges that the people's invidious motive did not invalidate the commandment itself. Moreover, he determines that *mishpat ha-melech* is not a condemnation but a prescription for kingship. The commandment has particular application for the Davidic dynasty, which is never to terminate, and whose kings are to be held in greatest awe. Yet, there is to be not merely a symbolic but a highly substantive regime. The king is to be designated before Amalek is destroyed and the Temple is built. This is a royal task: "Thus we did until their destruction was completed by David."[43] But the responsibility (for destroying Amalek) is not completed, and must be continued in the future. "It applies to those on whom it is imposed, and they must fulfill it as long as [any of those against whom it is directed] exists."[44] While this is a Torah commandment, and the king's responsibility for fulfilling it derives from a proof-text,[45] it is plain that such a task cannot be defined in religious terms only and must take on political form. Maimonides does recognize the deterrent nature of the Torah in relationship to kings. He not only reiterates Deuteronomy 17:18 concerning the king's writing a scroll of the Law, but he stresses that it "must be corrected by the court of seventy-one from the scroll in the Temple court."[46] This is presumably to prevent deviations from the authoritative text, thereby enabling the king to arrogate greater power to himself. This is the most stringent deterrent imposed on the king. Maimonides also emphasizes the restictions against royal excesses—wives and concubines, drinking, sexual excess, horses, and especially personal wealth, all of which incurs flogging.[47] The restraints and especially the penalties that dramatize the king's subservience to the law tend to stress his nonabsolutist role although the principal restrictions apply to defections in his personal life. But as a public, political, and military figure, especially in times of national emergency, he enjoys a far wider range of latitude, as will be seen.

Traditional concern for limiting the king's power is expressed in the requirement that he must be appointed by a prophet, but this applies only to kings not from the tribe of Judah. Other limitations applying to all kings, whether Davidic or non-Davidic, include, in addition to those from the Torah, the requirement that even a slight biblical precept takes precedence over a royal edict.[48] Yet, immediately following that requirement comes another open-ended provision to the effect that "if the exigency of the hour demands it," the king may set aside basic law (proper evidence, warning a culprit, two witnesses) "in order to preserve the stability of the social order."[49] This concession provides latitude for the king both to set aside religious law and to expand his prerogative to encompass a vast area of the political sector. If he is ordained to wage Israel's wars and to make his own law in the interest of the social order, the limitations on his power become more symbolic than substantive. The extent and intensity of his punitive powers during "the exigency of the hour" (the perennially elastic recourse of rulers in all times) include the right to wholesale and lingering hangings in order to "put fear in the hearts of others."[50]

Since war is no isolated event in the history of nations and ancient Israel, and thus represents a state of almost continuous "exigency," the rather detailed wartime prerogatives of the king establish his extensive political and civil powers. He may impose taxes "for his own needs or for war purposes." In peace as well as war, he establishes customs duties. Maimonides then adds the sweeping observation, "From these verses [I Samuel 8:17, Deuteronomy 20:11] we infer that the king imposes taxes and fixes custom duties and that all the laws enacted by him with regard to these and like matters [sic] are valid, for it is his prerogative to exercise all the authority set forth in the section relating to the king."[51] In peace as in war, the king may draft men into military service, press into his service "all the craftsmen he requires," take women to be his concubines and cooks. He may confiscate private property in anticipation of war. He may seize a tenth of the yield of grain. To him belongs the property of those executed by his decree. All this appears more like the prerogative of an absolute monarch than one confirmed by the Torah. In fact, Maimonides uses Scripture (I Samuel 8) to validate this authority. Instead of citing this famous passage as a warning against royal abuse, as it was intended, he makes it comply with reality and converts it into a legitimized prescription for Jewish kingship.

In his *Hilchot Gezelot V'avedot,* Maimonides advances the case for virtually unlimited confiscatory kingly power.

> If a king becomes angry with one of his servants or ministers among his subjects and confiscates his field or his courtyard, this is not deemed robbery and one is permitted to benefit from it. If one buys it from the king, he becomes its owner and the original owner cannot take it away from him. For the law permits them to confiscate all the property of those ministers with whom they are displeased, and the king has therefore canceled the owner's original right to it, so that the courtyard or field in question is regarded as ownerless, and if one buys it from the king, he becomes its lawful owner. But if a king takes the courtyard or field of one of the citizens contrary to the laws he has promulgated, he is deemed a robber, and the original owner may recover it from anyone who buys it from the king.

We note that Maimonides follows the principle that this is "the law of all kings."[52] This is based on his commitment to the application of *Dina D'malchuta* to all nations, including Israel. Also, only if the king breaches his own laws does he become culpable, but the laws have great confiscatory latitude. Other examples of kingly prerogatives follow:

> If a king decrees that whoever pays the fixed tax due from any individual may compel the one delinquent to work for him, and then an Israelite comes and pays tax due from some other impoverished Israelite, he may make him work more than would be usual, for the king's law is binding. But he must not make him work like a slave.
>
> If a king cuts down trees belonging to a private individual and makes them into a bridge, it may be crossed. Similarly, if he demolishes houses and makes from the material a road or a wall, one is permitted to benefit from it. The same rule applies in all similar cases, for the king's law is binding.[53]
>
> Regarding any of these or similar murderers who are not subject to being condemned to die by verdict of the court, if a king of Israel wishes to put them to death by royal decree for the benefit of society, he has a right to do so. Similarly, if the court deems it proper to put them to death as an emergency measure, it has the authority to do as it deems fit, provided that circumstances warrant such action.[54]

The wartime powers of the king are equally formidable. He receives a thirteenth of all conquered provinces in perpetuity. He is entitled to the royal treasures of conquered kingdoms. He acquires half of the war booty and has first choice. He may keep all the land he conquers. "In all these matters he is the final arbiter."[55] He may break through private property during a campaign "and none may protest." There are, nevertheless certain limitations imposed on him. For a war to expand Israel's borders and to "enhance his greatness and prestige," he requires the consent of a court of seventy-one.[56] Not so in the case of wars against the seven nations, Amalek, and the wars of defense against aggressors. But since the lines of demarcation between required and optional wars are rarely clear, the king's authority becomes awesome, especially so when his mandate is "to uplift the true religion, fill the world with righteousness, break the arm of the wicked, and fight the battles of the Lord."[57] The undefined limits of "battles of the Lord" are not reduced by the rule that "the primary reason for appointing a king was that he execute judgment and wage wars."[58] The sole authority for this is the Samuel passage where the people, not divine law, determine the king's role, and Samuel warns against its application. To reinforce his views on the power of the king, Maimonides cites Keritot 5b as proof that a rebel against the king may be executed. That citation deals with Zedekiah's rebellion against Nebuchadnezzar, a foreign king.

Rather than make a case for a king heavily subordinate to theocratic rule, as Weiler insists, Maimonides, by the power of his own dictum, envisions a "King-Messiah" who is a military regent with far-ranging powers. To be sure, he is under the aegis of the Torah, but as we have observed, the surveillance of the prophet has been lifted from him. He is subject to divine and Torah authority, but in the political-military area, except in the case of nonrequired war, he is virtually unrestricted. In light of this, we can see his *Hilchot Melachim* as a response to those who had issued scathing denunciations of kings and had even dared to question kingship.

Maimonides does not present more comprehensive or precise specifications for kingly government, but he goes far beyond limiting himself to reiterating the Torah's requirement of a king. It is, in fact, noteworthy that in a time when Jewry was deprived of sovereignty, Maimonides enunciated as extensively as he did the political role of the king. It is particularly noteworthy that he both built on rabbinic sources and made independent judgments that expanded rather than reduced the kingly role. Even more, he transferred vital tasks to the king and recognized the need for the king to be primarily responsible for the people's security, "to perform judgment and wage wars."[59] Maimonides did not share the misgivings of some of the earlier scholars who accused even David of bringing ruin on the people because of excessive power.

In V:8 Maimonides shifts from the term "king to King-Messiah" *(ha-melech ha-mashiach,)* to whom, significantly, is assigned one thirteenth of all conquered provinces. Yet he concludes *Hilchot Melachim* (and the *Mishneh Torah*) on a sublime spiritual note. In chapters eleven and twelve, the King-Messiah is endowed with spiritual and moral qualities. Having restored the people and defended it successfully in war, the king will undergo a profound spiritual transformation, and the people with him. The future king will model himself after David, who was the first messiah and who saved Israel. God's holy spirit will rest on him once his kingdom is established and the ingathering has occurred. While this is not mentioned in *Hilchot Melachim,* the king will also be a "great prophet." (*Hilchot Tshuvah* IX:2). He will study Torah and observe the commandments. He will teach the people, determine pedigrees by means of the holy spirit, and purify Levites. Nations will come to hear him, and "the earth will be full of the knowledge of God as the waters cover the sea."[60]

Two factors are noteworthy. First, the last two prerogatives (pedigrees and Levites), assigned by Maimonides to the king, are functions that others would not delegate to him but rather to a judge or a priest. For Maimonides, the holy spirit invests the king and none other with a special authority, and the king alone purifies the Levites. This represents a concentration of spiritual and temporal authority in the king's hands. Second, the king becomes the figure in whom the messianic expectations of the people are concentrated and also transformed into a historical, naturalistic setting. Maimonides dismisses others who expect the Messiah to "perform signs and wonders, bring new things into being, revive the dead." Kingship and messianism converge, and in the process the messianic element, as understood by some of the people, becomes attenuated and partly politicized. Maimonides is by no means the first to use the term "King-Messiah," but he invests the term most systematically with great political content. He nevertheless fuses the political king with the moral Messiah in whose times "there will be neither famine nor war, neither jealousy nor strife," but rather abundant blessings, comforts within the reach of all. The one preoccupation of the whole world will be to know the Lord. Israelites will be very wise, and they will "know the things that are now concealed and will attain an understanding of their Creator to the utmost capacity of the human mind."[61] Thus, there will be a spiritual transformation of humanity, and Israel will enter into a higher intellectual-theological consciousness.

All this is by way of stressing that kingship is not an end in itself but a means of attaining social-political goals that in turn are, in the Maimonidean perception, instruments leading ultimately to spiritual goals. Yet until the postrestoration times of spiritual fulfillment are achieved, the underlying principle of Maimonides is that kingship represents the fulfillment of the people's demand of Samuel for a king who would judge them and wage their wars. Kingship may not be an end itself, but as a goal and as an instrument it is endowed with far more than temporary powers, and within the historical structure for which it is designed, it is a consummation to be sought. This is not a contradiction because Maimonides insists that all this will be in a naturalistic setting. He reveals his attempt at fusion when he speaks of "two messiahs, the first, David; the later messiah, a descendant of David, who will achieve the final salvation of Israel."[62] While his two Messiahs represent a past reality and a future expectation, he endows one aspect of the future Messiah with the mighty achievements of King David, while ascribing more than political prowess alone to him. At the beginning of Chapter XII, he insists that "the world will follow its normal course," but at its conclusion he describes a new age in history, to be sure, in which a radically transformed humanity and Israel will emerge. Maimonides transposes the two Messiahs into a single, twofold Messiah, a warrior-deliverer of the people to its land, and also a harbinger of a higher age. Does one aspect cancel out the other? Not if we recognize that the prerequisite for the new age of the Messiah must be the waging of "the battles of the Lord" that will precede "the whole world serving the Lord with one accord."[63] When Maimonides decrees that whoever disbelieves in the coming of the Messiah denies the Torah and Moses, he refers to his own perception of the Messiah. And *that* Messiah, his spiritual qualities notwithstanding, does not differ markedly from the "King-Messiah" of IV:8 and the rest of that chapter. Together with the pursuit of the ways of Torah, he "fights the battles of the Lord,[64] restores the kingdom of David, rebuilds the sanctuary, gathers the dispersed of Israel."[65] None of these can be achieved without recourse to political and martial skills. Maimonides underscores this in his comment concerning Bar Kochba, about whose career he makes three significant comments—that the great Akiba regarded him as the Messiah, that "all the wise men of his generation shared this belief," and that Bar Kochba's alleged messiahship was disproved when he "was slain in [his] iniquity.'[66]

Maimonides must have been aware that Akiba's colleagues did not unanimously believe in the messianic role of Bar Kochba. Bar Torta's statement to Akiba that "grass will grow from your cheeks" before the Messiah comes clearly reflects less than unanimity on the issue and challenges the assertion that "all the wise men" considered Bar Kochba to be the Messiah. By taking a historically erroneous position, Maimonides reveals what appears to be an internal conflict, but he is really consistent. He seems to acknowledge on one hand that Bar Kochba had the necessary qualifications to be the Messiah, the chief qualification being military-political, but that on the other hand he failed because of his ultimate military-political defeat, not because he had not produced early, convincing signs of his qualifications. In victory and defeat, Bar Kochbas's pretentions are judged by Maimonides in terms of his martial prowess. Evidently Akiba judged him by related criteria. Had Bar Kochba triumphed and then succeeded in rebuilding the Temple and gathering Israel's dispersed in fullfillment of Maimonides' prescription, he would have been "the Messiah beyond doubt."[67] It can be assumed that that man who had minted coins and established political jurisdiction would have reconstituted a political commonwealth and would not have been content to abdicate in favor of a theocratic hierarchy. The specifications for kingly rule, as defined by Maimonides, enabled him to write so positively about Jewish history's near encounter with a messianic advent. It is therefore particularly difficulty to accept Gershom Weiler's observation that Maimonides "does not advocate the establishment of a political society based on the Torah." This also supports the assumption that in writing about a "political" king, Maimonides was envisioning the future and naturalistic reconstitution of a Jewish kingdom.

One might argue that a king who is subject to flogging for violating the law of the Torah must be unconditionally subservient to it. If he multiplies wives, horses, or silver, "he is flogged."[68] It should be noted that all of the transgressions cited are biblical.[69] Except for specific violations of biblical restrictions, the king otherwise enjoys enormous latitude, particularly in his political powers. The biblical restrictions, together with the rabbinic penalties that are prescribed, serve to highlight the lack of restrictions in the political areas. (Other restrictions deal with the king's marital life and eligibility to marry, illustrating all the more the gulf between the subordination of the king to the religious rules of the Torah and his freedom in political matters.) The rule against acquiring silver seems to be contradicted by *Hilchot Melachim* IV: 7, 8, 9 where he is given access to land and booty. Despite the Torah's explicit prohibition of going to Egypt, Maimonides makes allowance for it.

As Maimonides brings the *Mishneh Torah* to a close with *Hilchot melachim u'milchamot*, his ultimate conclusion deals with the nature of the *melech ha-mashiach*. One of Maimonides' purposes is to portray the Messiah as a flesh and blood being, a historical, nonmiraculous, and non-wonder-working king altogether different from any eschatological being, both in Jewish and non-Jewish thought, like Jesus, of whom he speaks disparagingly. The basis for such a concept of a Messiah can be established only in a political system at the center of which is the king. For the king to be also the Messiah, both his biblical and talmudic credentials need to be established. The king with whom *Hilchot Melachim* opens turns into the Messiah at the close. He has been the Messiah from the beginning, waiting to be so proclaimed at the end. But this comes about by Maimonides' daring, unilateral declaration about the Messiah's naturalistic being. This is of a piece with his opening declaration about kingship. In the face of contrasting rabbinic positions, he takes the one that validates his political system and codifies it. While he has rabbinic precedent for making kingship mandatory, his authority concerning the Messiah is more meager, essentially because *that* issue is theological, not halachic. But Maimonides, linking it to kingship, gives it a measure of halachic authenticity, since the role of the king as defined by Jewish law is strikingly related to that of the Messiah.

In the face of countervailing evidence, what leads Maimonides to dogmatically determine that kingship is mandatory in Israel? Obviously, he made a judgment based on what appears in Sifre and in Sanhedrin 20b, and later in Pesikta Rabbati and Midrash Tehillim (in abbreviated form). While the formula embodied there became accepted as a basic principle, it was also challenged, as we have indicated. An answer lies in his philosophic system. For Maimonides, even if the halachic foundations of the kingship principle may have been frequently questioned, that principle, though enunciated in a legal code, was profoundly linked to his philosophic-political formulation and related to his perception of man as a political being.

Maimonides may be considered a forerunner of political Zionism. This raises the issue of whether he believed in a historical restoration of a Jewish commonwealth. His references to Bar Kochba and his stress on the king in naturalistic, noneschatological terms strongly presents his commitment to the idea of a king and a Messiah who would stand within the historical order. Is there anything additional and more concrete than that? In his *Iggeret Teman* he writes to the threatened Jews of the community of Yemen that a time of oppression will be followed by the Messiah who will suddenly appear incognito in the land of Israel after prophecy has been renewed. He will undertake military campaigns and achieve victory, proving to the world that Israel's redemption is at hand. This is the only place where he specified the signs of the Messiah's advent, yet it is compatible with his naturalistic views. Even the renewal of prophecy is presented as a form of human perfection achieved through a natural process.[70] Nevertheless, Maimonides says nothing about the role of the people in bringing about redemption. Only God and the Messiah will be the dominant actors, and Blidstein speculates that the mention of any other factors such as a popular uprising could only bring harm to the oppressed Jews of Yemen.[71]

While the people's active participation seems to be missing from the eschatological expectations of Maimonides, still certain concrete realities are present. They are the role of the King-Messiah and even more, Maimonides' detailed exposition of the place of the king in his thought. Linked as it ultimately is to the messianic expectation, Maimonides was writing both about a future age and in its behalf. His naturalistic bent vividly concretizes his expectations all the more for a restored Jewish political order under a powerful king, acting as the head of the people within the historical process.

Notes

1. Leo Strauss, "Maimonides' Statement on Political Science," *Proceedings of the American Academy for Jewish Research*, Vol. 21–23, 1952–1959, p. 117.
2. Ibid., p. 119.
3. Moshe Ventura, Introduction to *Millot ha-Higayon*, pp. 10–11.
4. Strauss, "Maimonides' Statement," pp. 117–118.
5. Ibid., p. 118.
6. Ibid., p. 119.
7. *Guide of the Perplexed*, Pines translation, Chicago, 1963, II:39, 90.
8. Strauss, "Maimonides' Statement," p. 124.
9. Strauss, "Maimonides' Statement," p. 125.
10. *Guide of the Perplexed*, II:40, p. 382.
11. Ibid., II:40, pp. 383–384.
12. Ibid., III:27, p. 510.
13. Ibid., pp. 510–511.
14. Ibid.
15. Ibid., III:28, p. 512.
16. Ibid., p. 513.
17. Ibid., III:51, p. 524.
18. *Sefer Ha-Mitzvot*, number 173.
19. Ibid., p. 183.
20. Based on Shevuot 14b–15a.

21. *Hilchot Sanhedrin* I:3.
22. Sanhedrin 5a.
23. *Perush Ha-Mishneh*, Bechorot 4:4.
24. *Hilchot Melachim* IV:10.
25. *Hilchot Edut* XI:9.
26. Gerald Blidstein, *Ekronot Mediniim b'mishnat harambam*, Ramat Gan, 1983, p. 88.
27. Ibid., p. 115.
28. *Hilchot Melachim* III:6.
29. Ibid., p. 259.
30. Ibid.
31. Ibid., p. 115.
32. *Hilchot Sanhedrin* II:4–5.
33. Ibid., p. 135, citing *Hilchot Mamrim* II:4.
34. Sanhedrin 46a; *Hilchot Sanhedrin* XXIV:4.
35. Blidstein, *Ekronot*, p. 129.
36. Ibid., p. 133.
37. *Hilchot Talmud Torah* III:1.
38. *Hilchot Melachim* II:5.
39. *Sefer Ha-Mitzvot*, number 173.
40. Blidstein, *Ekronot*, p. 163.
41. *Hilchot Gezelah v'avedah* V:14; *Hilchot Z'chiya u'matanah* I:15.
42. *Hilchot Gezelah v'avedah* V:12.
43. *Sefer Ha-Mitzvot*, number 187.
44. Ibid., numbers 188, 189.
45. Deuteronomy 25:19.
46. *Hilchot Melachim* III:1.
47. Ibid., III:2–6.
48. Ibid., III:9.
49. Ibid., III:10.
50. Ibid.
51. Ibid., IV:1.
52. Ibid., V:13.
53. Ibid.
54. *Hilchot Retzichah* II:4.
55. *Hilchot Melachim* IV:10.
56. Ibid., V:2.
57. Ibid., IV:10.
58. Ibid.
59. Ibid.
60. Isaiah 11:9
61. *Hilchot Melachim* XII:5.
62. Ibid., XI:1.

63. Ibid., XI:4.
64. Ibid.
65. Ibid., XI:1.
66. Ibid., XI:3.
67. Ibid., XI:4.
68. Ibid., III:2–4.
69. Deuteronomy 17:15–20.
70. Gershom Scholem, *L'havanat ha-raayon ha-meshichi B'Yisrael,* Tel Aviv, 1976, p. 183.
71. Ibid., p. 245.

IX

—Isaac Abravanel (1437–1509)

Abravanel is the first theocrat in medieval Judaism to explicitly reject Jewish kingship as divinely commanded. He is the first in rabbinic Judaism to develop a systematic and reasoned refutation of it and to attempt to do so through a critical analysis of biblical texts. He is also a radical theocrat who not only denies even a subordinate place to the king but insists on the direct governance of Jewish affairs by God. Yet he appears to argue that while the Torah does not ordain kingship, it is nevertheless a permissible concession to the moral weakness of the people. There is a gap between the theory that kingship is not required and the need to confront the biblical provision for establishing kingship. Yet this paradox is no different from that which we find in I Samuel 8 and in Deuteronomy 17:14 ff.

Abravanel deals with Jewish government in his commentaries on Deuteronomy, Chapters 16–18 (composed in the 1460s and revised and completed in 1495, according to Netanyahu); I Samuel Chapter 8 (1483); and Exodus 18:13 (1505). Since Abravanel alludes in his Deuteronomy 16 commentary to *prior* comments in I Samuel 8, which are substantially repeated in the Deuteronomy commentary, we shall analyze the Samuel passage first.

While prior commentators accepted kingship as a commandment, they found fault with the way in which the request was made of Samuel. They wanted a king to lead them into idolatry,[1] but if this were so, says Abravanel, God would not have acceded to their request. The rabble justified the demand in order to be "like all the nations."[2] They wanted to usurp the role of the judge by asking for a king to judge them.[3] They made the request while Samuel was still alive.[4] Abravanel contends that if having a king was indeed a mitzvah, it should not have been postponed to the time of Samuel but should have been obeyed upon entering the land. "How could they [for so long] have transgressed this commandment?" Not one of the commentators answers this. Abravanel therefore concludes that the true sin of the people was not in the rationalizations of the commentators but in the very request for a king. Abravanel now cites a more formidable argument by Don Paolo of Burgos. A king may be chosen either by submitting to the laws of the Torah or by establishing his own laws arbitrarily, as among other nations. The Torah ordained the first course, but the people requested the second. ("So that we might be like all the nations.") Thus, when the sinful request was made, Samuel warned them of its consequences. His litany of royal abuses fits Aristotle's definition of a tyrant. But why didn't the people cast off the king after having suffered the consequences of his tyranny? Because, says Don Paolo, the king had already been anointed by God's command and the anointment cannot be annulled. Abravanel rejoins: Since the people requested a king in place of Samuel's wicked sons, would they have demanded yet another tyrant who would arbitrarily impose his own law? Certainly not, and if they had really wanted a tyrant, they would not have come to Samuel for one. Having disposed of the spurious explanations, Abravanel turns to two more substantive questions. First, is a king necessary for the government of other nations? If so, is he required in Israel? The very question is daring because it renders problematic the basic mitzvah of Deuteronomy 17:14–15. In order to address the second issue, Abravanel must confront the first one, since it involves the question of "like all the nations" in contrast to Israel's differentiation.

Is kingship mandatory for the nations? Aristotle and his colleagues think so, and believe that the relationship of the king to the body politic is like that of the heart to the body. According to this concept, kingship requires three attributes—unshared authority, continuity with nontransference of office, and absolute power. But this definition is wrong, maintains Abravanel, because (a) it is demonstrably possible to have collective rule; (b) there is no reason why rulership cannot change periodically, even annually, more frequently, or less frequently; (c) power can and should be curtailed by law through majority rule. It is more difficult for a single person sharing power with a group of rulers to transgress than for a single, unlimited ruler. Likewise, the tendency toward political folly is greater in a single authority. "Behold the lands governed by kings, and observe their abominations. Each does what is right in his own eyes, and the earth is full of violence because of them, and who dares say to them, 'What are you doing?' But today we see many lands governed by temporary rulers selected every three months. The law is defined for them in a limiting manner, while as for those who govern the people while waging war, no one may resist them unjustly."

We should note that Abravanel recognizes the special power of leaders during war. In the context of political rulers whose period of service is limited and who are subject to controls, those engaged in warfare do not undergo such restrictions. Thus, Abravanel provides for great latitude for leaders in wartime, thereby qualifying his preference for limited rulers. "If any one [of the rulers] trespasses even in a minor matter, others will take their place." Abravanel contrasts the Roman Empire, ruling tyranically and ultimately being subdued (despite absolute kingship or in consequence of it) with the governments of Venice, Florence, Genoa, and Bologna, who have no kings but are governed by leaders selected for fixed periods. Those cities are governed justly, proving that kings are not necessary. In fact, kings are destructive. "It is amazing how the king is compared to God. Kings are like the sea. There is no remedy for their wrath, and whoever goes among them is like one going in the midst of death. . . . When Solomon [Proverbs 28:2] declares, 'When the land sins, its rulers increase,' he speaks of princes who are lords of the land and not the judges and leaders (who govern by Torah)." When the king is just, the leadership of those around him will be improved, as was the case of the Bet Din of seventy, but if he is evil, his evil is mitigated by the leaders around him who are temporary, as in Aragon. "When God gave kings to the world and its inhabitants, this accursed leprosy came so that a man could arise and restrain his people and lead them like asses."[5]

Abravanel now turns to the issue of kingship in Israel. In addressing this question, we must inquire about the relevance of the prior issue to this one. Does kingship among the nations have any bearing on kingship in Israel and does it in any way fall within the purview of Jewish concern? We should, in the first instance, not disregard Abravanel's personal experience with monarchy, which, while not always traumatic (as in Portugal), found him a victim of exile and expulsion from Spain. Even more, the disaster befalling all of Spanish Jewry certainly helped evoke his enraged verdict on kingship, whose unchallenged tyranny could bring disaster to an entire people. In addition to the political and moral reasons for the harsh condemnation of kingship was the prevalent opinion, articulated by Abravanel, that kings (evil as well as just) were ordained by God. This presents a paradox for Abravanel, who advocates the abolition of kingship and who yet resists (like Aristotle) the assassination of tyrants, since they derive their authority from God. Once Israel has a king, to rebel against the king is forbidden since they had entered into covenant with him, and "the king on earth is in place of God in the world." Rebellion against the king is like "putting forth one's hand against the glory of God." This applies to kings of other nations and of Jews. In the latter case, the prohibition is reinforced by "You shall set up a king whom God shall select."[6]

Thus, even if kings are a "leprosy," they must be suffered, by Israel as well as the nations. But as for Israel, Abravanel contends that it is so radically different from the nations that even if kings were necessary for them, they would be superfluous for Israel. Likewise, if as Abravanel had attempted to demonstrate, they were not required among the nations, how much less were they required for Israel. Among the nations, kings are required to fight a nation's enemies and defend its land, to establish norms for the body politic as Aristotle indicates, and to punish offenders by extralegal measures as situations require. Other nations need these criteria because they lack divine laws and are not protected by divine providence. But "the Israelite nation (*umah*) does not require these criteria for kings because God fights its battles, and no king need make its laws, since it has the Torah. (Note: Although Strauss defines "*umah*" as construed by Abravanel as a religious body, it is clear from the context that it also carries political implications.) As for extralegal punishment, God assigns this to the judges and to the Sanhedrin. "The Bet Din punishes legally and extra-legally according to the needs of the time."[7] (This is contrary to Maimonides' judgment, which gives this power to the king.) Abravanel argues that Israel's uniqueness and kingship are contradictory.

Abravanel takes a position radically opposed to Maimonides and, in a measure, to those expressions in the tractate Sanhedrin. Maimonides in *Hilchot Melachim* categorically designates the king as the people's warlord and even defines his role in the waging of war. So do the rabbis. Likewise *Hilchot Melachim* gives the king special latitude in exacting punishment under exigent circumstances. Maimonides' influence on Abravanel was great. Yet, while not naming him in this instance, he clearly takes issue with him by transferring authority to the judges, and thus departs radically from Maimonides' political views.

An examination of Sanhedrin 46a will demonstrate this point. Abravanel cites only a portion of the passage in order to uphold his position and the results are misleading. It reads,

> 'Eliezer ben Yaacov says:' "I have heard that the Bet Din may flog and punish not in accordance with the Torah as long as it does not transgress the Torah, and only for the purpose of building a fence around the Torah. There is the incident of one who rode a horse on Shabbat in the days of the Greeks. He was brought to the Bet Din and they stoned him, not that he deserved this, but because the time required it. In another case a man had intercourse with his wife under a fig tree. He was brought to the Bet Din and flogged, not because he deserved it, but because the times required it."

The complete passage is hardly a confirmation of Abravanel's reference that the Bet Din punishes according to the requirements of the time. As he cites it, it appears to be a halachah. However, it is only a recollection by one scholar who does not attribute his recollection to anyone in particular. Then, of the two incidents described, we cannot even guess at the extraordinary circumstances prompting the punishment of the second man. Nor is there indication that a king reigned at that time. As to the first incident, it occurred "during the time of the Greeks" who governed the land of Israel—when there was no Jewish king. It demonstrates only that extralegal punishment was exacted by the Bet Din in the absence of a Jewish king. It therefore does not support Abravanel's argument, which implies that the king could not punish extralegally. It indicates only that when there is no king, the Beth Din acts in his place. Had there been other evidence, Abravanel would have adduced it. The absence of such evidence and the unconvincing proof that he does bring would appear to refute his own argument.

This break, however, is not only with Maimonides but even with those theocrats who acknowledged the rule of the king as responsible for the nation's security. He buttresses his thesis by the dogmatic assertion,

> Kings . . . were not required in Am (the people) Yisroel. From what we have observed . . . they rebelled against the light in

> Israel . . . as in the case of Jeroboam who caused the people's exile, and also (in the case of) the kings of Judah who at the end imitated [the kings of Israel] until Judah was exiled. . . . Not so do we see among the judges of Israel and their prophets, all valiant, God-fearing, truthful, not one veering from God. All this proves that the kings in Israel were harmful, not beneficial. . . . The Rabbis hinted at this (Zevachim 102a) "Ulla said that Moses our teacher sought kingship but it was not granted to him." . . . It was not the purpose of this scholar to state [merely] that Moses wanted kingship and lordship over Israel and that God denied it to him, but that God chose, not a king over Israel but a prophet, a leader and judges like Moses; all of which proves that a king is neither required nor beneficial in Israel. When you know this you will understand the meaning of the prophet Hosea (13:10, 11), ("Where now is your king . . . whom you demanded, give me a king: I will give you a king in my wrath.")

It does not apply, as Nachmanides states, only to the kings of Israel and not to those of Judah.

The Hosea passage, which refers explicitly to the Samuel event, means you corrupted yourselves by seeking a king whom God consequently gives, out of anger, since your help comes from Him, not from the king. The people of Israel did not ask for a king as soon as they settled in the land (*ki tavo el ha-aretz*), and since this was a foolish request when it was finally made, they were commanded *not* to make their own selection but to depend on God's decision. This is the essence of the command, to leave the selection to God if they are unwise enough to want a king. The passage in question is to be construed exactly like Deuteronomy 21:10. "When you take the field against your enemies . . . and you see among the captives a beautiful woman and you desire her . . . you shall bring her into your house . . ." This clearly does not say, you are commanded to capture a beautiful woman and lust for her, but rather if you do, there are certain limiting responsibilities incumbent upon you. Similarly, Deuteronomy 4:25, "Should you, when you have begotten children . . . act wickedly and make for yourself a sculptured image . . ." This is certainly not a command to act wickedly and make graven images. Thus the issue is not that the request is a mitzvah but an act of the evil inclination; the mitzvah is not the demand for a king but that if the demand is made, the selection must be by God, from the midst of their brethren, in no other manner. If there must be a king because of the people's demand, he is to be limited and under God's control.

"There are five proofs for this." (a) If indeed God had commanded that they ask for a king while his selection was not in their hands, what was the point of their asking? (b) If it was a mitzvah to say, "I will set a king over me," how could the people have been told to say "like all the nations," especially when God wanted them *not* to be like all the nations? (c) The opening phrase in the verse is not a mitzvah but a declearation of what could happen in the future, and a prescription of what to do when that occurs. (d) If the request for a king is a mitzvah, so is the selection of a king by God and so is the limitation to "your brethren." (e) If the people had made the request in order to fulfill a mitzvah they would have phrased it differently, as "Give us a king, as God has commanded Moses." Instead, they phrased it quite contrarily anbd defiantly, "so that he might judge us, like all the nations." Therefore, this was an act of the evil inclination.

Abravanel adds that the king was not required for conducting Israel's affairs, since God fought for the people, their leaders conducted their affairs according to the Torah, and they were under the guidance of the prophets. Their sin was in rejecting divine kingship and preferring human kingship. It was to the credit of Joshua and the God-fearing Judges that they did not raise up kings. Abravanel cites Sanhedrin 20b to prove his point and to refute Maimonides, who in *Hilchot Melachim* approves the observation of R. Yose that the "bill of particulars" in I Samuel 8 indicates all the permissable acts of the king. Abravanel states, "The simple meaning does not indicate this and shows that the truth is according to R. Judah (who says that the passage is intended to threaten and frighten the people) . . . since [Deuteronomy 17:20] says, 'so that his heart not be lifted up above his brethren and that he turn neither right nor left from the command.'"[8] Further, the term "practice of the king" as used in I Samuel 8 is a euphemism for "evil judgment." If it were a recitation of what was permitted to the king, if "he will take your fields," represented a legal act, why couldn't King Ahab legitimately expropriate Naboth's field without requiring Jezebel to find a pretext for executing him?

> The request for a King was not a sin explicitly denounced by the Torah. . . . I have said that it was permissible [*dvar reshut*],

> deriving from the evil inclination. It is not a transgression forbidden by the Torah. Thus, after requesting him [the king], and not abandoning him, they were like one who immerses himself in a ritual bath while holding on to an unclean reptile. It [consequently] sufficed that they obey the command [only] to take a king selected by God.

God would not abandon Israel in any circumstance and He tolerated human kingship, while reminding the people that He was the true King. Thus, He selected David, knowing him as God-fearing and observant of the mitzvot, and "made a covenant with him and his seed forever . . . even while the people persisted in their sinfulness."[9] David was selected for the people's own good.

The style of "I will take a king" is unprecedented among all other mitzvot. "It would have been sufficient to say 'You shall take for yourself a king,' since this is the essence of the mitzvah."[10] Also, the reference to "all the nations" is unusual, since we are commanded not to imitate them. Conversely, if this phrase is acceptable, why wasn't it used for selection of judges, whom the nations also have?[11]

Abravanel turns to his primary position: "In the time when there was a king [in Israel] he would appoint" [the Bet Din] (Ibid.). The Bet Din may judge in accordance with the needs of the hour. He adds, "Since the king was not required in Israel (*umah yisraelit*) . . . judgment was given to the courts, and judgment according to need of the hour was given to the Sanhedrin. . . . Ha-rav [Maimonides] in the weakness of his opinion, wrote that . . . [judgment in] extraordinary matters was in the hands of the king. This derives from his opinion that the king is required, but this is not my opinion."[12]

Concerning Sanhedrin 20 and Jose's argument that Samuel defined the prerogatives permitted to the king, Abravanel argues that Judah bar Ila considered it only a threat. He says, "Maimonides in *Hilchot Melachim*, Chapter 1, decided accordingly to Jose." But, argues Abravanel, the simple meaning of the text contradicts Maimonides and shows that the truth is according to Judah, who says it was intended not to endorse *mishpat ha-melech* but to intimidate the people with it. Since Deuteronomy 17 recalls nothing of this (the "permissible" prerogatives), it teaches instead that according to the Torah the king is not permitted to do the things Samuel enumerates.

Abravanel finds himself in a dilemma. He denies that the Torah requires a king but, facing up to historical reality and to Scripture itself, he must acknowledge that kingship is not forbidden. Here is encapsulated both Abravanel's and the Bible's ambivalence. But if kingship is tolerated, it commands a significant measure of authenticity and acceptance, and Abravanel's outright repudiation of it becomes problematic. Like many of his predecessors, he does not circumvent the ambivalence, but grants the king a role, however subordinate he might be in the Torah's hierarchy of leaders.

While some before him denounced and even rejected kingship, he takes a position that directly defies Maimonides and the sources on which he bases his *Hilchot Melachim*. In a sense, Abravanel's explanation of the institution of kingship as a concession to popular weakness is similar to Maimonides' skepticism about the value of sacrifices (even though they are divinely mandated), as a means of deflecting the lust for sacrifice. The absolute evil of kingship, together with the people's craving for it, results in a mitigating event by which kings, under divine limitation and in the providential case of David and his line, are allowed to rule. The reference to the acceptability of kings does not represent a contradiction in Abravanel's thought, not merely because the weight of the evidence opposes that conclusion but because the true contradiction is between biblical theory as he sees it and the historical reality of kingly rule. Having demonstrated that Israel could endure without a king, he attempts to explain why, despite this and under the sway of evil impulses, it was allowed to have a king. Nevertheless, he makes clear that the authentic leadership of the people resided among the judges.

Abravanel declares that in the wilderness Moses, at the urging of Jethro, created the ideal Jewish government that became the prototype for the most desirable kind of Jewish polity, which the Republic of Venice was to emulate centuries later. "He led them like a king and a righteous judge."[13] As Abravanel perceived it, a vast judicial system was instituted, involving great numbers of specialists dealing with a wide range of litigation—civil, criminal, fiscal, and their subcategories. He refers to the network of judges who sometimes sat in huge numbers and sometimes in small numbers, enabling the system to work with dispatch. As a result, people had confidence in the judicial system because the courts were not clogged with deferred cases. This was due to certain procedures instituted by Moses in contrast to Jethro's advice. Instead of appointing the judges, he allowed the people to select them. Also, despite Jethro's advice, he did not insist on "God-fearing, truthful men and haters of unjust gain" but only "men of valor," because "all of them were holy, with God in their midst." Finally, while Jethro advised him to select men only for adjudication, Moses selected military officers as well.

For Abravanel, while Moses' rule was tantamount to kingship, he did not assume that prerogative. He believed in a system in which the entire people participated and in which all the people were qualified for the highest national service. In addition, Abravanel perceived the judicial and military system as linked in the structure of national well-being. There is no suggestion that the military leaders were to be selected by the people nor that they were to replace God as the primary warriors, but rather that like the judges, the rules of law and of the sword were interrelated. Abravanel conceived of an idyllic system under which the people did not require centralized authority as invested in the king and whereby the judicial process alone preserved internal tranquility. This was also a conception of an inherently godly community that did not require the onerous restraints of kingship and whose members could both provide the necessary qualified judges and be content with their jurisdiction. Obviously, this was a paradigm neither of Israel in the wilderness nor of the Venetian republic. A more pointed issue is whether Abravanel superimposed the Venice of his day on ancient Israel. He had cited the city-state elsewhere in his ruminations about the dispensability of kingship, but these are illustrations of his antikingly thesis rather than the roots from which it springs. He was antiroyal and found contemporary realities to buttress his convictions. "The scholars did not go into the depths of the mitzvah [concerning kingship] and its roots, since they accepted it as a positive mitzvah to request a king, but this is not my opinion . . ."[14]

Abravanel criticizes Maimonides for designating kings to both wage battle and do judgment, based on the demand by the people that the king "should judge us and do battle," but, says Abravanel, it was because of this statement that the rabble spoiled the request, as indicated in Sanhedrin.[15] As a result of the popular request, the people under Solomon had to supply food for his vast household, maintain his forty thousand horses and twelve thousand horsemen, and provide for the vast number of people who came from abroad to see him. "This was a great burden and heavy toil. . . . He imposed annual taxes upon them for his wars." Concerning his son, Rehoboam, he planned to make their burden even heavier and to enslave them for their entire lives.[16]

The essence of Abravanel's argument is that although kings are not required in Israel, and yet the people in their sinfulness secure a king, two conditions must ensue. First, he is to be selected by God and must be subject to His regulations. Second, he cannot be dethroned, even if he is a tyrant, because God has selected him. The issue Abravanel leaves unanswered is—if kingship is so evil, how could God permit it even if the people demanded it? What other evil institution does the Torah tolerate even if the people hanker after it, especially when the stigma of idolatry seems to hover over it? Since Abravanel confronted the issue theologically, he could not consistently resolve the problem. Nevertheless, he presented the issue so that it could be perceived as an unreconciled confrontation between the national will for kingship and the religious-ethical resistance to it, with the latter submitting reluctantly and imposing restrictions. Abravanel is not a rebel but a harsh critic of Jewish kingship. He does not abolish kingship, he rejects it. He rejects it as a principle, and acknowledges it as a disagreeable reality.

We can see Abravanel's position on kingship as a confrontational response to Maimonides. This is particularly significant because Abravanel was once devoted to Maimonides, Abravanel "accepts the literal teaching of the 'Guide' . . . That literal teaching is . . . at least the framework of Abravanel's own philosophy."[17] According to Strauss, the divergence can be traced to Maimonides' rationalism and Abravanel's antirationalism (due, Strauss would argue, to the latter's failure to penetrate the secret and disguised meaning of the former) and to the former's perception of Judaism in political terms and the latter's non-political perception. Maimonides, like the Islamic philosophers, influenced by Plato's "Laws," was "deeply driven to interpret revelation more precisely as an ideal political order. . . . They had to assume that the founder of the ideal political order, the prophetic lawgiver, was not merely a statesman . . . but a philosopher of the highest authority. They had to conceive . . . of Moses or Mohammed as philosopher kings."[18] While Maimonides attempted to harmonize philosophy with revelation, the thought of Abravanel, "however deeply he may have been influenced by . . . the philosophical teaching of Maimonides . . . was determined, not by philosophy but by Judaism as a tradition based on a verbally inspired revelation."[19] For Maimonides, the basic beliefs of Judaism are construed in terms of political philosophy, "interpreting Judaism as a whole as a perfect law in the platonic sense." Abravanel rejects this approach and denies the *Guide's* assertion that the greatest sector of the Torah's law deals with the "government of the city."[20] Prophecy does not bother with politics and economics. Not Moses but Jethro organized Israel's juridical structure. "Abravanel's depreciation of political philosophy, which is a consequence of his critical attitude toward Maimonides' rationalism, thus implies a decisive limitation of the content of political philosophy."[21]

Abravanel theoretically dismisses the king and converts the Messiah, whom Maimonides merges with the king, into an eschatological, miracle-working being whose advent brings catastrophe and the end of the world, preceded by a disastrous war in which God, not Israel, will be the direct victor. Unlike Maimonides' view, Abravanel's Messiah will not be a martial or a political figure.

The unpolitical character of Abravanel's Messiah is illustrated by the contrasting interpretations by him and by Maimonides of the passage in Exodus 13:17ff. explaining why God did not lead the people of Israel directly through the territory of the Philistines. According to Maimonides, this was for the purpose of teaching them courage. According to Abravanel, God wanted to drown the Egyptians and since there was no sea on the way to the Philistines, He routed Israel differently. This unpolitical proclivity is attributed by Strauss to Abravanel's submission to Roman, Greek, and Christian thought. His account of the innocent life "in the field" during man's first period is "literally taken over" from Seneca.[22] Strauss adds that his criticism of Cain as the founder of the first city appears first in Josephus.[23] Strauss also points out that Abravanel, in the spirit of Josephus and the Church Fathers, treats life in the city, private property, and authoritarian government as the result of rebellion against God's natural order.[24] "His criticism of political organization is truly comprehensive."[25] The reasons for this, according to Strauss, are Abravanel's antirationalism and his belief in miracles, manifested by Israel's natural condition in the wilderness where the people were sustained by God. That natural condition will be restored during the messianic age. Thus Abravanel diverges from Maimonides' Aristotelian perception of man as a political creature. Instead, he sees man's political existence as essentially sinful in origin and only reluctantly granted to man by God.[26] At his best in the past and in the future, he relies on God's miraculous powers.

Strauss refutes Abravanel's position on two major grounds: first, that Abravanel studiously follows the ideology of Christian thinkers;

second, that Abravanel flies in the face of Jewish tradition, which is promonarchical. Strauss, in addition, argues that Abravanel's supernatural ideology is opposed to Maimonides' rationalism. Strauss contends that in order to consistently oppose Jewish kingship, Abravanel denies that the Messiah will be a king but that instead he will be a prophet and judge. Thus, instead of synthesizing king and Messiah as Maimonides does, he separates them, rejecting the first and redefining the second. By way of enforcing his position that rabbinic Judaism was almost monolithically promonarchical, Strauss acknowledges that "as far as I know, the only medieval commentator who, in his commentary on Deuteronomy 17:14ff, expressly understands that passage as conveying a permission is Ibn Ezra."[27]

Strauss observes, "Both the Jewish and the Christian tradition, and in particular both the Jewish and the Christian Middle Ages, were in favour of the monarchy. Anti-monarchical statements are, in both traditions, exceptional up to the humanist age." Also, "the Jewish Bible shows not the slightest sign of an anti-monarchist tendency. The immediate origin of Abravanel's anti-monarchist conclusions from his theocratic premises has to be sought for, not in Jewish, but in Christian sources."[28] Aquinas (1225–1275), says Strauss, provides the model for Abravanel's view of Jewish government that is transposed from the description of the Jewish constitution in *Summa Theologiae* to a hierarchy ranging from the democratic element (local judges elected by the people), to an aristocratic element (Sanhedrin), to a monarchic element (Moses and his successors). This is the government human. The government spiritual also has three degrees—the Levites, the priests, and chief in the hierarchy, the prophet. It should be noted that when Abravanel speaks of Moses as king, it is in a prophetic sense. Following the Christian tradition, says Strauss, Abravanel defines the government human as greatly inferior to the government spiritual that is governed by priests and prophets.

That Abravanel, like other Jewish, Christian, and Moslem thinkers, was engaged by their intellectual environments is not at issue, just as the thesis that Maimonides' political outlook was affected to an extent by Al Farabi is not at issue. Nor do these observations detract from the Jewish significance of Abravanel's or Maimonides' positions. But this does not necessarily suggest that Abravanel was dominated by Christian thought. For one thing, the Christian world was split on the issue of the relative powers of church and state, the world of the spirit and the world of the imperium. The issue was more involved than promonarchy or antimonarchy; rather the question was of the relative power between kings and popes, and the question of the restraints under which they ruled. This was equally true in the debates within Judaism about the king, not only whether he was required, but his role, his legitimacy, and the degree of power that should be allowed or denied to him. Early in the development of Christianity, churchmen differed markedly on these issues. We should examine the debate within Christianity to determine whether, given the difference within it, Abravanel can justifiably be perceived as primarily subject to its influences.

St. Augustine (354–430) declared, "If justice be put aside what are kingdoms save instances of robbery on a large scale?"[29] The Church Fathers saw government as a consequence of original sin, a condition that cannot be corrected. Augustine developed this idea in the duality of the city of God and the earthly city. His position was that authority came into the world as a punishment of God over fallen man. Chrysostom (347–407) wrote, "Because of our depravity there was need of government."

But, unlike St. Augustine in the West, Basil the Great (330–379) in the East saw political power as a "natural need of man" that would have been necessary for society regardless of original sin. "The ruler is not only God's minister for good, but he also beareth not the sword in vain . . . princes and magistrates are the avengers of the law of God. The ruler is also God's minister to execute wrath, but both functions of the ruler appear necessary, according to Basil, for the safeguarding of the common good."[30] "Basil . . . is certainly convinced that the power of the Imperium on earth is legitimate, is derived from God and must be obeyed from a religious obligation."[31] But he also contends that the closer man comes to God the less need there is for the imperium. God is the source of imperial power. "The Lord constitutes and disposes kings, and there is no power except it be constituted by God." Church and state are coexistent, one for man's spiritual bliss, the other for his temporal happiness. The spiritual is superior to the temporal, but the heavenly zeal of both is the same, since both are of God.

Nine centuries later, the issue persisted. For Thomas Aquinas, "the State was accepted as a true value in its own right. . . . Man is not born free, but subject to his group. . . . Social balance . . . is the achievement of civilization, that is, the living like a citizen within a State."[32] In his *On Kingship*, Aquinas states, "The greatness of kingly virtue appears in this, that he bears a special likeness to God, since he does in his Kingdom what God does in the world: . . . Kingship is the best way to rule the people if it is not corrupted" (*Summa Theologiae*). Yet he also writes "There is a higher priesthood by which men are guided to heavenly goals. Consequently, in the law of Christ, kings must be subject to priests."[33] Yet while Thomas Aquinas regarded the state as subordinate to the church, he nevertheless recognized secular authority both as an entity and a good in its own right. He thereby contributed to the emergence of national consciousness. Like Aristotle, Aquinas saw human life as social and organic. Man is not born free, but subject to his group. Whereas Augustine saw human nature as doomed, and reprieved only by unmerited grace, Aquinas saw human nature "endowed with its own proper goodness, including rights which sin could not abolish."[34]

Prominent among Strauss' indications of Christian influence on Abravanel is Jerome's Vulgate translation of Deuteronomy 17:14ff. He charges that Abravanel's interpretation of that passage "is directly opposed to that of the Jewish tradition[and] is in substance identical with that implied in the Vulgate."[35] The operative portion of the passage reads: "Eum constitues, quem Dominus tuus elegerit de numero fratrum tuorum. . . ." An analysis of Jerome's translation does, in fact, reveal a permissive, not a mandatory attitude toward kingship. "Eum constitues" carries a different emphasis than *som tasim* and lays stress not on selection by the people but on God's choice. "You shall (if you request) select him whom God will choose from among your brethren."

Yet, the suggestion that Abravanel depended on such a source is gratuitous, since it overlooks the Jewish tradition of controversy on this verse that, as we have seen, was subjected to a wide range of views on Jewish kingship. One could pursue with equal congency the speculation that Jerome may have been influenced in his version through his association with Jewish scholars during his long sojourn in the Land of Israel, among them Rabbi Chanina.

Abravanel did not have to stand on the shoulders of Christian scholars. He found ample ground within Jewish controversy concerning kings.

At times, Abravanel does cite a Christian authority approvingly, and Strauss points out a similarity between Abravanel and Nicholas de Lyra (1270–1340). But here again, as with Jerome and the Jewish scholars with whom he studied, the influence of Jewish scholarship on de Lyra must also be taken into account. Most significant is Graetz's statement: "If from the voluminous writings of Nicolas de Lyra, the best Christian exegetist, all [that is] borrowed from Rashi were to be excised, the part left, which he himself composed, might be comprised in a few pages."[36] In reading de Lyra, one is impressed with the resemblance of his perceptions on kingship to earlier rabbinic commentators, rather than Abravanel's dependency on de Lyra. He refers approvingly on Don Paolo of Bourgos, who argued that a king could be selected by popular request either to obey the Torah or to arbitrarily make his own laws. The people's motives in the selection of Saul were for a king who would be disobedient. But this was not an original idea of Don Paolo. It has its origin in early rabbinic literature. Indeed, Abravanel also strongly disagrees with Christian scholars (*chachmay ha-notzrim*) who, for example, argue that Samuel was at fault in the matter of kingship because he did not originally prevent his sons from acting corruptly and thus he incurred the people's request for a king.

The second argument by Strauss that "both the Jewish and Christian tradition were in favor of the monarchy" is excessively simplistic, as the debates within Judaism and Christianity attest. We cannot accept Strauss' assertion that "the [Jewish] scholars did not go into the depths of the mitzvah [concerning kingship], since they accepted it as a positive mitzvah." Yet we know that Abravanel was not only familiar with but cited the controversy over kingship as it appears in Sifre and in Sanhedrin. He could well have referred to the halachic predominance of the prokingship position. He could also have referred to the codification of that position, particularly in Maimonides. But when he cited prior invidious references to the people's sinfulness in requesting a king, he could not have been unaware of his rabbinic predecessors. If he meant to say that Abravanel was the first to systematically subject kingship to critical scrutiny, he was correct. If Abravanel had been the first rabbinic authority to renounce kingship in defiance of an entire body of prior opinion, one might be permitted to indulge in a charge of acquiescence to Christian philosophy and theology. However, we know that he was in one Jewish tradition, that suspicious of kingship, which is obscured by Strauss' insistence on monolithic rabbinic thought concerning kingship.

Moreover, it has been noted that Christian speculation about kingship was no more monolithic than Jewish thought on the subject. While Abravanel was conversant with Greek and Christian philosophy, and could very well have been affected by descriptions of the hierarchies of government, he did not require external validation for his views. Unlike Maimonides, the protagonist of Judaism as a polity, Abravanel pursued the less pronounced currents of Jewish apolitical belief. In doing so, he was diametrically at odds with those Christian thinkers who advanced the cause of Christian kingship. Like Abravanel, they were engaged in a debate within Christianity in which they advanced their own political views against the apolitical views of their opponents. The hierarchical system in the human and divine governments, which Strauss ascribes to Christian thought and which he claims that Abravanel appropriated, is not essentially un-Jewish except in nomenclature and philosophical systematization. The development in the Torah of the categories and rule of judges, priests, prophets and kings, and their further expansion in rabbinic law is, if anything, a model for its absorption into Christian civil and religious thought, including that of Aquinas.

Abravanel was certainly not in agreement with Aquinas who wrote, "The greatness of kingly virtue appears in this, that he bears a special likeness to God, since he does in his kingdom what God does in the world; wherefore in Exodus the judges of the people are called gods, and also among the Romans the emperors received the title Divus."

Abravanel cannot be properly compared with Christian thinkers because the latter came to develop the principle of two separate but coequal powers. The attempts by one to subject the other were reconciled by the establishment of two authorities under God. Abravanel did not attempt to resolve the issue by division, but rather through a radical unitary process. As medieval Christian thought on kingship develops, there is a clear polarity between church and state. While the ultimate authority for both comes from God, their temporal jurisdictions are separate and subject to contention, each with the other. In rabbinic thought, the principle of separation of powers is not so precisely pronounced. It is dealt with through the principle of subordination, with temporal authority flowing to the king in Maimonides, to the judges in Ha-an, and with authority draining away from the king in Abravanel—all into a unitary system.

JEWISH SOURCES OF ABRAVANEL

Having ascribed Christian influences to Abravanel, Strauss concludes quite contradictorily that "the sources . . . are for Abravanel, not so much the historians, poets and orators of classical antiquity, but the literal sense of the Bible—and Josephus. . . . Thus we conclude that Abravanel's view of the Jewish government as a whole is taken over from Josephus."[37] This represents an ambivalence in which Strauss faults Abravanel both for his dependence on Christian thought and for being "fundamentally determined by the Jewish tradition."[38]

The conclusion by Strauss that ultimately Josephus is the source of Abravanel's singular position is an indication of the weakness of his "Christian" argument. It seems to suggest that the claims to Christian origins of the "unpolitical" position is after all rooted in Judaism.

There is a fundamental weakness in this argument. To equate the priestly theocracy of Josephus with the judicial theocracy of Abravanel presents two contrasting and contradictory advocacies. As we have already indicated, Josephus wanted to see the continuation of the Temple cult under the benign protection of Rome. Abravanel stressed the capability of the Jewish *umah* to manage its own affairs precisely because of the superior capability of the judges who were to govern in accordance with the Torah, and under God. Rabbinic thought, while aspiring toward reconstitution of the Temple cult, certainly did not embrace the more atavistic hopes of Josephus for the concentration of national internal power in the hands of the priests. That John Milton prefers Josephus to the "tenebrionibus Rabbinis," rabbinical obscurities (as Strauss points out) in no way identifies Abravanel or the rabbis for that matter (a la Gershon Weiler) with Josephus.

Strauss' argument that the Bible is entirely promonarchical is qualified by our earlier findings. Nor is his argument that rabbinic literature is overwhelmingly monarchical convincing. Strauss does not fully take into account the strong negative rabbinic attitudes toward kingship. That rabbinic sources accept Deuteronomy 17:14 as a mitzvah does not fully encompass the range of response toward it. For the tradition to openly renounce a Torah mitzvah is unthinkable, and the fact that some sources, such as Deuteronomy Rabbah did just that is far more significant than the affirmation of kingship. Equally significant is Ibn Ezra's comment that kingship is only permissible, not mandatory. Maimonides' dogmatic assertions suggest the need to assert the mandatory character of kingship in the face of contrary and wavering opinions in rabbinic thought. In addition, the shift of emphasis from the authority of kings to that of judges (*Haran*) and silence where clear assertions about kingship might be expected (*Kuzari*) point to ambivalence at least, and even profound skepticism if not about the mandatory character of kingship, then certainly about its utility.

According to Strauss, for Abravanel to successfully disprove kingship as a mitzvah, he must overcome the fact that according to "the earlier commentators . . . Deut. 17:14 ff did express such a command (for a King)."[39] The Strauss argument is that Abravanel alone holds out against the concept of kingship as a mitzvah. Against him, he cites Nachmanides, Moses of Coucy, Gersonides, Bachya ben Asher, Moses Chayim Alsheich, Samson Raphael Hirsch, Buber, and Menasseh ben Israel, who says, "This opinion is highly consistent with the words of Scripture, but it is not accepted by many because it is opposed to the beliefs and the tradition of the ancients."[40] Yet it has been noted that Nachmanides is not merely contradictory but essentially resistant to kingship; Alsheich reduces kingship to divine anticipation of the people's sinfulness; Gersonides ascribes much Jewish suffering to kingship.

Both Bachya and Moses of Coucy acknowledge kingship as a mitzvah, and then proceed to disparage it because of the unworthy motivations of the people. We address ourselves to Strauss' observations on Menasseh ben Israel, who is also adduced as witness against Abravanel. Menasseh ben Israel is cited as an authoritative advocate of Jewish kingship. But an analysis of the quotation cited by Strauss reveals that Menasseh asserts there are two sets of opinion on the subject.

Hirsch converts the king into an etherealized, depoliticized moralist.

Buber's view on monarchy is best presented when he speaks of "the ancient opposition to subjugation to a man which demands mastery over him and his family. There are men who . . . bring to this stubbornness a tendency that . . . converts it into dependency on God the King, and they do this by . . . renunciation of rulership. . . ."[41] This position is anticipated in Mendelssohn's *Jerusalem*, where, in discussing I Samuel 8, he writes, "The people persisted in their resolution . . . and they experienced everything the prophet had foretold them. Now the polity was undermined . . . State and religion ceased to be identical."[42]

Of special interest are the only three exceptions to his assertion that Strauss recognizes—Targum Yonatan, Rashi, and Ibn Ezra (although his prime example is Ibn Ezra). We have already noted that

Targum Yonatan, unlike Targum Onkelos, does not present Deuteronomy 17:14 as a command to have a king but rather as a command "for instruction before the Lord." Strauss acknowledges that Ibn Ezra "simply says that the passage expresses a permission . . . [and that] Rashi does not say anything on the passage." It is noteworthy that he gives no further attention to these highly significant data in a brief note, giving the impression that these represent the only exceptions. Yet, Rashi is not totally silent in his note on Sanhedrin 20b. Of greater significant is Ibn Ezra's comment that refutes, Strauss who identifies Abravanel with Nicolas de Lyra's observation that Deuteronomy 17:14 "non est Praeceptum, nec simplex concessio." (is not a command but a concession) Did Abravanel necessarily depend on Nicolas when Ibn Ezra's position was known? Was the "point of view of Abravanel identical with that of Nicolas," or was it rather informed in part by Ibn Ezra and other Jewish scholars?

In addition to the material already cited, Shimon Federbush asserts that "the Torah did not command the selection of a king, only that if the people insist on a king, he must be Jewish."[43] He cites approvingly Rabbi Nehorai (Sanhedrin 20b), "This commandment was made because of the complaints" of Israel who insisted on being like all the nations. These words, "like all the nations," are words of disparagement, as Samuel's response indicates. Federbush cites Ovadia Sforno who states that kingship is not desirable, but if the people obstinately request a king, there are restrictions to his power, but asking for a king was a sin. It might be added that if Deuteronomy 17:14 is indeed a mitzvah, it is the only one extracted under pressure and out of the people's base desire. Thus, concludes Federbush, the laws concerning the king are intended primarily to circumscribe his power.

He then indicates that the use of *Ki* in other laws in the Torah means "if" and not "when" and that by analogy Deuteronomy 17:14 is to be construed accordingly. Citing Rabbi Ishmael, he indicates that in the law of the Sotah, the husband is certainly not commanded to suspect his wife; the passage, "You shall enslave them forever" is not a command; Leviticus 21 does not require the defiling of the high priest's sister; the law concerning the captive woman permits but does not require her captivity. Also Federbush cites Akiba's view that blood revenge is not required but the Torah tires to limit it through the cities of refuge.[44] Federbush draws an analogy to Maimonides' concept of sacrifices that were not required but permitted and restricted to only one place and only for the service of God. This is based on Leviticus Rabbah 22: The Israelites, lusting for idolatry in Egypt would bring their sacrifices to Seirim (demons) . . . God said, "let them (instead) bring their sacrifices to Me in the Tent of Meeting and thus be removed from idolatry. . . ." Also, concerning levirate marriage, Maimonides says that it is not a law but a limitation placed on Jews because of a pre-Sinaitic practice that the Torah limited by *chalitzah*.[45]

In *all* of these, *including* kingship, says Federbush, the Torah considered the weakness of the people, but being unable to eliminate the practice, circumscribed it. Declaring the issue irrelevant now as for many centuries in the past, Federbush declares that it is legally impossible to set up a king, since this requires the consent of a prophet and a Bet Din of seventy ordained scholars.[46] Since both prophets and Bet Din have lapsed, the law has long been a dead letter.

It appears both that Abravanel's basic sources for this theme were Jewish and that (as we have already observed) rabbinic Judaism did not unanimously and unequivocally endorse kingship as a mitzvah.

In continuing our study of Abravanel's political philosophy, we find that for him, the greatest human affliction is the political system. The generation of the tower of Babel sinned for the same reason that Adam and Eve sinned, and also Cain and his descendants: God had provided all the natural resources by which humanity could sustain itself. They were not content with this but lusted after superfluous matters, resulting in the spoiling of the earth and the necessity for hard labor "as the Moreh wrote."[47] "Cain chose to engage in mechanical (malachutiim) matters and thus became a farmer . . . despoiling his land, and his intellect became subservient to his bestial portion."[48] On the contrary, Abel was content with "natural matters." This accounts for the Patriarchs, Moses, and David being shepherds. Because of his antinatural and his animalistic bent, Cain built a city and taught his sons crafts connected with city building, "mixing mechanical matters with the work of God."[49] The sin of the generation of the tower was similar. They were not content with what God had bounteously provided but were bent on applying their craftsmanship to building a city

> so that they could unite there and make themselves governmental (institutions) . . . believing that their ultimate good was the unification of the governments [*kibutz ha-medinot*], so that

> there might prevail among them cooperation and social relationship [which they considered] the ultimate goal of humanity. . . . [But this] resulted in violence, theft and bloodshed, which did not obtain when they lived in the field. . . . Ham and his sons . . . incited the people of their generation to pursue superfluous crafts in the building of the city and the tower so that they might attain rule and authority over other people.[50]

If all this was evil in God's eyes, why did He not forbid it to Israel? He foresaw that they too would become steeped in the same kind of lust. Therefore He decreed rules by which they could justly and decently pursue their unnatural life,

> as in the case of the king, which was contemptible to God. But when He saw that they would nevertheless choose [a king], He decreed that his selection must be by His prophets and from among his brethren. . . . All the days that the Israelites wandered in the wilderness under Divine Providence, God sustained their needs with natural things—manna and quail, the well, their garments and sandals and the clouds of glory, not crafted things.[51]

Abravanel therefore concludes that the true sin of the people was not in the rationalizations by the commentators but in the very request for a king. It was in the wilderness that Moses, at the urging of Jethro, created the ideal Jewish government that became the paradigm for the best kind of Jewish polity.

ABRAVANEL'S MESSIANISM

In Abravanel's world, belief in messianism and the miraculous were no deterrents to rigorous political thought. In an era where the idea of kingship was both resisted and espoused by theologians, from Augustine on one side to Aquinas on the other, additional factors prompted Abravanel's politics. His theology did not cause him to abandon the political order but to structure it on lines radically different from the system of Maimonides. This rejection of kingship did not involve the rejection of government, only the reordering of the hierarchies of rulership.

We can get a more persuasive perception of Abravanel's views on kingship by examining his outlook on messianism, which is as diametrically opposed to Maimonides' as his views on kingship differ from those of Maimonides. Abravanel's Messiah is not a king, even a superior one, in the context of Maimonides' definition. Maimonides' king is informed with a carefully defined and naturalistic messianic character. Conversely, Abravanel's Messiah is endowed with the kind of kingship that more approximates the ultimate Kingship of God than the kingship of men. Abravenel's Messiah is by definition irreconcilable with a human-historical king, even if he is a King-Messiah.

Abravanel rejected the idea of the Messiah as a warrior. In his discussion on Bar Kochba, he distinguishes between what he considers the authentic Jewish use of the term Messiah and its less acceptable use by the prophet Isaiah when he speaks of Cyrus. Thus he states that Ben Kochba did not involve himself at all in the matter of executing judgment, which is the special task of the King-Messiah, as it is said, "He shall judge the poor in righteousness." He adds,

> Akiba knew that the King-Messiah must be from the seed of David and ben Koziba was not. . . . It was the intention of Rabbi Akiba that ben Koziba would be God's destructive agent to inflict vengeance upon the enemies of his servants since the destructive agents of God are known as Messiah . . . like Cyrus, who destroyed Babylonia. . . . It was known among the people that before the Messiah son of David would come, the Messiah son of Joseph would come not to execute judgment and righteousness but only to fight the battles of God. . . . Therefore when Rabbi Akiba saw the wonders and heroism performed by ben Koziba among all the lands of the Romans, he thought in his heart that he [ben Koziba] was the representative of providence, the Messiah of the God of Jacob, in the matter of war and vengeance on the enemies alone.

Abravanel states that in reading extensively in Roman history, the accounts of Bar Kochba's campaigns are far more detailed than the rabbinic accounts, and they explain more specifically the devastation he carried out among the Romans. He emphasizes again that the messianic role played by Bar Kochba was only that of Messiah ben Joseph and that the overwhelming body of rabbinic opinion was opposed to him. The rabbis rejected the idea that he was even Messiah ben Joseph because even that status would suggest that the Messiah ben David would soon follow. How could Akiba have thought that bar Kochba was the forerunner of the true Messiah? "Who knows if it was not because of this sin that Rabbi Akiba was put to death, since his death was more difficult than that of the others executed by the government." Abravanel also rejects the notion attributed to Akiba that the ten tribes would return with the coming of the Messiah. Abravanel therefore forecloses a political consummation in the messianic age.

In *Sefer Yeshuot Meshico,*[52] completed in Naples in 1497 "at the time of our expulsion, and the height of our troubles," Abravanel presented an anti-Maimonidean messianic perception:

> We have seen in many places in the Talmud the statement by Samuel that the only difference between this world and the days of the Messiah is [liberation] from servitude to other Kingdoms. . . . The great scholar Maimonides, referring to this passage at the end of his Mishneh Torah and in other places interprets this to mean that in the days of the Messiah nothing in the natural order will change, only that the servitude of Israel to other nations will pass, and the words of prophecy that contradict this are [only] figurative. . . . In order to raise [his own scholarly] stature in this matter, he did not mention [Samuel] by name lest it be said that this is the word [only] of one individual, and it was cited in the name of scholars as though all of Israel's scholars agreed to this. This is very astounding because the prophets testified as one that in the days of the Messiah, God would perform for His people great wonders beyond the natural order. . . . God's spirit resting in him, striking the earth with the rod of his mouth, not breaking a reed, bringing forth judgment in truth, all are perfection beyond the natural order. What they predicted concerning revenge upon the enemy and the destruction of the nations in miraculous ways and what they predicted about the success of the land beyond the natural order . . . as well as the elimination of the evil urge, the circumcision of the heart, the spread of wisdom throughout the land without study by children or adults . . . the acceptance by all the nations of the unity of God . . . and the greatest of all miracles, resurrection which is to come close to the ingathering of the exiles . . . all of these are doubtlessly beyond the natural order. . . . How, then, could Samuel deny [all this]? From such a statement the denial of resurrection is a necessary result. . . . (The reference to) "Servitude of nations" means that the nations will become submissive to the King-Messiah."[53]

Further,

> Messiah ben David . . . will suffer during the conquest of Eretz Yisrael and during the wars of the nations until he will miraculously, in his days, revive the dead, that is the banished of Israel who are the "dead" of the Exile. He will revive the spirit of the lowly. . . . He will pray for the dead, and his leadership will bring tranquility and quiet, honor and glory in the salvation of the people. . . . The light that was created [at the beginning] . . . [and was hidden due to the eruption of evil], will be restored to the Messiah and his generation.[54]

During creation, the true Messiah "was not created until the sixth day. Because of his wisdom and perfection it was said, "in the image of God He created him.' "[55] Compounding his eschatological view of messiahship, Abravanel speculates on the tradition that the Messiah will come only after all souls have left their bodies. He also discourses on the proximity of the time of resurrection to the advent of the Messiah, "when the souls are gathered into the bodies."[56]

Abravanel thus presents a melange of supernatural and mystical notions as well as a reference to vicarious atonement, and even natural events that he construes as miracles. In all cases, however, especially by referring to the Messiah's preexistence, he strives to differentiate his transnatural and transhistorical Messiah from Maimonides' naturalistic, historical Messiah.

Abravanel indulged in mathematical calculations concerning the coming of the Messiah. Basing himself on various prophecies, he related them to the expulsions from England, France, Germany, Spain, Sardinia, Sicily, and other places, and authenticated his Messianic speculation by this. "From the day that Judah was exiled . . . there befell them in the lands of Edom and Ishmael great oppression, destruction and forced conversion . . . but expulsion . . . was unheard of . . . until the year 5020 since the creation, and the beginning was in an island called the End of the Earth, that is England."[57]

A compelling contrast between the supernaturalistic bent of Abravanel and the naturalistic-historical approach of Maimonides can be found in their respective interpretations of Isaiah 24:17–20 and Joel 3:3–5. Concerning the first, Maimonides writes:

> I do not think that there has been anyone in whom ignorance, blindness, and the inclination to adhere to the external sense of

figurative expressions and of rhetorical speeches, have reached such a point that he thought that the stars of the heavens and the light of the sun and of the moon have been changed when the kingdom of Babylon came to an end, or that the earth was removed from its center, as was stated. All of this is merely a description of the state of someone put to flight; for without any doubt, he sees all light as black, finds everything that is sweet bitter, and imagines that the earth has narrowed for him and that the heavens are closed over him.[58]

Concerning Joel 3:3–5, Maimonides writes:

As for the passage in Joel: And I will show wonders in the heavens and in the earth, blood, and fire, and pillars of smoke. The sun shall be turned into darkness, and the moon into blood, before the great and terrible day of the Lord come. According to me the most probable interpretation is that he describes the destruction of Sennacherib before Jerusalem. If, however, you do not wish to accept this, it may be held to be a description of God before Jerusalem in the days of the King Messiah, though the only things mentioned in this passage are great slaughter, the burning of the fires, and the eclipse of the two luminaries. Know that every day in which a great victory of a great disaster comes to pass is called the great and terrible day of the Lord.

The notion toward which we are driving has already been made clear; namely, that the passing-away of this world, a change of the state in which it is, or a thing's changing its nature and with that the permanence of this change, are not affirmed in any prophetic text or in any statement of the Sages either.[59]

Concerning the Isaiah passage, Abravanel states:

In the time of the future redemption God will punish the hosts on high from above. . . . Abraham Ibn Ezra interpreted this to refer to the angels who were the guardians of the nations. . . . God will subdue their strength and influence. . . . The extinction of the lights and the cleaving of the stars will be renewed in those days. In my judgment, the prophet proclaimed by this that God would be king over all the earth . . . and the kings of the earth would cease to reign. . . . God in His own providence will reign on Mount Zion and in Jerusalem.

Concerning Joel, he writes:

> Since prophecy in our nation was in the nature of [wondrous] signs and not by the way of nature, as the Rav (Maimonides) thought, therefore 'I shall place signs in the heavens and on earth' tells that their prophecies will be in the class of [wondrous signs] . . . God will perform in the midst of Israel as [he did] in ancient times. . . . There is no doubt that this is what Ezekiel explained concerning the war of Gog and Magog . . . that God will rain down from heaven fire and brimstone. . . . The sun will turn to darkness. . . . The Rav (Maimonides) interpreted this entirely allegorically.

Nevertheless, in Abravanel's world, and despite frequent inconsistencies that make him appear totally antipolitical, belief in messianism and the miraculous were no deterrents to his political thought. In an era where the idea of kingship was both resisted and espoused by theologians, from Augustine on one side to Aquinas on the other, additional factors prompted Abravanel's politics. His theology did not cause him to abandon the political order but to structure it on lines radically different from the system of Maimonides. His rejection of kingship as a divinely mandated institution did not involve the rejection of government, only the reordering of the hierarchies of rulership. In the face of contradictions, he clung to a demonarchized polity.

It would be exceedingly simplistic to write off Abravanel as a naive supernaturalist, leaving the Jewish people's well-being to God alone. One should not have expected that a financier and a counsellor of kings should have submitted to a totally transcendental view of government and politics. An accurate reading of his work reveals a more subtle dialectic. When he denigrates the king as expendable in the divine economy, (since God alone is the savior), he is careful to add that God works through his own designated agents, the judges. While he is probably inaccurate in defining their roles, he assumes that the judges were *both* military instruments and protectors of the divine law, preempting the king who, unlike the judges, was not mandated by God ("Judges and officials shall you establish" Deuteronomy 16:18). Thus the essence of divine protection over Israel is defined by the designation of human intercessors, not necessarily, nor always, by direct divine intervention. Abravanel thus arrives at this theory of sovereignty through utter rejection and suspicion of kingship as tyrannical, and through its displacement by a prior, more authentic, and divinely accredited instrument. The rule by kings is untrustworthy. Rule by sacred law under the judiciary (as Abravanel interpreted it) offers a surer guarantee against excess and usurpation. In his intellectual world, king and law are incompatible. By his nature, the king violates the law. But the law and the judge, mandated by God, are meant for each other. The judge and the judicial system are meant to rule. With similarly designated warrior-protectors acting under the law's restraints, the king becomes redundant.

Abravanel appears inconsistent in his attitude toward the kings whom he served. As was to be expected, he wrote that Ferdinand and Isabella "brazened their heart to humble the pride of Judah."[60] Yet he also refers to the kings of Spain as divine agents in advancing the time of redemption.[61] Then again, the kings of Naples "are gracious Kings."[62] Still there is an underlying consistency. For Abravanel, the divine strategy of Israel's salvation is at work, making all kings, good and evil alike, instruments in the redemptive plan. Thus, for Abravanel, kings become subordinate to his own vision, stated consistently, of the messianic and miraculous rescue of the Jewish people by the Supreme King (for Abravanel, impending between 1503 and 1573).

Finally, the question persists concerning the effect of Abravanel's personal experiences on his view of kingship.

Abravanel was certainly affected by his own and his people's traumatic career in Spain, and most certainly by his own wrenching experiences—exile from one nation after another, rejection by sovereigns whom he had faithfully served, falls from power and wealth. Against this gloomy background, he was to write a bitter confession of how history had threatened the foundations of his belief:

> In the days of the Redemption . . . I shall relate how I used to say in those days [i.e., in the times following the Expulsion] . . . all the prophets who prophesied about my redemption and salvation are all false. . . . Moses, may he rest in peace, was false in his utterances, Isaiah lied in his consolations, Jeremiah and Ezekiel lied in their prophesies, and likewise all the other prophets. . . . Let the people remember . . . all the despairing things they used to say at the time of the Exile.[63]

Yet, this very cry from the heart gives evidence that his and his people's tragedies did not ultimately determine his essential beliefs.

He was anything but a creature of historical determinism. Without discarding the compulsions of history, we must also look to the religious environment out of which Abravanel emerged as an undeviating, supernaturalist, fundamentalist, transnatural messianist. These fundamentally affected his antimonarchical views, which may only have been intensified but not formulated by his experience. His beliefs were indeed threatened but not destroyed.

Also, the lives of Maimonides and Abravanel demonstrate how conflicting perceptions emerged out of similar historical backgrounds. Although Maimonides and Abravanel lived in different imperial environments, they nevertheless encountered profound manifestations of national might. In differing degrees each experienced the effects of national and religious oppression on the Jewish people and on himself. Yet, each arrived at an opposite conclusion about Jewish kingship. Speculation concerning the possible effect of historical conditions on Jewish thought in this area are important, but not necessarily determinative. If anything, Abravanel's encounters with kings and history seemed to confirm rather than shape his religiopolitical outlook.

Notes

1. Sifre, Parashat Shoftim.
2. Tosefta, Sanhedrin, Chapter 2.
3. Nissim Gerondi, called Ha-Ran.
4. Nachmanides, Parashat Vayechi.
5. Abravanel, Commentary on I Samuel 8.
6. Abravanel, Commentary on Deuteronomy 17.
7. Sanhedrin 46a.
8. Abravanel, Commentary on I Samuel 8.
9. Ibid.
10. Abravanel, Commentary on Deuteronomy 17:14.
11. Ibid.
12. Ibid.
13. Abravanel, Commentary on Exodus 18.
14. Ibid.
15. Abravanel, Commentary on I Samuel 8.
16. Ibid.
17. Leo Strauss, "Six Lectures," p. 101.
18. Ibid., pp. 97–98.

19. Ibid., p. 104.
20. *Guide of the Perplexed,* Part III, Chapters 27–28.
21. Strauss, "Six Lectures," p. 105.
22. Ibid., p. 109.
23. Josephus, *Antiquities,* II:2.
24. Abravanel, Commentary on Genesis 11:1ff.
25. Strauss, "Six Lectures," p. 110.
26. Ibid., p. 111.
27. Ibid., p. 119.
28. Ibid., p. 122–124
29. St. Augustine, *De Civitate Dei,* New York, 1950, IV, 4.
30. Gerald F. Reilly, *Imperium and Sacerdotum,* Washington, D.C. 1945, p. 8.
31. Ibid., p. 27.
32. Thomas Gilby, *Between Community and Society,* New York, 1953, p. 24.
33. Aquinas, *On Kingship,* Westport, CT, 1986, pp. 62–63.
34. Gilby, p. 29.
35. Strauss, p. 120.
36. Graetz, *History of the Jews,* Vol. IV, p. 442.
37. Strauss, "Six Lectures," p. 127.
38. Ibid., p. 128.
39. Ibid., p. 119.
40. Menasseh ben Israel, Conciliator, p. 228.
41. Martin Buber, *Malchut Shamayim,* Jerusalem, 1965, pp. 143–144.
42. Mendelssohn, *Jerusalem,* London, 1838, pp. 160–161.
43. Federbush, *Mishpat Ha-meluchah Be-yisrael,* Jerusalem, 1952, pp. 39, 40.
44. Makkot 12b.
45. Maimonides, *Guide of the Perplexed* III:49.
46. *Hilchot Melachim* I:3.
47. Abravanel, Commentary on Genesis 11:1–9.
48. Ibid.
49. Ibid.
50. Ibid.
51. Ibid.
52. Abravanel, *Sefer Yeshuot Meshicho,* Koenigsburg, 1861.
53. Ibid., Chapter 7, pp. 56–58.
54. Ibid., pp. 59–63.
55. Ibid., First Iyun, Chapter 1, p. 20.
56. Ibid., p. 36, 37, 56.
57. Ibid., p. 46.
58. Maimonides, *Guide of the Perplexed,* II:29, p. 338.
59. Ibid., p. 344.
60. Abravanel, Introduction to *Ma'yanay ha-yeshuah,* cited by Yosef Hayim

Yerushalmi, *The Lisbon Massacre of 1506 and the Royal Image in the Shebet Yehudah*, Cincinnati, 1976, p. 56.

61. Abravanel, Commentary on Isaiah 4:36.
62. Abravanel, Introduction to Commentary on Book of Kings, cited by Yerushalmi, p. 58.
63. Abravanel, *Zevah Pesah*, Constantinople, 1505, fol. 35r.; Sasson, p. 692.

X

Philosopher-Troubadour of Record Judah Halevi (1086–1167)

When Maimonides composed *Hilchot Melachim* about a generation after Juah Halevi's *Kuzari,* it contained an unintentional refutation of Halevi's thesis. Always considered the forerunner of modern Zionism, "the most national and the most patriotic of all Jewish poets," as Michael Sachs proclaims him in *Die Religiose Poesie der Juden in Spanien,*[1] Halevi is, on the contrary, proponent of the priestly theocratic notion. Neither modern Zionists nor contemporary opponents of theocracy seem to have taken note of this fact. This may be due to a heavier emphasis placed by some on his Zionist poetry where references to persecution, the adoration of the land of Israel as a place of refuge, and occasional nostalgia for the kingship are expressed. ("I am in Arab chains . . . With whom could they [Christendom and Islam] compare your [Zion's] anointed kings? . . . I dream of the return of your captivity" (from "My heart is in the East," *Ode to Zion*).

Yet, in his poetry, kingship is infrequently referred to as an emotional abstraction, while the Temple and the priesthood are fervently evoked.

My God, Thy dwelling-places are lovely!
It is in vision and not in dark speeches that Thou art near
My dream did bring me into the sanctuaries of God,
And I beheld His beautiful services;
And the burnt-offering and meal-offering and drink-offering,
And round about, heavy clouds of smoke.
And it was ecstasy to me to hear the Levites' song,
In their council for the order of services.

I awoke, and I was yet with Thee, O God,
And I gave thanks, and it was sweet to thank Thee.[2]

In his *Kuzari,* the yearning for kingly restoration is absent. His devotion to the land is prompted by religious factors, not oppression, while Ha-levi's priestly theocracy is explicit and detailed. An elaborate edifice is erected, one of whose major premises is the theological interdependence of land and religion, whose source is Sinai, continuing in steady progression through a chain of religious categories exclusive of the kings. They are barely mentioned. David who is mentioned incidentally, Jannai (who is held up to censure), and the Khazar king are the sole exceptions. Like Ha-Ran, Ha-levi does not repudiate kingship but, while addressing himself to the vast edifice of Jewish law which does confront the issue as a halachic matter, he does not engage the problem at all. Yet his silence, accompanied by explicit excursions into Jewish governance, unmistakably defines his position.

For Halevi's *Kuzari,* the land of Israel was the soil on which Israel, the "superior grapevine," could flourish amidst messianic anticipation. In his philosophical thinking there was little place in that spiritual ambiance for the rule of kings. *Galut,* imposed on the land, is not only a condition of oppression but of an alien way of life. It is the land's special nature that endows Israel with its superior religious faculty.[3] It manifests itself because of the Holy Land's natural environment and because of its special climate. Israel is thereby possessed of a particular religious capability not found among other nations.[4] Halevi stresses the primacy of the supernatural divine providence that, as Julius Guttmann puts it, manifests "itself in reward and punishment, (and) exists only for Israel, not only in the Biblical past but continuing into the present."[5] This kind of protective providence explains the virtual absence of the king who, among other nations, is the primary factor insuring his people's welfare.

For Halevi, the primary role of the land of Israel is for the restoration of the Shechinah, for the pronouncements of the prophets, for the site of the Temple and the sacrifices, for the fulfillment of festivals and Sabbaths in their highest form, all of which await the return of "the chosen people." The land has a special relation to God. "Pure life can be perfect only there. Many of the laws lose their force for him who does not live there."[6] "Our Torah is bound to the law of Moses at Sinai or from the place which God will choose, for 'Torah will go forth from Zion' [where] judges, officials, priests and Sanhedrin will be established."[7] Nowhere in the *Kuzari* is the land referred to as the place where Jewish government will be restored. Instead, the emphasis is upon the full restoration of the religion so that the advent of the Messiah will be advanced.

Speculation beyond that consummation becomes irrelevant because Israel's destiny would be in God's hands. What is essential is for Israel to return home. "If we provoke and instill love of this sacred place . . . we may be sure of . . . hastening the [messianic] goal. . . . Jerusalem can only be rebuilt when Israel yearns for it to such an extent that we sympathize even with its stones and dust."[8] Yet for Halevi there was a system that constituted the governance of the people, and for the restoration of which he yearned—the Temple cult, allied in his mind with the prophetic order. The purpose of the laws concerning the Temple was to "create a workable system, in order that the King [God] could 'sit enthroned' there."[9] So paramount is the Temple system that qualified Jews stand ready to enter into its service as soon as it is reinstated. "Were we today to be commanded to offer sacrifices, we would know how to slaughter . . . how to sprinkle the blood . . . and what the priests are obliged to do."[10]

No equivalent thought has been given to preparation for administering a future state.

Halevi compares the divine power immanent in the Temple with the reasoning soul that governs the human body.

> It is beneficent, desirous of doing good to all. Where a being is found well prepared to receive its guidance, it does not refuse it nor hesitate to shed over him light, wisdom and inspiration. If, however, the order is distorted, this light . . . is then lost. Hence, if the whole order of sacrificial service . . . is to be performed in utmost purity and holiness . . . all this expresses His pleasure in the beautiful harmony prevailing among the people and its Priests, and His readiness . . . to dwell among them in order to distinguish them."[11]

For Halevi, the Temple system with its priesthood is the way by which Israel's life is governed and kept in spiritual equilibrium. A perfect system like this presumably requires no other form of government. Yet Halevi does anticipate the question whether this suffices to govern the people, and his response is the Torah, from which there proliferated scriptural and prophetic wisdom, embodied in priest and prophet. "Both were, so to speak, the people's councillors, seers and admonishers, its secretaries and chroniclers; they therefore were the head of the people."[12] The governmental chain of command derived from God through the Temple system and was administered by God's priests and prophets. Halevi exercises care to exclude the reign of kings. Obedience is through prophets, none other. (He) "sent Moses with his Law, and subsequently thousands of Prophets, who confirmed his Law by promises to those who observed, and threats to the disobedient."[13] "The restoration of the people is dependent on the resotration of the Temple which is its heart, and our leader, King and ruler . . . is the living God."[14] Elaborating on this theme, Halevi expands the hierarchy of government to include judges, officers, priests, and Sanhedrin. As to the central official, "we are commanded to heed the judge who is appointed in every generation. . . . Whoever disobeys the priest must die. . . . Disobedience to the priest or judge is the greatest of offenses."[15] Halevi refers to the men of the Great Assembly who were succeeded by a long line of priestly descendants, referring in passing to King Jannai who is admonished not to infringe on priestly prerogatives. "His friends prejudiced him against the sages, advising him to . . . scatter or kill them. . . . He expelled the sages, among them Simon b. Shetach . . . [who later] returned . . . and restored tradition to its former condition."[16] This rare, and invidious reference to a king is significant.

By way of stressing the Kingship of God alone, and the centrality of the Temple to the people's fortunes, Halevi compares Israel with the other nations who, he suggests, have attempted to emulate Israel in building sanctuaries to their deities, but God did not reveal Himself to them. They have sought to induce prophecy to no avail. When they sinned, no special divinely activated punishments ensued. Not so Israel, which has felt God's displeasure in the Temple's destruction and in its exile just as it experienced His presence through its existence and through the prophets; and in these manifestations He asserts His Kingship.

Halevi's sense of exile is prompted not by political conditions but rather by a positive yearning for the land of Israel and, with equal intensity, a rejection of "Greek [philosophical] wisdom." This theme appears with special poignancy in his poem, "L'maan beit Elohenu."[17]

A recently discovered fragment of a letter in which the poet discusses the motives for his voyage to the land of Israel sounds this note as well. The letter was sent to Shmuel Hanagid, in Egypt.[18] The poet writes "concerning my thoughts which sent me forth from my dwelling place." In the course of the letter he writes,

> Neither Israel nor Judah is bereft. In his days (will come) . . . wise men, disciples, masters of the Torah and masters of Mishneh, Israel, his elders, his officers and judges, his servitors and those who seek his presence, his servants and those who stand in His presence, and of the three assemblies (the Synagogues of Cairo and Fustat), . . . the heads of the exile, masters of the Law, my princes and my scholars, who are honored by me. May God answer them day and night and may all the people come in peace to their place.

Here Halevi presents the galaxy of Jewish notables, but the absence of the king who is to rule in the future Zion is apparent.

NOTES

1. Sachs, *Die Religiose Poesie der Juden in Spanien,* second edition, p. 300.
2. *Selected Poems of Juah Halevi,* Philadelphia, 1928, p. 9.
3. Halevi, *Kuzari,* Oxford, 1947, II:12.
4. Ibid., II:97.
5. Julius Guttmann, *Philosophies of Judaism,* translated by David Silverman, New York, 1964, p. 128.
6. Halevi, *Kuzari,* V:24–28.
7. Ibid., II:20.
8. Ibid., V:27.
9. Ibid., II:26.
10. Ibid., III:57.
11. Ibid., II:25.
12. Ibid., II:28.
13. Ibid., I:11.
14. Ibid., II:32.
15. Ibid., III:39.
16. Ibid., III:65.
17. *Selected Poems of Judah Halevi,* p. 14.
18. Cambridge Library, T=S Loan, Box Two 25.

XI

Advocate of Judges—Ha-Ran (1290–1380)

Nissim ben Reuven Gerondi (Ha-Ran), who lived in Spain at a time when Christian clergy in Aragon and Barcelona were becoming increasingly hostile, followed in the tradition that subordinated the role of the king. Intended or otherwise, his diminution of royal authority constitutes a response to Maimonides. His is the first in Rabbinic literature to attempt to go beyond only asserting the theocratic principle, but rather seeks to define its application. His is not only a theology of theocracy but a politics of it. Frequently referred to by Abravanel, he became the channel through which Abravanel entered upon full rejection of Jewish kingship. For Ha-Ran, the *shofet* (judge) assumes far greater authority than the king who serves primarily as the civil arm of the Torah in those areas not under the Torah's direct jurisdiction. In this sense, Ha-Ran is a forerunner of those who perceive the secular arm of a Jewish government as essentially secondary to religious authority. This is a modified theocratic principle that recognizes the need for a secular agency to fulfill the day-to-day functions of government, but only with the surveillance of religious authorities guarding against encroachment in its domain as well as violation of the sacred principles of the Torah. This blueprint for modified theocracy is defined in his eleventh lecture, based on Deuteronomy 16:18, "Judges and officers . . . and they shall judge the people righteously." Referring to the statement in Pirke Avot in behalf of government, he resorts to a radical transposition of *malchut* (government) to "judges," and declares, "It is known that the human species requires a judge to adjudicate among its parts, because otherwise people would swallow each other alive."[1] Ha-Ran states this as a categorical principle for all society, not only Jews, and invokes Deuteronomy 16:18 as claiming greater authority than Deuteronomy 17:14. He does not pose this issue in a vacuum but contemplates the reestablishment of a Jewish political entity in which his vision could be realized. "Every nation *(umah)* requires a political establishment . . . and Israel requires this as do the other nations." The additional Jewish reason for this is to restore the full application of the Torah's laws, even where they have no political relevance. "The laws of the Torah [must be established] on their base, so that those incurring flogging may be punished and those incurring death by the Bet Din for violating the Torah's laws [may be executed], even if in the transgression there is no loss to the political community."

Ha-Ran acknowledges the necessity for a king in Israel, apparently to serve with the judges as another arm of government, but he leaves no doubt that kingship is not of primary importance, since only the judges are informed with "the divine effluence." Necessary as it is, kingship is subordinate because it is not sacramental.

By social necessity, kingship shares authority with judgeship. Judgeship's boundaries are defined, yet it occupies a more determining position because the fulfillment of the Torah is more compelling than preserving the social order whose governance in any event is under the Torah's supervision. Aryeh Feldman, editor of the work's standard edition, comments, "The social order requires policing which does not derive from legal justice but requires legislation which derives from that side of government which has the power to impose authority. . . . Therefore two legislative arms are required, social justice in the hands of the judges, and police legislation which has the power of the government and the monarchy for the purpose of public stability." This is supported by Ha-Ran's statement that if offenders are not punished by the government, crime would increase and the social order would deteriorate; "therefore God ordained the selection of kings" to preserve the stability of society."[2] The reference to public stability and the consequent need for the enforcing arm of government derives from the statement, "pray for the peace of the government." It recognizes the aggressive nature of man that later Lutheran theology develops into the concept of government as a restraint of innate human sinfulness. It is for this "intimidating" reason that, as Sanhedrin 20b indicates, it is a mitzvah to select a king. This thesis reflects the struggle for ascendancy within Christendom between church and state in which each gained the upper hand for a time and then settled down to an uneasy division of powers that proved unworkable.

Ha-Ran's thinking is predicated on that aspect of rabbinic thought found in the Midrash concerning the "guardians of the city" *(neturei karta)* who are identified not as the watchmen or other security personnel, but rather as the scholars.[3] The intent of this Midrash is to clarify the rabbinic view not merely that the preservation of the community depends on its scholars but that the other functionaries serve in subordinate positions. Those officials primary purpose is to preserve the scholars and the God-fearing. Because of that, they play no collaborative role in the true preservation of the city.

In this context, the king does have extralegal powers, because as chief law enforcer he must be endowed with such authority. Thus, while the halachah requires the warning of a potential offender, the king may act without warning in all matters of national interest. Yet, while the selection of a king in Israel is on a par with the selection of kings elsewhere,

> the selection of judges is unique and more necessary in Israel, as scripture states: "They shall judge the people with righteous and true judgments. . . ." Just as our Torah is distinguished from the customs of the nations by commandments and statues, the commandments' concern is not with proper functioning of society but rather with the dwelling of the divine effluence in our nation . . . both through visible signs such as sacrifices . . . and through other commandments whose purpose is not revealed. Our Torah is distinguished from the ways of other nations who have no concern with such matters, only in the proper functioning of their society. . . . As to the proper functioning of our own society, the king will provide what [Torah law] lacks [in this regard].[4]

Feldman adds, "It is important that we relate the purpose of these matters to the ultimate goal, the divine matter, but as to the rules of society, we can depend on the [civil] law and the power of the king."

For Ha-Ran, "the proper functioning of society" is far more limited than it is in a secular society. As he defines it, it is confined to preserving law and order, while the "divine matter" consists of maintaining the national religion and personal and public morality and guarding the vast network of social and domestic relations, all of which come under the jurisdiction of the (religious) judges. The relative status of the *Neturei Karta* and their deputies could not be identified more clearly.

In this context, the ultimate sin of the people who requested a king was in their attempted transfer of power from the judge to the king. "Give us a King so *he* may *judge* us." In addition, the people wanted to be "like all the nations" insofar as they desired that their primary law be an expanded civil (not theocratic) law, as among other (non-theocratic) nations.

> They wanted the legal system between persons to be under the King's control . . . and they said to Samuel, "Give us a King to judge us like all the nations." . . . They wanted that which pertains to the political order . . . to derive from the royal side rather than the judicial side. . . . At that time Israel inclined more toward the perfection of their political society. . . . They preferred the improvement of their natural condition to the presence of the divine principle among them. . . . [Through] the law of the king, he can do as he pleases . . . because the Judge is more subservient to the laws of the Torah than to the king. That is why [God] warned and commanded the king that a second scroll of the Torah must be with him. . . . These warnings are not required of the judge because his power is limited to the law of the Torah alone.[5]

Ha-Ran explains the Samuel event and the Deuteronomy 17:14 law in terms of a tension between God and people that is resolved in favor of a monarchy limited by the Torah. Explicitly, the king is needed as a guardian of the public welfare. Just as explicitly, the urge for a king was too great to successfully resist, as Ha-Ran clearly acknowledges. Hence, the need to restrain the king as much as possible. If the people's desire for a king is overwhelming, he must be God's choice through a prophet, not the people's wish, according to Sifre, Piska 157. Because of a king's lust for power, the Torah imposes restrictions on him—he must not be arrogant, nor acquisitive, since the monarchy is not his but a gift from God. "It is known that those most susceptible to this are kings, because they lust after acquisitions in order to wage war and pursue their own interests. Most of the kings of Israel failed in this matter."[6] In order to control him as much as possible, the law requires that the king, unlike a judge, may not deviate even from a slight precept of a prophet, since judges are not bound by prophets.[7]

There is then a moral basis for the restraint of the king—the fear of abuse of power. Ha-Ran's position is based on the belief that the judges, acting under the control of God, would not fall victim to this abuse.

In Ha-Ran we find the development of a systematic theological basis for theocracy under the rule of Torah but also a system of government in which the theocratic system works through its major human component, the judiciary. Power is thus transferred from one absolutism to another.

Notes

1. *Drashot Ha-Ran,* Jerusalem, 1950.
2. Ibid., p. 190.
3. Pesikta d'Rav Kahana, ed. Mandelbaum, New York, 1962, pp. 249–262.
4. *Drashot Ha-Ran,* p. 190, 191.
5. Ibid., p. 193, 194.
6. Ibid., p. 204.
7. Ibid., pp. 202–203.

XII

Orthodox Modernists Federbush

It would be helpful to learn what contemporary Jewish thought says on the subject of kingship and statehood. Two authorities have been selected because, while committed to rabbinic tradition, they ascribe great weight to kings and civil authorities. Also, they recognize the need for viewing the issue in light of new realities concerning the modern state, yet arrive at divergent conclusions. They are Rav Avraham Isaac Kook (1865–1935) and Shimon Federbush (1892–1969).

HaRav Kook

In the charter Hilchot Melachim in *Mishpat HaCohen,* HaRav Avraham Isaac Kook explicitly states that the rules concerning the king are not limited to ceremonial functions doing him honor,

> but everything having to do with the nation, every act in time of emergency (*hora'at sha'ah*) for the purpose of forestalling evil doers, is included in the rules of kingship. The king has the right to deal with them as he sees fit even when it is of no benefit to him or his honor but when it is for the good and the honor of Israel. . . . The power of the king's rule derives from his own honor and authority. . . . Joshua slew Achan and David slew Hagar the Amalekite by their own authority.

Kook then adds the highly significant point that when an optional war is declared with the authorization of the Bet Din, it is also done because of the norm of the kingdom. "Just as a Bet Din is required for declaring such a war, so is a king required."[2] From what follows, it appears that of the two, the king is the greater requisite. The distinctive role of the king is noted by Kook's observation that an optional war by "a judge which is not in accordance with the public's will is forbidden."[3] Kook not only follows in the path defined by Maimonides but expands on it, seeing the king as a political figure functioning in a historical situation and claiming his authority from historical exigencies. Prior restrictions on the designation of the king are likewise relaxed by Kook. The biblical requirement that a prophet choose the king is in effect annulled in favor of kings who were selected with the approval of the nation, in the absence of a prophet. Not only was this done in the time of the Hasmoneans, but "even if Israel were to have set up a king without a prophet he would be king in accord with the rules of kingship."[4]

This also applies when, as a result of the exile or historical crises, there is lack of certainty as to who is in the order of Davidic succession. This is precisely how the royal Hasmonean dynasty was established.[5] This view is a radical departure from the opposition to that dynasty by the rabbis who argued that it was illegitimate and usurped power. But Kook, who argued that the Maccabean uprising was technically unauthorized because it was not legally declared, and yet justified it because of its emergency nature, likewise justified the Hasmonean kings as necessary for their time, despite the absence of a prophet. This is reinforced by his dictum, "Whoever leads the nation judges in accordance with the rules of the kingdom, for [it is] necessary for the nation, required for the time and for the stability of the world."[6] "When the leader of the nation is designated for all its needs . . . by the consent of the people and the consent of the Bet Din, he certainly stands in place of the king in matters related to the nation's laws."[7] Unlike Federbush, Kook assumes the existence of a Bet Din. Yet he does not cavil at the elevation of the Hasmoneans to kingship without benefit of a Bet Din. Kook cites Maimonides to the effect that the exilarchs in Babylonia stood in the place of the kings. He adds, "But those who were accepted for the sake of the nation in its general and territorial governance, as were the Hasmonean kings . . . are not inferior to the exilarchs. . . . When a leader of the nation is designated by the general consent and the consent of the Bet Din for all its needs in the sense of royal rule, he certainy stands in place of the king. . . ."[8] It should be noted that the identification of exilarchs with kings is hyperbolic, insasmuch as the former enjoyed only the autonomy that was permitted by the Babylonian rulers.

Kook's strong support of kingship, following and strengthening the Maimonidean position, illustrates further the internal division within rabbinic literature on this subject. As we have observed, the latitude afforded the king by the concept of special circumstances limits the theocratic impulse that is generally imputed to rabbinic thought. This is further demonstrated by the subordination of the judge to the king in military matters and even more by the king's capacity to assume power by popular consent, not by the prophet's designation, thereby avoiding the biblical requirement. Kook's identification of leadership in exile as encompassing the totality of Jewish life and also as equated with kingship demonstrates the broad extent of powers he ascribes to both exilarchs and the king. Finally his acceptance of the Hasmonean dynasty, a radical departure from many rabbinic views of that dynasty, reveals a perception of kingship fully compatible with historical reality and the unfolding of modern Jewish statehood.

SHIMON FEDERBUSH

Shimon Federbush was an advocate of separation between civil and religious authority in Judaism. The king, although limited by Jewish law, exercises extensive power, while religious law has long since lost its claim to enforce its decrees through government. Thus, in a contemporary context, the state legislates while religion persuades. Yet, Federbush perceives not two coequal and cogoverning Jewish authorities or halachic authority serving as a check on government, but two different entities, separate yet related, with the state alone accountable for all but ecclesiastical law. Federbush begins with the thesis that with the creation of the state of Israel, it has become necessary to search old Jewish political and social law for the clarification of issues confronting statehood.[9] As will be noted, he demonstrates the capacity of Jewish law to generate civil law, but not to administer it. The Torah's vision for the state was the moral development of the people so that it could become "a kingdom of priests." The embodiment of the moral impulse in Judaism was the messianic king, foreseen by Isaiah, who would be a humble man of God. Fanatic nationalism was to be eliminated, and in the messianic age the state would become superfluous. In Jewish tradition, these expectations are foreshadowed in the limitations placed on the king. The Shabbat may be violated for a newborn infant, but not for a dead King David. A scholar takes precedence over a king in the redemption from slavery because the former is less easily replaceable. Interpreting Maimonides leniently, Federbush argues that the king may expropriate only in time of emergency and must compensate the owners.[10] Thus, the king is not an absolute ruler in Jewish law.

Not only the kings but the priests and religious authorities in general are restricted by Jewish law. In fact, Judaism makes a clear separation between both authorities. The kind of theocracy that imposes a priestly form of government was not ordained in biblical Judaism. From the time of Moses and Joshua until the last kings of Judah, political rule was separated from priesthood. "The first Hebrew kingdom was intended to be a Torah-kingdom" in which the king was to govern in accordance with the Torah, but in reality, political government and religious government branched off into two realms, each of which, according to the Torah, must be obeyed. This applied during the first and second commonwealths, and during the latter the Sanhedrin sat in the chamber of hewn stones and judged priestly matters.[11] Originally courts were expected to follow Torah guidance, but there arose an entire category of issues, enumerated by Nachmanides, concerning political and social matters such as dealing with one's neighbor and relations with women, children, and one's enemies.[12] Other examples from Nachmanides are the ten conditions ordained by Joshua, all of which limit private interests for the benefit of the community. Just as new conditions require new judicial treatment, they also demand special responses by the king. Nachmanides states that while certain laws are followed by judges, according to the Torah, the king supplements what is required by the nation. Federbush adds the radical observation, "Judgment is divided between the power of the judge and that of the king. The rule of the king is not as subordinate to the Torah as is the judge."[13] The Torah avoids specifying those areas of law that fall under the purview of civil government, thus giving the king great latitude. Maimonides greatly expands the circle of authority of governmental law by including matters of state and civil and criminal law. All the military legislation and matters of national defense derive from the king's authority, i.e., permissible war, expropriation for the general good, taxes, draft in time of crisis, international relations, designation of officers "in order, of course, to fulfill the religious law.[14] "In sum, any law which the King enacts for all, and not for the benefit of a single person, is not theft."[15]

The passage "in order, of course, to fulfill the religious law" would seem to suggest that the civil order must be governed by halachah. However, Federbush indicates both in the foregoing and in what follows that while he wishes the state to conform to the spirit of the Torah, he does not wish to see it enforce laws in the realm of religious authority. The fulfillment of religious law refers to its intent, not its specific content, as will become evident.

Two crowns of authority (kingship and priesthood) were united only in Hasmonean times, and the rabbis were dissatisfied with this. In consequence of this,

> The observance of religious laws cannot be transferred to political control, since the political regime is concerned only with statutory law and guards over them through the compulsion of punishment, while religious mitzvot are according to halachah and are moral mitzvot alone which do not incur any human penalty. There is no civil penalty today for any of the mitzvot of the Torah, due to the abolition of ordination, and an unordained court cannot judge concerning [religious] laws affecting punishment and fines. The mitzbot of the Torah are today moral laws for which a court of law cannot impose punishment and it is therefore not permissible to transfer to the government any authority for coercing the population with laws . . . based on mitzvot of the Torah. The government has broad powers in legislation between a citizen and the state, but such legislation is beyond the borders of the Torah's judgment. . . . The religious mitzvot are valid in the areas of moral influence and spiritual education. All who see in religious Judaism the principles of the religious existence of the Jewish people . . . must establish a religious authority in Israel which will have spiritual power. . . . (The religious elements) must demand that the government . . . do nothing to interfere with the Torah-life of believers. . . . (Likewise) observant Judaism must . . . influence the government to be permeated with the spirit . . . of Torah and Prophecy, and that its political legislation be based on the righteous foundations of the Torah.[16]

It would appear that this last statement creates a broad opening for civil legislation designed to enforce biblical law, but Federbush forestalls this by stipulating that the enforcement of religious law should not be entrusted to nonobservant parties.[17] Thus his understanding of Jewish principle of theocracy differs markedly from theocracies elsewhere. Other theocracies are both unsuccessful and destructive, and alienate those who reject them. Religious coercion, says Federbush, should not be defended on the fallacious ground that religion and nationalism "came down joined from heaven."[18] Judaism's democratic spirit is manifested in the acceptance of religious law as an act of free choice. Spinoza argued that the government of the early Israelites from the political aspect was democratic, since they did not transfer their rights to a man but to God, and also voluntarily accepted the Torah and its political law.[19] "The king conducted national affairs in accord with previously determined principles," as in Deuteronomy 17. The Talmud expands this principle by stating that only such laws as the people can sustain may be enacted.[20] If the people refuse to accept such law, it is inoperative. In addition, national leaders are designated by national assent. This really means not that the people choose the king, but that they only endorse God's selection.

The Panhalachic authority of the king is further supported by the principle of *dina d'malkhuta dina,* which applies to Jewish as well as to foreign rule. This principle permits the king to act in areas beyond the Torah for the greater good, as Maimonides and, in recent times, HaRav Kook proposed. This is contrary to Abravanel who argues that the Sanhedrin can punish under extraordinary conditions, thereby invalidating the need for a king, but Maimonides and others including Federbush declare that the king alone or the government's ruling authority (in his absence) may do this, not the Bet Din, except rarely.

Despite this, the king's power is not absolute and is predicted on popular consent. The absence of laws in the Torah prohibiting rebellion against a king or treason against the state are construed by Federbush to be confined only to rebellion against God, not a mortal king whose office is regarded with displeasure by the Torah. This last observation is consistent with Abravanel. Only resistance to "the spiritual rule of Israel's government is considered decisive."[21] Even the uprising against Moses did not entail death at the hands of a human court. The first enactment against rebellion is in the Book of Joshua (Chapter 1:18) where the law concerning disobedience to Joshua is essentially proclaimed by the people's leaders.[22] While the king does not have the Torah's authorization to punish rebels, the people may legislate special laws to this effect. Federbush cites the

Chatham Sofer who, striving for a precedent for this principle, arrives at "rebellion against the government is punished by virtue of Israel's ban [against looting] in Joshua's time." On the same principle of government by popular sanction, the king may not confiscate the property of a rebel.[23] All this applies, however, only to a king designated by a prophet or accepted by the people. If neither of these conditions is met, the people do not have to obey and whoever disobeys is not a rebel.[24] Similarly, Ha-Ran rules that the principle of *dina d'malkhuta* applies only to a righteous king, but an unjust expropriation is not law but extortion.[25] Hence, Federbush derives the thesis that when there is no prophet, kings are given their authority from the power assigned to them by the people. The ultimate test of this is their capability or disability to withhold or grant the power of punishment against rebels. The king is therefore *allowed* great powers but their application resides in the people.

This raises the issue of who may govern when there is no king. This issue bears on who succeeds the king or even preempts him. Is it the judges or the priests or is it an authority that stands in place of the king? Federbush cites various authorities. According to Nachmanides, any authorized person may declare war. During the exilic period, authority was granted to leaders to "govern" in matters of fiscal, communal, interpersonal, and sometimes even capital issues. Rabbi Gershom said in this context, "Whoever is designated over the community is like the mightiest of the mighty, and Jephthah in his generation is as Samuel in his." The same principle is stated by the Shulchan Aruch[26]: "The leaders of the city . . . have the power to do what they see fit in order to limit the generation's lawlessness." Federbush concludes that two sets of laws, Torah-based and non-Torah based, continued throughout the exile, to the extent that issues were sometimes determined not in accordance with the Torah. He cites Sanhedrin, concerning Shimon b. Karcha, who argued that some issues may be decided by a judge in accord with his own perceptions and not necessarily in accord with the Torah.

Yom Tov Vidal of Tolosa (fourteenth century) contends that the Torah intentionally did not discuss details of civil and fiscal laws, setting down only general principles based on eternal moral concepts and leaving the rest to future lawmakers who would judge according to changing conditions.[27] Rabbi Judah declared, "everything is in accordance with the years, the places, and the time."[28] Joseph Albo, the author of *Ikarim*, wrote, "The oral Torah was not transmitted in writing because it cannot suffice for all times; therefore general principles were given to Moses, so that the scholars in every generation might derive from them new matters."[29] Rabbi Zvi Hirsh Chayut goes further by observing that most of the halachot in Seder Nezikin and Baba Batra are not based on the Torah. All the laws there are the result of the rabbis' reasoning and prevailing practices as well as the understanding of human nature.[30]

On the strength of these opinions and precedents, Federbush demonstrates how the principles of Torah and halachah can be applied to current issues in the Jewish state: taxes; a free market versus a controlled economy; export-import; civil rights; laws dealing with territory (conquest, settlements, land development, ecology); economics (economic equality, restrictions on private property, anti-poverty measures); labor (protection of the non-Jewish laborer, protection of the Jewish laborer, standard of living, strikes and lockouts, unions); warfare (military law, draft and requisition, declaring war, making peace, conduct of war, rights of the conquered, laws of blockade, neutrality); euthanasia.

While Federbush advocates the independent role of civil government and bases this on Jewish precedent establishing prior existence of law not derivable from Torah, he also propounds the possibility of establishing modern law on halachic principles. Can this be achieved without subordinating the state to the rule of halachah, and thereby bringing about the very results to which Federbush objects, the end of separation between the legislative state and the persuading, not coercive, religion? Or is he advancing the employment of biblical and rabbinic principles alone, from which contemporary laws derive? This would be more compatible with his separatist position, but other questions emerge. Would the contemporary laws be considered halachic or civil? Would they be the product of a civil judicial system or rabbinic influence? On the strength of his support of the principle of "a kingdom of priests," that is, the prevalence of the *spirit* of Jewish morality within the state, it is permissible to conclude that Federbush seeks the development of civil law as related to the spirit of the halachah and anchored in contemporary application as defined by current needs and realities.

Certain illustrations follow.

a. The issue of preventive war. Some consider this like an optional (aggressive) war that requires prior consent, but Rabbi

Judah considers it a mandatory war that does not require the assent of the Bet Din and for which all are obligated. The law conforms to those who relate a preventive war to an optional war, because the issue is too critical to entrust to a national or military government. Nations tend to justify aggressive wars on the pretext that they are about to be attacked. Therefore, it is necessary to subject the matter to the impartial inquiry of judges and to determine whether there are sufficient signs of preparation for war. "The ruler may not declare [war] without the opinion of the judicial [branch of] government."[31]

b. Peacemaking. The refusal to make peace with a national enemy is worse than murder.[32] Even the seven idolatrous nations may be permitted to make a pact of peace with Israel, despite the Torah's express prohibition.[33]

c. Private property. A system by which there are no restraints on the economy is "not approved by the spirit of Israel's Torah . . . [which] commanded the limitation of private ownership through moral restrictions for the benefit of the society."[34] Federbush cites Rav Kook (*Anu l'geulat ha-aretz,* Sifriyat Torah v' avodah). "It can be confidently assumed that if all of the Torah's social and economic laws were to be strictly observed, and without concessions, the property system could not exist."[35] Federbush continues, "A coalition government which depends on coercion, on unrestrained rule of men over others, on repression of personal autonomy . . . such a rule of collective tyranny is totally opposed to Judaism's doctrine of righteousness."[36]

Notes

1. Abraham I. Kook, *Mishpat Ha-Cohen,* Jerusalem, 1937, p. 335.
2. Ibid., p. 349.
3. Ibid., p. 350.
4. Ibid., p. 336.
5. Ibid., p. 337.
6. Ibid.
7. Ibid., p. 344.
8. Ibid., p. 338.
9. Shimon Federbush, *Mishpat Hameluchah b'Yisroel,* Jerusalem, 1973.
10. *Hilchot Melachim* III:8, IV:6.
11. Federbush, p. 46.
12. Nachmanides, Commentary on Exodus 15.

13. Federbush, p. 48.
14. Ibid.
15. Ibid.
16. Ibid., p. 28.
17. Ibid.
18. Ibid., p. 30.
19. Spinoza, *Tractatus Theologico Politicus,* Chapter 17.
20. Baba Kamma 79b.
21. Federbush, p. 82.
22. Ibid., p. 83.
23. *Hilchot Melachim* III:8.
24. David ben Zimra on Hilchot Melachim III:8.
25. Federbush, p. 87.
26. Chosen Mishpat, *Hilchot Dayanim,* 2.
27. *Magid Mishnah,* 1509.
28. Taanit 14b.
29. Albo, *Ikkarim,* Jewish Publication Society, 1930, III:14.
30. Federbush, p. 54.
31. Ibid., p. 203, 204.
32. Yevamot 79a.
33. Tanchuma, Parashat Tzav; Federbush, p. 219.
34. Ibid., p. 133.
35. Ibid.
36. Ibid., p. 134.

XIII

Summary—Jewish Concern about Power

The debate over kingship has taken place within a broad spectrum of political conditions in the world where Israel dwelled. Yet, the dominant factors influencing the controversy reflected both external and Jewish, internal conditions. Not until the modern age did outer and inner conditions converge through Zionism.

It may have been assumed that exilic Judaism, committed to the idea of supernatural intervention, waited resignedly. This is only partly valid. Lively concern in rabbinic literature over kingship demonstrates that a part of the Jewish consciousness was alerted to the possibilities of political renewal. Thus we encounter a powerful subliminal component—the impulse to repair the Jewish past, through the king or other forms of sovereignty.

The impulse was expressed by eruptions of messianic movements in which human initiative superceded divine action. And the identification of the king as a flesh and blood redeemer, as articulated by Maimonides, was to serve as a foreshadowing of political Zionism. Thus, despite Judaism's apparent expulsion beyond history, the debate manifests an irrepressible yearning for restoration.

Our study illustrates the alternating acceptance, rejection, and ambivalence of rabbinic thought about kingship. It also reflects considerable caution even among those who consider kingship a mitzvah. Unlike one aspect of Christian thought, kingship is not apotheosized. Stobaeus (fifth century) wrote that "the king stands to the state in the same relation as God to the world."[1] And Ambrosiaster (fourth century) wrote, "Dei enim imaginem habet Rex" ("Truly the king has the likeness of God").[2] Counterparts of these views are not to be found in rabbinic thought.

Those sectors of rabbinic thought that can be identified more or less with the position of Maimonides or Abravanel represent well-defined views on Jewish government as embodied in the role of the king. The first perceives the Jewish national polity as the product of the collective need, rooted in the social impulses of men, but also as a necessary result of biblical and rabbinic insight. It is rational and humanist in that the social order is recognized as requiring human structures and human leadership, even if subject to divine direction and mandate. A major aspect of government—national security—must abide under human control. In this respect, Maimonides leads Jewish thought into modernity and opens a path leading ultimately to Zionism. Maimonides and certain of his predecessors recognize that Jewish government is required not only for security against external forces but also to correct destructive human impulses within society itself. Thus, Jewish kingship, while frequently accepted as necessary and mandated, is nevertheless deplored by some because of the moral shortcomings of both the people and its kings.

Yet as we examine the various currents of rabbinic thought, we note that even where it affirms kingship, it strives to circumscribe it and to assign to it subordinate status in favor of other modes of governance. (This is consistent with Deuteronomy 17:14 ff., which establishes kingship but is careful to subject it to limitations. It is not inappropriate to refer to kingship in Israel as a constitutional monarchy, at least in theory.) To characterize this as "theocracy" does not do justice to the intent of some aspects of rabbinic thought. We have already noted that "theocracy" encompasses a wide range of options in Jewish governance, and we have also noted the rabbinic renunciation (with the possible exception of Halevi) of the priesthood as the people's governing body. Preponderately, "theocracy" in rabbinic thought refers to governance by the judiciary, in accordance with Jewish law. This is most systematically presented by Ha-Ran. It is not our purpose here to evaluate the consequences of this principle as it has been used in present-day Israel by its more zealous proponents. We would rather examine this principle in terms of its earlier projection by rabbinic thought as a Jewish alternative to kingship. What did it oppose in kingship? What did it espouse in his own brand of "theocracy"?

Even when Jewish kingship is approved in Scripture and in rabbinic thought, there, is the constant assumption that only God, not the human king, is the ultimate source of loyalty. Loyalty to God implied the capacity to disobey the king if he has contravened the Law. Though chosen by God (not by direct intervention but by prophets or judges), kings in Israel were neither divine nor endowed with divine attributes. Because kings among Israel's neighbors were deemed to be gods, loyalty to them readily became idolatry, a condition that Jewish religious literature quickly grasped and recoiled against. Even when kingship became firmly established in Israel, and accepted both in Scripture and among the people, the primary concern over it was not dispelled. Kaufman correctly describes the replacement of a loose confederacy of tribes by a more centralized kingship, but nostalgia (justified or not) for premonarchical times persisted. For better or worse, kingship was grafted on to Israel's polity generations after it had emerged among its neighbors.

Since the rabbinic mainstream could not totally reject a kingship believed to be rooted in divine law, they deprecated it and sought (ambiguously in most cases) an alternative form of governance. That task was predicated on the assumption that Israel was not "like all the nations," and could be effectively governed and protected on its own soil without the conventional authority of the king, even if he were to reign under restricted conditions. For Ha-Ran, the judges could fulfill the primary functions of government. For Abravanel, it was the judges together with the people themselves, living a pastoral existence and waiting for divine intervention in history. Abravanel favored dismantling human institutional structures though the fusion of democracy and supernaturalism. Yet even he did not go as far as to dichotomize human existence into the Augustinian City of Man and the City of God. Even he did not construe the social order as rigorously divided between what belonged to Caesar and what to God. Those who advocated kingship and those who deprecated it agreed on the unitary form of Jewish government in which the human and the divine were functionally united. The source of contention was not the nature of the unity but the instruments who would be responsible for sustaining it.

Rabbinic thought had misgivings about kingship by virtue of its reading of Scripture. While there was yearning for restoration, there was also apprehension over the excesses of kingship. The apprehension was grounded in belief in the kingship of God before whom and before whose power earthly kingship dwindled. The proponents of absolutism of the state are far more prevalent in non-Jewish philosophy and theology than in rabbinic literature.

To be overwhelmed by power, civil and religious, was to confirm Israel in its distrust of power, that of others as well as its own. "With the coming of the Messiah, kingdoms will cease from the earth."[3] Absolutism revealed its demonic proportions. Out of this, Israel learned to pray earnestly for the welfare of the government and passionately for speedy deliverance from bitter exile. Israel was enveloped not only by power itself but by conceptions of power that did violence to the prophetic view. One of the earliest philosophical contributions to political absolutism appears in Plato's Law. He writes:

> The greatest principle of all is that no one should ever be without a commander. . . . Nor should the mind of any one be accustomed to do anything on his own initiative . . . but in war and in peace he should look to and follow his leader. . . . In a word, he should teach his soul . . . never to act independently. . . . There is no principle, nor will there ever be one, which is superior to this, or better and more effective in ensuring salvation and victory in war. And we ought in time of peace from youth upward to practice this habit of commanding others, and of being commanded by others.[4]

Early Christian views of the state stand midway between prophecy and philosophical absolutism. For our purposes, the critical question is: What kind of judgment does early Christianity make upon the state? It is a judgment always conditioned by the conviction that the state is willed by God. While the Christian must always be critical of the state, his moral resistance is aroused when it infringes upon the realm of God; but, as Cullman puts it, he must "obey every State as far as it remains within its bounds."[5] This division of the sacred and the temporal makes the New Testament judgment equivocal and plants the seeds for a latter-day collapse of Christian morality through submission to the demonism of the Nazi state. True, the early Christian is taught to recognize the "beast out of the abyss," but the state becomes a beast only when it leaves its natural and allotted haunts to prey in forbidden preserves of exclusive Christian prerogatives. Luther's submission to the state on all matters except Scripture is illustrative. When the beast prowls, it is still God's instrument serving His vengeance. Also, the nature of Christian resistance, even when the beast invades the sacred terrain of God, is ambiguous.

Cullman says, "Of the totalitarian claim of the State which demands for itself what is God's, Paul does not speak directly."[6]

This ambiguity is heightened by two other factors. One is the expectation that the entire historical system of the world would be shattered and that the state, a temporary institution, would then be displaced by God. This eschatological hope reduced, if it did not abrogate, the early Christian's moral resistance. The other factor, stemming from a different set of premises, related on the naive assumption of the intrinsic benevolence of the state. Commenting on Romans 12:3–4, Cullman states: "Only he who does evil has to fear the State . . . not he who does good."[7] Thus the judgment to which the early Christian is summoned is a patchwork of real but circumscribed concern over the possible excesses of the state, and credence in the essential fairness of the civil powers. The judgment to which the early Christian is summoned is not the judgment of which Jewish prophecy speaks. It lives in a different realm. "In the world's opinion, [judgment] takes place in that which is visible, either as a cosmic catastrophe (the apocalyptic view) or in catastrophes within history (the exception of the Old Testament prophets and, in part, of Judaism). In reality the judgment takes place in the decision of men toward Jesus as the Revealer of God."[8]

It is no historical accident that during the Middle Ages, despite theological efforts to limit the power of the ruler, the weight of opinion shifted to the absolute sovereignty of kings. Doctrines of church leaders like Gregory VII (1020–1085) stressed the claim of the Church to "govern and control the civil state . . . the State must be baptized, disciplined, directed, and formed and enslaved by the supernatural society of the church."[9] Nevertheless, the fundamental source for royal sovereignty was the Paulist doctrine that "the powers that be are ordained of God," and resistance to these powers meant damnation. Gregory the Great even denied the right to judge or criticize a king. This political rigidity was part of the broad deterministic system of medieval theology. Herbert Muller writes: "Medieval thinkers, even the saints, seldom took seriously the possibility of basic social reform. They preached charity to the poor the more earnestly because they assumed that poverty and suffering were also ordained by God."[10]

It was during such a period that a Jewish scholar, destined to be jailed and held for ransom, dared to challenge the very suppositions of power. Out of the bleakness of Jewish existence, he dared, and out of the prophetic tradition, he dared. Commenting on a juridical matter involving Jewish and Christian litigants, Meir of Rothenberg demolished the infallibility of the dogma of *dina d'malkhuta* when he decreed: "This is not the law of the kingdom *(dina d'malkhuta)* but thievery of the kingdom, and it is no law."[11] Other medieval rabbis declared: "The law of the king is law, the law of the nation is not law to us."[12]

It remained for Hegel to elevate the concept of the state to its ideal condition. "The State is the actually existing, realized moral life. For it is the unity of the universal, essential will, with that of the individual. The state is an institution not consonant with the Judaistic spirit, and it is alien to the legislation of Moses."[13]

Our discussion of the contemporary implications of Jewish power emphasizes the contrast between the prophetic conviction of the mutability of power and an alien conviction of not only its immutability but its claim to divine origin. The state is made absolute. It is stratified beyond the possibility of mutation. Thus, in our own time, Karl Barth can say, "Every State, even the worst and most perverse, possesses its imperishable destiny in the fact that it will one day contribute to the glory of the heavenly Jerusalem, and will inevitably bring its tribute thither."[14]

When the state is absolute, when, in whatever idiom, it becomes an embodiment or an agent of the Universal Spirit, Israel cannot abide with it, whether on its own soil or on the soil of Diaspora. The truly absolute state knows, even if many Jews may not, that the people Israel must be totally expunged if the absolute state is to survive.

Historical events now make it possible for Israel to react more freely to power and to alien views of power. The rebirth of Israel the state opens the way for a renewed dialectic of prophecy and power, and offers again an opportunity for a creative confrontation of both. Once more, the old dichotomy, arrested by exile, can be resumed. The discourse between State and Diaspora, the encounter of Israel and the world, and the identity and destiny of *all* Israel hang largely on issues of power to which prophecy directed much of its attention.

The State of Israel has transformed rabbinic theorizing about sovereignty into a compelling need for social and political resolutions. The restorative time of Jewish nationhood confronts Jews with issues once barely contemplated. Yet, in a broad configuration, the ancient debate continues in an altered idiom. In a sense, the struggles dividing Israel are modern transmutations of old issues. They do not represent an abrupt break with the past, now that Israel has come into being. To the contrary, they reflect a continuum. The times have changed, but the drama with its familiar scenes and cast of characters in new costumes and dialects has not. Once more, supporters of the Torah lay claim to control over the sovereign.

Just as kingship emerged tardily in ancient Israel, both as a reality and later a dream, so has Jewish statehood now emerged late from the people's troubled dream. Both kingship and statehood have been objects of debate and anguish over power and limitation upon it, but except for some dissenters, their legitimacy has not been challenged. As we have seen, rabbinic thought was wary of monarchy and sought to restrain it, perhaps to transcend it. This ancient tendency now challenges an age where nationalism as a saving value comes under increasing distrust. Together with the ineradicable striving for national restoration, the search for a redeeming Jewish polity as set forth by Maimonides, the supreme political figure in religious thought, has not ceased in Judaism. Today, this issue is no longer theoretical but urgently real, both in Israel's internal spiritual struggle and in its confrontation with its adversaries. The wariness of power, yet the sense of its necessity, have been age-old Jewish preoccupations. These absorb us now with renewed intensity.

The resumption of national existence represents not only relearning polity but discovering for the first time the bewildering complexity of modern statecraft. The radically unique component in today's Jewish nationhood is its rise to power, a power born of utter powerlessness verging on annihilation. Jewish power differs from other such national manifestations in its transition from near physical extinction (not merely territorial loss as in the case of some defeated nations) to both physical renewal and the assertion of territorial independence. Israel might not have emerged except through the crematoria. Nor, in the light of Israel's brief history, could the malignancy of the Shoah have metastasized in the presence of a Jewish state. This should be pondered by those who would rather see Israel dismantled than morally tainted.

Now that power has become Judaized, it presents the Jewish world with inescapable dilemmas, perhaps more portentous than for most nations. The making of war entails risking national existence once and for all. David Ben-Gurion had to remind his nation that Arabs could sustain unlimited defeats but Israel could not afford to lose a single war. The making of peace involves courting grave hazards that inhibit the nation's will. The very inhibitions that impede peace raise concurrent dilemmas about the treatment of subject people living under occupation. Can the dispossessed be governed without repression? Can they be permitted limited autonomy without feeding their political expectations? Can they be liberated without risking retaliation? From these dilemmas must emerge decisions, planned or improvised. Are the perceived rights of the Jewish majority compatible with the needs of the Arab minority? What are the prospects of successfully imposing those rights? What are the potential consequences of coercion—indefinite rebelliousness? the captivity of the captors? final and sullen submissiveness? Can there be a benevolent occupation? Can this lead to a harmonious relationship? Transcending all other questions, can Judaism survive a triumphant Jewish state? Still, powerless people do not have to make moral or political decisions. In today's world, powerless people have no decisions to make, except to indulge in theoretical speculations.

We know that all is anything but well. The Zionist enterprise and with it the Jewish enterprise are imperiled. The democratic instruments and the ancient values that have animated them are in jeopardy. Democracy is under attack within Israel and therefore in the Diaspora. As a possible consequence, democracy is hard put to cope with the most ominous assault on the Jewish people in more than forty years. Profound democratic values and antidemocratic values confront one another in modern Judaism. "The whole head is sick and every heart is ailing; from head to foot no spot is sound."

Is there a way out? Two proposals present themselves, one for our internal trauma, one for the external assault. The first, which has already been examined, suggests a way of coping with the conflict of the authoritarian halachah with the democratic political system. It has been suggested by Federbush and Berkovits, among others, that Jewish law in the private sector should be used only to persuade and not to coerce. In the public sector, the spirit of Jewish law, which is malleable enough, can inform current issues of state from labor relations to property rights to international affairs. Federbush cites Albo, who wrote, "(only) general principles were given to Moses so that scholars in every generation might derive new matters from them" (Ikarim, book 3). Federbush adds, "A government depending on coercion . . . is totally opposed to Judaism's doctrine of righteousness."

Second, in respect to the Palestinian insurrection against Israel, we must consider the possibility that Israel might choose to abandon its democratic structures and values in order to save its physical being. Though we shrink from the prospect, we note that other democracies have taken this road before. The halachah also makes provision for national emergency under the rubric of *horaat shaah*. Under this circumstance, even laws of the Torah, such as the two witnesses principle, may be suspended. In extremity, Israel may be faced with such a decision fortified by both political and halachic sanction.

But we must consider the possible consequences. Once the fragile instrument of democracy is suspended, particularly by a tiny nation whose enemies will never relent despite its draconian actions, what hope will there be for the renewal of democracy in Jewish life? The triumph of antidemocracy would be overwhelming and, from the point of view of its supporters, validated by the Torah. Let us not linger on the perilous political consequences alone. What would the voiding of democracy do to the Jewish people? There could be, together with a frenzied, wagon-circling rush of loyalty by many to Israel, massive falling away. There could be a Masada mentality and post-Sabbatean defection. There could be irreparable splits and alienation. No calls to loyalty could arrest those trends. For many, Israel, which promised both rescue for the homeless and, almost as compelling, the creation of a new, spiritually liberated Jew, a new Judaism established on the principles of the Jewish democratic spirit, would no longer be credible. Do we have the ingenuity to quench the fire and to preserve the very justification for our collective being? Did we come all this way only to surrender our hold on the very values, the sacred values, that gave us reason to want to endure?

The struggle goes on. In the moral and political trauma that Israel together with the entire Jewish people now endures, issues deriving from our discussion must be confronted. Both the nature and the future of all Jewry depend on how they are to be resolved. Should the Chosen People suspend this title when its political interests stand in jeopardy? Can chosenness be tentative and conditional, or perhaps only the attribute of Exile? Can the modern use of unlimited power and absolute chosenness coexist? Can or should Jewish sovereignty differ from that of "all the nations"? Is the social morality of the Torah applicable to a modern Jewish state? Which version of the Torah?—not to oppress but rather to love the stranger in our midst? or to show him no mercy? Jewish existence thus ultimately depends not only on tactics but on values, religious-moral values.

There were prophets who did not seek the surrender of power, or the withering away of the commonwealth, but rather containment of the one, transformation of the other. The king is to become a wonderful counselor, a righteous judge, a champion of the afflicted. He is "to restore the order of society which the monarchy itself had dissolved."[14] Yet he is not to be an eschatological phantom, but a monarch. The people is not to be disembodied, but a living community. "Israel was still to be regarded as a community bound together by nature and history . . . really a people in the proper sense of the word."[15]

But if the people was to endure, the content of its existence had to be altered. Replanted in its land, Israel would undergo both a renewal and a radical change. The neglected covenant would be reestablished and more deeply imbedded in the people's life. It would be Sinai all over again. "As I entered into judgment with your fathers in the wilderness of the land of Egypt, so will I enter into judgment with you . . . and I will bring you into the bond of the covenant."[16]

Prophecy joined the hope for national redemption to that of the world. One was a precondition of the other. One was antecedent to the other. Israel now stands in an unbroken bond with the world, a bond of conflict and tension, but also of irrevocable concern with the fate and destiny of nations. The interaction between Israel and the world was a reality and a principle of Jewish existence in preexilic times. Today, national peril might yet release this principle as a living force. But only if wisdom prevails.

Notes

1. Frank Gavin, *Seven Centuries of the Problem of Church and State*, Princeton University, 1938.
2. Ibid.
3. Midrash Zuta, Shir ha-Shirim, ed. Buber, p. 2.
4. Plato, *Laws*, 942.
5. Oscar Cullman, *The State in the New Testament*, New York, 1956, p. 70.
6. Ibid., p. 65.
7. Ibid., p. 58.
8. Rudolf Bultmann, *Theology of the New Testament*, New York, 1955, Vol. 2, pp. 31–32.

9. Frank Gavin, *Seven Centuries of the Problem of Church and State*, p. 3.
10. Muller, *Freedom in the Western World*, New York, 1966, pp. 98–100.
11. *She'elot u-Teshuvot Maharam b. R. Barukh*, Budapest, 1895.
12. Hegel, *Philosophy of History*, New York, 1944, pp. 38, 197.
13. Barth, *Community, State, and Church*, New York, 1960, p. 125.
14. Pedersen, *Israel*, Copenhagen, 1926, III, p. 91.
15. Gerhard von Rad, *Old Testament Theology*, New York, 1962, p. 190.
16. Ezekiel 20:36–37.